GROUP RELATIONS WORK

GROUP RELATIONS WORK

Exploring the Impact and Relevance Within and Beyond its Network

Volume IV

edited by

Eliat Aram, Robert Baxter,
and
Avi Nutkevitch

Routledge
Taylor & Francis Group

LONDON AND NEW YORK

First published 2015 by
Karnac Books Ltd.

Published 2018 by Routledge
2 Park Square, Milton Park, Abingdon, Oxon OX14 4RN
711 Third Avenue, New York, NY 10017, USA

Routledge is an imprint of the Taylor & Francis Group, an informa business

British Library Cataloguing in Publication Data

A C.I.P. for this book is available from the British Library

ISBN 9781782201977 (pbk)

Edited, designed and produced by The Studio Publishing Services Ltd
www.publishingservicesuk.co.uk
e-mail: studio@publishingservicesuk.co.uk

CONTENTS

v

PART III
EXPLORING VARIATIONS IN THEME AND/OR DESIGN
OF GROUP RELATIONS CONFERENCES

PART IV
POST-CONFERENCE REFLECTIONS

Eliat Aram, PhD, the Chief Executive of the Tavistock Institute of Human Relations, is a Chartered Scientist Psychologist (BPS), a UKCP registered gestalt psychotherapist, and has been one of the pioneering members of the Complexity and Management Centre of Hertfordshire University. She works with organisation and community change agents, exploring how to work in the unknown, in conditions of high turbulence, uncertainty, and ambiguity. She has a special interest in the dialectic between leadership, ethics, and aesthetics, using a participative design approach. She brings expertise in creating spaces for difficult and creative conversations and facilitating a process out of which change and growth may emerge. In her commitment to developing a learning culture, she oversees the Institute's professional development programmes and is a keen practitioner in group relations, the Tavistock enterprise's core "learning through experience" practice. In that role, she regularly staffs and directs group relations conferences nationally and internationally. Since 2007, She has directed and made innovations to the Tavistock Institute's flagship GR conference, "Authority, Role and Organisation", otherwise known as the "Leicester" conference.

Robert Baxter, MD, is a retired professor of psychiatry at the University of Louisville, where he was Director of the Division of Child and Adolescent Psychiatry and Executive Director of the Bingham Child Guidance Center. He is a Fellow of the American Psychiatric Association and the A. K. Rice Institute for the Study of Social Systems, and a member of the American College of Psychiatrists and the American Academy of Child and Adolescent Psychiatry. He formerly served on AKRI's Board of Directors and was its President for eight years. He also directed AKRI's National Conference for four years and chaired its Training and Certification Committee for several years. He continues to consult to boards of directors of healthcare organisations while dividing his time between Bonita Springs, Florida and Santa Fe, New Mexico.

Jaume Benavent i Guardia, MA, Pedagogy (University of Barcelona), MA, Human Resources Management and Process Consulting (UB), Professional Development Programme (IOD, Belgium), is Project Manager and Organisational Consultant of the Innova Institute for organisational and social innovation, Barcelona. His practice is mainly orientated towards the facilitation of innovative transitions for a wide range of companies, work groups, and professionals. He is an adviser of managers and entrepreneurs on their work roles, especially in family-owned businesses, and he runs management development programmes. He has been the organiser and staff member of numerous group relations conferences (Cuba, Holland, and Catalonia).

Colleen Brent, MSW, is a clinical social worker in private practice as a therapist and organisation and group consultant in San Francisco. She teaches group relations as an Associate Clinical Professor in the department of Psychiatry at the University of California San Francisco and is a senior faculty member in the Community Psychiatry Residency in San Mateo. She is a member of AKRI and GREX, and a former Board member of GREX. She has been involved in AKRI and group relations work since 1973 and has served on many conference staffs.

Jolita Buzaityte-Kasalyniene, PhD, is associate professor at the Social Work Department, Vilnius University Faculty of Philosophy. She teaches research methodologies, youth work, and social pedagogy in social work and education study programmes on the Bachelor and Master levels. Currently, she is a head of the Social Work Department. She is a member of the National Board of Social Work, established as an independent advisory board for the Ministry of Social Security and Labour. She is a member and former chair of the Lithuanian Scouting Association. She is a representative of the Vydunas Youth Foundation (Chicago), and a founder of group relations in Lithuania.

Sandra Carrau Pascual, MA, Sociology of Organizations (University of Barcelona), Post-graduate Management in Human Resources (University Pompeu Fabra, Barcelona), is Project Coordinator and Organisational Consultant of Innova Institute for organisational and social innovation, Barcelona. She is a consultant for organisations and processes to integrate diversity in work teams. She advises about leadership roles, especially for health and social care professionals. She is an organiser and staff member of group relations conferences (UK, Cuba, the Netherlands, and Catalonia). Currently, she is researching and developing work around femininity and masculinity in organisations and its effects on leadership roles.

Gouranga Chattopadhyay, DPhilSc., is a founding trustee of Group Relations India and an independent consultant with commercial and government organisations and NGOs. He has taught and worked as a consultant to organisations and as staff in GRCs on five continents, including as a UN Adviser in East Africa. He is an honorary Fellow of four national and international learning organisations. His professional publications include five books and 112 journal articles to date, six volumes of poems in English, and the English translation of a Bengali novel. His English translation of some songs and poems of Tagore was published in 2015.

Hanna Fisher is a child psychotherapist in the UK, trained at the Tavistock Clinic; she specialises in the treatment of adolescents and patients with complex medical symptoms. She has worked and published in Italy and is currently practising as a psychotherapist in the British public mental health service. She is a PhD candidate at the Psychoanalysis Unit at University College London. She has developed a special interest in group relations as an application of psychoanalytic thinking and has worked in several conferences as a translator, a member, and a junior consultant.

Franca Fubini is a psychoanalytic psychotherapist, group analyst, and organisational consultant. She is a founder member of Social-dreaming.it (Italy), a trustee of the Gordon Lawrence Foundation (UK), and a senior consultant within mental health institutions, both in Italy and in the UK. She has lectured at Rome, Perugia, L'Aquila University in the field of psychology and human resources. She is Senior Fellow of University College of London (UCL). She has served as consultant and director of the Italian group relations conferences (Authority, Leadership and Innovation—ALI, and Energy, Creative Collaboration and Wellbeing in Organisations—ECW). She is a member of IL NODO group (Italy), of OPUS (UK), and of ISPSO. She is the convener of the Listening Post in Rome. She has contributed to the creation of "Blossoming in Europe", a programme which has connected, for ten years, European countries through the medium of cultural and art events.

Bernard Gertler, PhD, is an organisation consultant, psychotherapist, and psychoanalyst in private practice. Dr Gertler received his PhD degree in clinical psychology from the City University of New York, is certified as a psychoanalyst by the William Alanson White Institute, and holds a qualification in organisational consultation from the Tavistock Institute. He is a faculty member and a supervisor at the White Institute and was a faculty member and co-director of the White Institute's Organization Program. He is a Fellow of the A. K. Rice Institute for the Study of Social Systems.

Vivian Gold, PhD, is a clinical and consulting psychologist in private practice in Los Angeles, California. She is an Associate Clinical Professor at UCLA in the Department of Psychiatry and Bio-behavioral Science. She is a Fellow, an associate, and past board member of the A. K. Rice Institute for the Study of Social Systems. She is a past president of GREX, the West Coast Affiliate of the A. K. Rice Institute. While living in Israel in the 1980s, she was a founding board member of OFEK, the Israeli Association for the Study of Group and Organisational Processes. She has worked for fourteen years at the VA Greater Los Angeles Healthcare System in a unit treating addictions. She currently specialises in work with trauma and on the application of group relations to intergroup issues.

Seth Harkins, EdD, is chief executive officer of the Philip J. Rock Center and School in Glen Ellyn, Illinois. He is a career educational administrator, having served in a variety of leadership roles in public and private education. He has been adjunct professor and assistant professor of education at National Louis University, Chicago, for thirty years. He has been active in group relations conference work since 1985. He is a member of AKRI and is the past President of the Chicago Center for the Study of Groups and Organizations.

Charla Hayden, MA, is an independent organisational consultant to national and regional health care systems and for-profit organisations such as international manufacturing firms, local technology start-ups, and regional food distribution systems. Currently, the core of her work is facilitating the increased effectiveness of executive groups and the coalescence of groups whose members have diverse and often competing interests. She has held faculty or consultant positions at Oregon Health Sciences University, the Wright Institute, Los Angeles, the University of Southern California, and the Stanford Graduate School of Business. She currently serves as Vice-president of the A. K. Rice Institute for the Study of Social Systems.

Ruthellen Josselson, PhD, ABPP, is Professor of Psychology at the Fielding Graduate University and a psychotherapist. She is co-director of the Yalom Institute of Psychotherapy, for which she runs group therapy training programmes internationally. She has directed many group relations conferences, including three AKRI international conferences. She is the author, co-author, or editor of many books and articles, including a book on women and leadership entitled *Transforming Self, Transforming Institutions: The Life and Leadership Lessons of Faith Gabelnick*.

Oren Kaplan is a Professor of Psychology and Business, a clinical psychologist, and an MBA graduate in marketing. He is the Dean of the School of Business Administration and the Academic Director of the Management & Business Psychology MBA Programme at the College of Management, Rishon LeZion, Israel. He is a member of OFEK, the Israeli Association for the Study of Group and Organisational Processes.

Olya Khaleelee is a self-employed corporate psychologist and organisational consultant with a particular interest in organisational transition and transformation. She has been associated with the Tavistock Institute for over thirty years in developing group relations, both in the UK and abroad, has been on the staff of many conferences, and was the first female director of the Leicester Conference, which explores authority, leadership, and organisation from a psychoanalytic and systemic perspective. She was for many years director of OPUS: Organisation for Promoting the Understanding of Society.

Judith Levy, PhD, is Senior Teacher (retired) in the Department of English, Hebrew University of Jerusalem and an executive coach. She is on the faculty of the MBA Programme in Management and Business Psychology at the College of Management, Rishon Le'Tzion. She is a member and former Chairperson of OFEK, the Israel Association for the Study of Group and Organisational Processes, and is a member of ISPSO and OPUS.

Keren Lipinsky-Kella is a social worker and MBA graduate with expertise in business psychology, consumer behaviour, and corporate social responsibility (CSR). She is a faculty member at the School of Business Administration, the College of Management, Rishon LeZion, Israel.

Susan Long supervises research students and conducts organisational research at a variety of universities, including INSEAD, MEICAT, University of Melbourne, and Crossfields. As an organisational , she works with organisational change, executive coaching, board development, role analysis, team development, and management training. Her experience of working with people as individuals and in groups and organisations gives her a broad perspective on management practices. She is a member of the board of the Judicial College of Victoria and of Comcare's advisory board for the Center of Excellence for Research into Mental Health at Work. She was the founding President of Group Relations Australia and a past President of the International Society for the Psychoanalytic Study of Organisations.

Mary McRae, PhD, is an associate professor of applied psychology in the Department of Applied Psychology, New York University, where she teaches courses in Group Dynamics and Cross-Cultural Counseling. Her scholarship involves the study of racial and cultural dynamics in groups and organisational life. She is a licensed psychologist with a small private practice. She has worked as a consultant doing group and organisational work nationally and internationally. Her publications include articles, chapters and a book titled *Racial Cultural Dynamics in Group and Organizational Life: Crossing Boundaries*. She has served on the board of AKRI and is a Fellow.

Luca Mingarelli is a social entrepreneur and clinical psychotherapist (ECP). He is Chairman and CEO of Fondazione Rosa dei Venti, Director of Therapeutic Communities for adolescents, consultant to profit and non-profit organisations, and a faculty member in psychosomatics.

He is Vice Chairman, Il Nodo Group, a member of OPUS. He was Co-director of the "Energy Creative Collaboration and Wellbeing in Organizations" and of "Learning from Action", group relations events. He has written the book, *Difficult Adolescents, an Autobiography of a TC* (2009). He has been a staff member in national and international group relations conferences (Perù, Canada, UK, Serbia). He is also a basketball coach and journalist.

Ilana Mishael, MSc in Organizational Behaviour, MA in Social Work—clinical track, graduated from the International Programme in Organisational Consultation and Development: a psychoanalytic–systematic approach. She is an independent organisational consultant, supervisor for financial, service, and industry organisations, and a therapist at the mental health centre "Lev HaSharon" in Pardesia and at a private clinic in Tel-Aviv. Prior to transitioning into consultation and therapy, she served as a human resources director at leading organisations. As a member of OFEK, the Israel Association for the Study of Group and Organizational Processes, she took roles as an administrator and as a consultant in group relations conferences.

Avi Nutkevitch, PhD, is a clinical psychologist, a training analyst, and an organisational consultant. He is a member of the Israel Psycho-analytic Society and teaches at the Israel Psychoanalytic Institute and other postgraduate programmes for psychotherapy. He is a founding member and former Chair of OFEK, the Israel Association for the Study of Group and Organisational Processes. He is currently Co-Director and Faculty of the Programme in Organisational Consul-tation and Development: a Psychoanalytic–Systemic Approach. He holds a senior teaching position in the MBA programme of the College of Management in Rishon Le'Tzion.

Richard Morgan-Jones was originally educated at Cambridge, Oxford, and Exeter Universities in anthropology, theology, and educa-tion. He is a training psychoanalytic psychotherapist with the British Psychotherapy Foundation. He is a member of the British Psycho-analytic Council and of OPUS, and an elected board member of ISPSO. He is an organisational consultant and coach as well as a clinician. In all these roles, he has an eye for the dual experiences of being a body and mind that belongs to the larger body and mind of the family, group, workplace, and society. This reveals old wounds recycled, growing pains, and strategic opportunities that challenge the energy for creative living. He directs Work Force Health: Consulting and Research, whose work is explored in: *The Body of the Organisation and its Health* (Karnac, 2010), an exploration of how organisations get under the skin.

Dr Hüseyin Özdemir, DiplOec, is a member and co-operating partner of the International Coach Federation (ICF); a member and co-operating partner of SIETAR; and Senior Coach of the Germany Coaching Association DBVC. He is a senior organisational consultant, management trainer, executive coach, and Director of oezpa GmbH, Academy & International Management Consulting for Strategic Organisational Development, in Bornheim-Walberberg (Cologne–Bonn), Germany. He is Programme Director of oezpa Leadership—OD and Coaching Programmes as well as of group relations conferences. He has published numerous books and articles about his experiences. He is a senior lecturer on leadership and organisational development at the following institutions: Fresenius University Cologne (lecturer and co-operating partner), European School of Management and Technology (ESMT), Germany, and Lorange Institute of Business, Zurich (lecturer and co-operating partner). He is a co-operating partner at the Tavistock Institute of Human Relations, London, and President of ILAC (International Leadership Academy—Cooperation of Business Schools and Academics).

John B. Robertson, Jr., MD, is the co-owner of the Center for Family Psychiatry PC and Attention Deficit Center in Knoxville, Tennessee. He is certified by the American Board of Psychiatry and Neurology in three areas: general psychiatry, child and adolescent psychiatry, and addiction psychiatry; his medical practice is quite diverse. Awards include selection by peers multiple years for Top Doctors of Knoxville. Group relations work includes serving as staff consultant for many AKRI-sponsored group relations conferences since 1993, conducting workshops, and presenting at AKRI national symposia and presenting at Belgirate IV.

Joan Roma i Vergés, MA Philosophy (University of Barcelona) and Social Psychology (UB), MA Organisational Development (CSP, La Jolla, USA), Professional Development Programme (IOD, Belgium), is President and an organisational consultant of the Innova Institute for organisational and social innovation, Barcelona. With a background of management experience, as consultant and professor, he specialises in transitional processes of organisations and its members around Europe, Latin America, and Africa. With extensive experience as organiser, staff and director of group relations conferences, he has been involved with experiential learning programmes for managers and consultants and applied research from the integrative "Organisational Transnovation" approach. He is a member of ISPSO and the "Organisation for Promoting Understanding of Society".

Jeffrey D. Roth, MD, is an addictions psychiatrist and group psychotherapist. He has directed ten group relations conferences on recovery from addiction. He is the past-President of the Chicago Center for the Study of Groups and Organizations, a Fellow of the American Society of Addictions Medicine, and a Fellow of the American Group Psychotherapy Association. He is the author of the book *Group Psychotherapy and Recovery from Addiction: Carrying the Message* and the editor of the *Journal of Groups in Addiction and Recovery*.

Anja Salmi, MD, is a psychiatrist, psychotherapist, and organisational consultant. She is a founding member and the Managing Director of Psychiatric Outpatient Clinic Egofunktio Ltd. Her experience and education contain a wide range of various psychological aspects from educational analysis to large group phenomena at the level of society. She has studied and published on psycho-biological gender differences, collective losses, and changes in generational and family structures. Within Egofunktio Ltd, she has been managing knowledge creation on health care organisations, their management, and connections with society.

Maija-Leena Setälä is an organisational psychologist, MSocSc, Lic, and a senior organisational consultant. She is the ex-President and a member of FINOD (Finnish Association of Organisational Dynamics). She is a lecturer in the Advanced Work Counselling Programme of Metanoia Institute and the Opus Listening Post Convener in Finland.

Yael Shenhav Sharoni, MA, is a clinical psychologist and organisational consultant. She is a member in training of the Tel Aviv Institute of Contemporary Psychoanalysis. She is a member and former Board Member of OFEK, the Israeli Association for the Study of Group and Organisational Processes.

Mannie Sher, PhD, is a principal social scientist and Director of the Group Relations Programme at the Tavistock Institute of Human Relations, London. He is a Fellow of the British Association of Psychotherapists and a practising psychoanalytical psychotherapist. He has published on subjects of consultancy, leadership, organisational development, ethics, and corruption. His latest book is *The Dynamics of Change: Tavistock Approaches to Improving Social Systems* (2013). He is a former member of the Board of the International Society for the Psychoanalytic Study of Organisations (ISPSO) and a member of the Israel Association for the Study of Group and Organisational Processes (OFEK).

David Sierra Lozano, MA, Organisational and Work Psychology (University of Barcelona) and Post-graduate Process Consulting (UB), is a partner and organisational consultant of Innova Institute for organisational and social innovation, Barcelona. He serves as a consultant for organisations and processes to create strategic vision. He is an adviser of managers and entrepreneurs on their work roles, especially on leadership roles. He is an organiser and staff member of group relations conferences (Argentina, Cuba, Holland, and Catalonia). He is currently researching and developing programmes that integrate perspectives of soft systems methodology, viable systems, and systemic contributions methodology through the "Organisational Transnovation" approach.

Maria Grazia Siri has a degree in Philosophy and is a psychoanalytic psychotherapist. She has served as host of Social Dreaming and is a member of Il Nodo Group of Turin. She is a trainee in the AIPPI school of the Tavistock method in Italy, a supervisor for training of Centro Studi Martha Harris Firenze, and a member of Centro Studi Martha Harris. She was a staff member of the GRCEnergy Creative Collaboration and Wellbeing ECW.

Gordon Strauss, MD, is Professor of Psychiatry at the University of Louisville School of Medicine, where he directs student psychiatric services for the university's student health service. He is a member and fellow of the A. K. Rice Institute for the Study of Social Systems (AKRI). He is also President of the Midwest Group Relations Center and a member of GREX, both affiliate centres of AKRI. He received advance training in organisational consultation from the Cincinnati Psychoanalytic Institute.

Rina Tagore has an MA (Psy) from Delhi University, India, and is a social policy planner and community development professional. She has worked in different capacities in local government in Auckland over the past ten years, as a principal policy analyst, community and social planner, and, currently, as a senior adviser in local board services of Auckland Council, New Zealand. Prior to that, she was programme officer with the Swiss Agency for Development and Cooperation in India. She has worked in group relations conferences in India and Leicester, UK, and has been an associate member with the Centre for Socio-Analysis, Melbourne, Australia.

Simi Talmi, MSW, is a psychotherapist, group facilitator, and organisational consultant. She is a lecturer at Haifa University in the Psychotherapy Programme and co-director of the seventh cohort, the Programme in Organisational Consultation and Development: A Psychoanalytic-Systemic Approach (POCD). She is a member of the Tel Aviv Institute for Contemporary Psychoanalysis and of OFEK, the Israel Association for the Study of Group and Organisational Processes.

Marianne Tensing has a Master's degree in education from the University of Tartu (Estonia) in sciences of sport and philosophy, and psychology from the University of Oulu and consultation at Metanoia Institute. She is an organisational consultant, a supervisor and coach in consulting methods, and the lead Advanced Supervisor in the Metanoia Institute programme. She is the convener of the International Listening Post in Estonia. She is a member of the Finnish Society for Organisational Dynamics (FINOD), a member of the Finnish supervisors' association (STORY), and a founding member of the Human Experience Research Institute.

Kay Trainor, DocConsOrg, is Principal Consultant and Executive Education Lead at Tavistock Consulting, part of the Tavistock and Portman NHS Foundation Trust in London. She is Director and member of the faculty of the Masters programme there in Consulting and Leading in Organisations: Psychodynamic and Systemic Approaches. She is also a member of the faculty on the EMCC accredited Executive Coaching course at Tavistock Consulting and a member of the Tavistock's Group Relations Conference Committee. Her doctoral research focused on the experience of managers and leaders in fourteen organisations in and around the City of London in the period leading up to the Lehman Brothers crisis.

Josef Triest, PhD, is a clinical psychologist and supervisor, training analyst of the Israel Psychoanalytic Institute (IPS), and an organisational consultant. He is a lecturer at Tel-Aviv University and co-owner of the Triest–Sarig private clinic. Since October 2014, he has served as the President of the Israel Psychoanalytical Society. He is a Member of OFEK, the Israel Association for the Study of Group and Organisational Processes, and Co-director of the Program in Organisational Consultation and Development: A Psychoanalytic–Systemic Approach (POCD). He has taken up a variety of roles in group relations conferences, including the director's role in some of them, and is the author of several papers in the field of group relations.

Gerard van Reekum is an organisation scientist, consulting to various institutions and industries in government and business in his native country, the Netherlands. Over the past twenty years, he has participated in group relations events in the Netherlands, UK, France, USA, and Belgium. On the board of Group Relations Nederland, he holds the role of treasurer. Through his writing, he aims to challenge and innovate the conceptual framework underlying group relations work.

Barbara Williams, EdD, is the Director of Bureau Kensington Consulting in Toronto and is an experienced consultant in the areas of strategic change, leadership development, and human resources management. She works and publishes in the area of psychoanalytic perspectives on learning, gender, and change. She is a guest of the Toronto Psychoanalytic Society, a member of OPUS, the International Society for the Psychoanalytic Study of Organizations, and a member of the Institute of Corporate Directors in Canada. She holds a doctorate in Adult Education from the University of Toronto.

FOREWORD

Brigid Nossal

This is a very important book to those of us in the field of group relations striving to make sense of our current state: in terms of our collective thinking (if I am permitted to call it that), our evolution as a field, and our systems psychodynamics. Like earlier editions in the series, Volume IV of *Group Relations Work: Exploring the Impact and Relevance Within and Beyond its Network* provides the opportunity to articulate and explore the development of this work. In this sense, it plays a crucial role in facilitating the sort of self-scrutiny and self-reflection to remaining relevant and meaningful to the organisations and societies to which we offer it.

The experience of reading the book mirrors my experience of the Belgirate IV conference itself. If I can use a dream-like metaphor, it was as if something was breaking down and dispersing into multiple shapes, like the ice on a lake fracturing and creating new forms, moving towards something more fluid—perhaps a new flow. This poses one of the key questions that seem to underpin this book: where is this flow taking us? Will the fundamental principles of group relations conferences (GRC) be diluted, leaving us nothing, or only an adulterated version of the discipline we hold so very dear? Or is the process something more akin to the spirit of group relations itself, fashioning openings and creative spaces for new learning? It seems to me that this is just one the debates going on between the lines in this book, with now an assertion of the importance of maintaining boundaries and now an alternative conference or event that explores what happens when you let them go.

This book enables a dialogue between reader and writers in which our habitual or under-examined assumptions can be challenged. I realise that a number of key questions about group relations have been floating around in my head for some time and these were met and entertained (if not answered) in some way as I wandered and wondered my way through the book. For example, how are we thinking about the role that the transference to authority figures (the staff) plays in GRCs and the extent to which they are enabling/disabling of learning that continues to be relevant to the organisations people find themselves in? Do we think enough about the impact of the way we take up our roles?

There is a general sense in this book (and at Belgirate IV) that we are engaged in pushing at the outer boundaries: geographically (with venturing into China), literally by challenging long-held assumptions about the boundaries between therapist and patient and the authority relations manifest therein (boundaries of space with a dream matrix in a playground on a boulevard, boundaries of long-held assumptions about the role of containment in creative discovery). In all of this pushing, there is the searching for relevance and for the adaptations that will meet the current context.

As with earlier volumes, the fact that the chapters are left to speak for themselves, much in the way the conference does, brings a liveliness to the experience of reading as well as providing something of the experience of being there for those who were not able to attend or for those who join the field in the future and wish to discover where we came from and how we got here. Most chapters stop short of saying (in any didactic way) what the implications of the thinking are for conference design into the future—rather, there are open-ended ponderings and some serious introspection. Again, we are challenged to engage with this thinking, this pushing at the boundaries and to consider, at each new frontier, what it means in application. This is a serious enterprise.

I was left wondering (as indeed I think we should), is it an *irritable* reaching, not after facts and reason, but a whole new paradigm?

While there is the assertion of fundamental shifts taking place in some manifestations of authority relations, as presumed to be exemplified in the Arab Spring and the supposedly "agile" organisation, alongside this is the fact that the psyche (e.g., the fundamental hypothesised architecture of the psyche as we have come to understand it, with its oedipal dynamics and object relations, its paranoid–schizoid and depressive functioning, etc.) has not changed or evolved in synchronisation with the pace of technological change as much as we might wish that it had. With the benefit of hindsight (the conference was in 2012), we must reframe the Arab Spring as the oft-cited exemplar of a fundamental shift in authority relations. While, in the west, it was hailed as a new and democratic order, enabled by social media, we now know that it led to the establishment of a more authoritarian rule and eventual social breakdown. That is, the celebrated first democratically elected leader in decades in December 2011 resulted in a conservative religious leadership that was ousted only a year later, resulting in a leadership vacuum, military rule, and increasing violence, mistrust, and uncertainty. Similarly, the much-publicised "occupy movement" offered as another example of the shift in authority relations seems not to have brought about fundamental change. Are we impatient with a psychic life that does not keep pace with the changes we see in other spheres of human enterprise: technology, engineering, and science, for example?

Perhaps we work with the assumption that because aspects of the model of the group relations conference were first discovered over forty years ago, they must be out of date. But have they reached their use-by date? Or were they more revolutionary than we care to acknowledge? Is this some sort of watershed era in the development of our thinking, or has it always been thus and this is the great beauty of the method? If this is an irritable seeking after a new paradigm, we are faced with just the same challenge we put to our members: there is the discomfort in not knowing—the hatred of learning from experience—perhaps the wish for an omniscient authority to relieve us of the agony of it all.

This book strikes me as an honest, earnest, deep, thoughtful enquiry into our method. On the one hand, it presents a sort of angsty identity crisis and, on the other, it offers many clear illustrations of the multiple useful and relevant applications of group relations in different parts of the world.

As Rina Tagore reminds us, group relations provides "a lens that challenges internal assumptions and those in the surrounding environment". Even the critiques of the conference presented here make use of this "lens" to make their case and, in so doing, they remind us of the sharpness, agility, and relevance of the method.

There is movement and flow of some kind, a pushing at the boundaries on one side and a reaffirming of them and their utility in effecting transformational change on the other. Long may these debates continue!

Introduction

Eliat Aram, Robert Baxter, and Avi Nutkevitch

This book, the fourth in the series covering the outputs of the conferences at Belgirate, which were anchored in the exploration group relations conferences, marks twelve years of exploration. As we reflect on the journey we have been through thus far, we are noticing the expansion of the boundary, of moving from focusing on the group relations conferences themselves to the network and beyond the network.

From one book to the next, we gain deeper and perhaps new understanding of what group relations is for us. The conference has demonstrated that group relations is beyond conferences, that it is an approach—with a theory, with a methodology—to work, to social problems, to life, perhaps.

The "Belgirate conferences" can be seen as a container for the exploration of these questions. When we started, more than twelve years ago, the conference was more structured and managed, but, from one conference to the next, we have increasingly let go of that. We have done that partly because of our increased trust and confidence in our small group work as the management team and partly because of our increased capacity to dialogue and collaborate with conference participants and respond, from one conference to the next, to insights that emerged from the last conference.

Over the years, we have noticed in the network an ever-increasing demonstration of its capacity to manage itself creatively and collaboratively and, hence, in this fourth conference, we moved from inviting parallel presentations to a call for papers that represents a shift in the responsibility and accountability for what this conference, and now this book, is to be about. The second shift was marked by the offer of the open space, where a number of conversations took place in the same space during the same time. Another change was a move away from assigning people to introductory groups at the opening of the conference to allowing people to self-organise into small groups both for the opening session and the application and review session at the end of the conference.

In putting the responsibility of developing the conference to the network and levelling out the structures, we faced resistance. The exploratory event seems typically to be the recipient of the resistance and criticism as well as ambivalence towards us, in particular with regard to our decisions, which have changed from one conference to the next, of how to take up our roles as management and administrative team (MAT) in the exploratory event. Looking back at our three other introductory chapters, we were interested to discover what we said in our introductory chapter to Volume II (pp. 9–10). We said there that we decided to stay together as a MAT group in the exploratory event because, at the time, we felt that our role as "hosts" was the prevailing one but we were also acknowledging some anxiety about separating and joining the rest of the membership.

In this fourth conference, we particularly aimed to offer opportunities for the network of people to study itself as a network. For that reason, and because we also matured as a MAT during these years, we changed our practice this time in the exploratory event and did not stay working together. Having established the container based on the principles of GR method, task, time, and territory, we allowed ourselves and the network the opportunity to co-create the exploratory event with a management in-the-mind, or possibly even more than that, participatory management.

However, our experience has been that, never the less, there is always a longing to make the Belgirate Conference into a group relations conference. Our stance has been, and remains, that this enterprise is not meant to have a GRC design and structure, but is about enabling conditions where exploration of GR method can take place.

We believe that one exploratory question in this conference has to do with how to take up authority, personal and in role, in a networked organisation. If we draw on the distinction made by Emmanuel Ghent (1990) between surrender and submission, we would suggest that the question of a member in a network is: how does one experience the network and being a member of it; do we experience ourselves as submitting to external authority, which in a networked organisation might need to be imagined or invented, or do we find the authority to surrender, to participate in the process as it unfolds in an active way?

This fourth conference is also about transition. Whereas, in the third conference, we put out for exploration the notion and meaning of succession, in this fourth one, we enacted the first stage in this process. During the third conference, we put out a question with regard to the future institutions to manage the enterprise called Belgirate, and our sense was that the network wanted the three sponsoring organisations to carry on, so they appointed successors for OFEK and AKRI and decided that the TIHR representative will remain as continuity and succeed for the sixth conference. Working with these successors, Gordon Strauss for AKRI and Josef Triest for OFEK, during the conference was also a dynamic to reflect on. We included Gordon and Josef in our pre-conference meetings as well as in the review meeting at the end, but during the conference they were left to manage themselves in the role of successors while maintaining a position as part of the membership.

As the organisation called Belgirate is maturing, there is the sense of loss, of connectedness, with which we also grappled in our process of succession, wanting to be replaced in the role of management, feeling that this is the right thing to do, but which is also always fraught with ambivalence and not wanting to let it go. Linked to this, age and ageing were more broadly present at the conference. The sudden death of Anne-Marie Kirkpatrick surfaced through telling of dreams in the morning reflections and associations sessions, dream about a grandmother locked in a tower in a hotel in New York City when the hurricane occurred, and other grandmother dreams. We are also aware that, in a conference with every three years' occurrence, one encounters the ageing in the other, sometimes in quite poignant ways.

Who came to Belgirate on this fourth iteration?

We had eighty-nine members including the MAT, three of whom were prevented from attending due to Hurricane Sandy. We had forty-six women and forty-three men, who represented nineteen countries including: Argentina, Australia, Canada, Denmark, Finland, Germany, Greece, India, Israel, Italy, Lithuania, the Netherlands, New Zealand, Norway, Spain, Sweden, Switzerland, the UK, and the USA.

In terms of age distribution, we had 20–29 (one person), 30–39 (two), 40–49 (twenty-three), 50–59 (thirty-one), 60–69 (twenty-five), 70–79 (eight) and unknown (two).

Out of the eighty-nine people, thirty-nine have directed conferences, seven have co-directed, eighty-three had been consultants, and thirty-five had been administrators.

Excluding the MAT, fifty-one participants took up roles in the conference: two held the morning reflections and associations session, eleven chaired keynotes or parallel presentations, two gave keynote addresses, thirty-three presented in parallel presentations, and four presented in the open space session. Including the MAT, there were fifty-six participants who held specifically authorised roles during the conference.

We are quite delighted with these data. We see this as evidence of the growing participatory, collaborative nature of the network that spans its geographical boundaries. This is evident also in the work surrounding some of the chapters in this book, both in the support offered around the preparation of the presentations and in the collaboration in the post-conference reflections.

This brings us to the question of how this book is organised. There are four parts in this book. The first, reflecting on the theory of group relations and its relevance to contemporary phenomena, comprises five chapters, including what was the keynote by Mannie Sher. The second, studying the relationship between group relations work and its impact in its cultural and geographical settings, comprises five chapters, including the keynote by Hüseyin Özdemir. The third section comprises four chapters, which explore variations in theme and/or design of group relations conferences, and the fourth section, with four chapters, offers some post-conference reflections written by participants following the conference and reflecting on their experiences and learning from them.

Finally, we would like to note that this book marks an ending of a ten-year collaboration among the three representatives of the three sponsoring organisations, and we would like to extend our special gratitude to all who have joined us and taken part in the birth and growth of this special project called the Belgirate conferences. In addition to the scholarly products and the contribution to the furthering of understanding and learning from group relations conferences, a precious friendship has developed between the three of us, which has enabled us to lead and contain this process with joy. For that, we are also grateful to all of you who participated, and who will continue to participate in future.

Reference

Ghent, E. (1990). Masochism, submission, surrender—masochism as a perversion of surrender. *Contemporary Psychoanalysis, 26*: 108–136.

PART I

REFLECTING ON THE THEORY OF GROUP RELATIONS AND ITS RELEVANCE TO CONTEMPORARY PHENOMENA

The Oedipus complex, creativity, and the legacies of group relations' intellectual parents

Mannie Sher

Summary

This chapter highlights two key conceptual elements that are core to our understanding of group relations conference dynamics and which are often ignored—Oedipus and Sphinx. It is argued that focusing on these two concepts should help distinguish between resolutions of conflict with authority based on the paranoid–schizoid position and those based on the depressive position. In the paranoid–schizoid position, resolution is based on victory of one party over another; in the depressive position, resolution is based on the acceptance of difference that includes tolerating weakness without withdrawing from the group process. This is especially relevant where the group's purpose is learning (Sphinx) and not a struggle over power and dominance (Oedipus). This paper also links understanding of these two concepts in group relations work to its application to social thought and social behaviour outside the group relations network.

Group relations has been at the centre of my professional life for over forty years, helping me address the challenges of organisational work and social and political process. I offer a few perspectives here on how I think group relations serves as an instrument beyond its network for understanding how individuals, groups, communities, and society conduct their affairs and, where possible, helping them to do so in better ways.

I am grateful to the organisers of the conference—Eliat, Bob and Avi—for the honour they have extended to me by inviting me to give the keynote address, thereby providing the opportunity to reflect on what group relations means for me and to offer a few thoughts on its development.

First, a brief personal history: as a young man in South Africa, I was an active member of a Jewish youth movement that later led me to live for a year on a kibbutz in Israel where ideas of the collective and the role of the individual in it were the topics of discussion and argument into the early hours. We were imbued with ideological imperatives that we believed were destined to change society and the national character. Our endeavours, centring on developing awareness, new knowledge, and integration, would be loyal to both South African and Jewish history and heritage, yet we would be revolutionary in breaking the mould of historical identities. The group, the community, the nation, the people were the focus of our youthful intellectual and political ideologies. Our daily thoughts, discussions, and actions were hugely influenced by them.

Writing about psychoanalysis, Rustin (1981) argues that seeking connections between the individual and the social are major reasons for the distance and latent hostility between psychoanalysis and general political and social modes of thought. He considers these two "systems of ideas" in tension with one another. I am positing a similar tension in "systems of thought" between group relations and organisational and leadership theory. Rustin implies that by emphasising processes involving individual minds and feelings, and an insistence on individual responsibility for them, certain forms of political commitment and social action can be undermined. I wonder if that is one reason why we are concerned about the relevance of group relations beyond its network. Rustin writes (p. 72),

> Political commitment and social action attribute agency and responsibility in a collective way; they generate responses to perceived wrongs; they are activities that are external in their objectives, and are open to other interpretations of inner motivation. Such externalisation of feelings can become frenetic and one's experience be deeply

structured by a split between the idealisation of the product of change
and denunciation of the evils of the present.

In this chapter, I take the view that connections between the
personal and the political are significant features of group relations
and are also consistent with applications of group relations theory to
economic, cultural, and social behaviour. I think we share a belief that
group relations and political movements outside our network will
develop future directions of society through political action that
depends also on understanding the capacity to live by meanings and
values that are more civilised, sociable, and altruistic and more equal
to the difficulties of life. Group relations can and ought to assist in this
process; without this capacity to live by meanings and values, the
experience of political commitment could become a very paranoid–
schizoid one. In our group relations view, the "freedom of constraints"
would be greater awareness and knowledge of unconscious defences
that prevent us facing what we know. That was the challenge I felt as a
young socialist in South Africa as we experienced the dismantling of
democracy. We had reached a crossroads where we had to face the
challenges of a redistribution of power and wealth. In short, we
believed the nation needed to undergo a process of redemocratisation.
In this process, for me, group relations later became powerfully instru-
mental in learning about resistance to the changes that were widely
recognised as necessary and inevitable.

In group relations, we believe that cognitive ideas of social behaviour cannot be separated from the pains inflicted by our biological
natures. Political and organisational theory must take account of these
facts and construct a frame of meanings that can be faced—matters of
pain, death, our sexual natures, the needs of infancy and nurture, and
inborn individual differences in natures and capacities. Kleinian object-
relations theory (Guntrip, 1961) is relevant here to the understanding
of natural needs and capacities of people. In the wider field of cultural
and organisational meanings, Kleinian theory offers a view of human
nature as being fundamentally moral. It also assumes human beings to
be constituted as social beings interdependent with others. Kleinian
theory is suffused with moral categories in its developmental concepts,
especially those of the paranoid–schizoid and depressive positions,
notably the concern for the well-being of others. Guilt in the Kleinian
"depressive position" is understood to arise from the recognition of

pain suffered by, or inflicted on, others and is an essential part of relatedness. Capacity for moral feeling, therefore, is the definable attribute which links human beings, not an unfortunate external constraint upon them. The attribution of moral capacity derives from the Kleinian view of the infant's early relationship with its mother. Individuality is shown to be not the starting point, but, rather, the result of a prolonged and delicate process of dependency. Innate concern for the well-being of the other, at a very deep level, appears to arise from the earliest lack of differentiation between self and other and from the process whereby this lack comes about. While committed to the development of individuality, object-relations theory starts from the assumption that social relationships are always primary. Bowlby and his colleagues provided experimental proof for the assertion that social relationships form the precondition for human cognition, as did Rosenfeld, in *Psychotic States* (1965), Bion, in *Experiences in Groups* (1961) and Meltzer, in *Explorations in Autism* (1975).

The theme of this conference was: "Exploring the impact and relevance of group relations work within and beyond its network".

I shall now describe the impact of ideas about the Oedipus complex and ideas of Sphinx on group relations within and beyond its network because I have been intrigued by the ubiquitous force of these two concepts. They are central to our thinking about group relations and are often poorly acknowledged. This follows developments in psychoanalytic thinking about the Oedipus complex, the metaphor used by Freud to describe the son–father psychosexual competition for possession of the mother, and the daughter–father competition, also for possession of the mother. Otto Rank, in developing object-relations theory, proposed that a boy's mother was the source of the superego. Rank's ideas of the centrality of the mother in the Oedipus complex were developed by Klein, who concentrated on the early maternal relationship, proposing that underlying the Oedipus complex there is an earlier layer of more primitive relationships with the oedipal couple. Klein's work lessened the role of the Oedipus complex with the concept of the "depressive position", in which the infant is able to experience others as whole and which radically alters relationships with others, bringing the good and bad aspects of the feeding mother and the withholding mother and leads to a corresponding integration of the ego. For the post-Kleinian Bion, the myth of Oedipus concerns investigatory curiosity—the quest for knowledge. Bion regarded the central crime of Oedipus as his insistence on knowing the truth at all costs (Parsons, 2000, p. 45). The achievement of the Oedipus complex is the child coming to understand something about the oddity of possessing its own mind and discovering a multiplicity of points of view (Bollas, 1987, pp. 86–89); Phillips, 1994, p. 159). For Britton, "the link between the parents perceived in love and hate can be tolerated in the child's mind and provides it with a capacity for seeing itself in interaction with others and for reflecting on ourselves, whilst being ourselves" (Britton, 1989, p. 86). Parsons (2000) proposes that the Oedipus complex is a life-long developmental challenge with new kinds of oedipal configurations that belong to later life. I hope that you can see these links with the development of psychoanalytic theory and how they bring me to our theme of group relations.

Lawrence (1997, p. 2) reminds us that Bion believed that the self-study of groups is a methodology that allows for the exploration of the group mind through observations that tend to fall into two categories: those that tend to centre on the oedipal situation, when related to the pairing group, and Sphinx situations when related to problems of the desire for knowledge, the function of learning, and scientific method (Bion, 1961, p. 8). The group relations method is directed at the study of the group mind that is based on the nature of psychic reality in the inner worlds of the individuals in a group and as the individual believes it is construed in the minds of others in the group. In psychoanalytic thinking, the study of the two-person relationship centres on Oedipus. Using psychoanalysis as a means of understanding the nature of thinking in groups, Bion talks about Sphinx. Lawrence (1997) argues that transferring insights from the psychoanalytic dyadic relationship to groups risks the danger that groups come to be understood in terms of the psychopathology of the role-holders constituting them rather than as potential "properties" of the group or system as a whole. This would be an over-simplification of the qualities of groups that try to bring thinking into being that transcends the individual.

A vignette from a large study group (LSG)

I am working with a white South African female consultant. A South African member links our roles to his own South African background and culture which was characterised, he said, by white authoritarian rule that spied on the people to see they did not get up to sexual mischief. Other members of the LSG continue with a theme of the consultants having other agendas—in particular, controlling the membership and the abduction and sale of children. Two Irish women take up the theme of the abuse of children in Irish children's homes. A man volunteers that he was in a children's home as a child where his main objective was to not attract the attentions of the male staff.

This vignette describes the feelings of helplessness and the phantasies of tragedy formed in infancy: for members of the LSG it has taken the form of fearing that their survival is at stake because the consultants appear engaged in a power-play with the weakest elements of the group.

In our group relations work, we know that a good interpretation does more than make the unconscious conscious. It offers the opportunity to integrate a newly found understanding into one's overall organisational structure. It is a corollary of the Oedipus complex that creativity requires that one comes to grips with the legacies of one's intellectual parents. Within the broad domains of group relations, there have been embarrassingly many attempts to kill off the line of heritage from Freud, Klein, and Bion to Rice, Miller, and Lawrence. The proliferation of schisms in group relations has often hidden a wish to murder the father (Lear, 1999, p. 125). Our work must continue to be a unique blend of creativity and faithfulness, bringing together in group relations understandings, on the one hand, of the Oedipus situation that involves a relationship with our "intellectual parents", and creativity on the other, of the Sphinx situation of acknowledging a need to learn and co-operating with others to assist in that learning.

A usual group relations conference structure reflects the different roles that members and consultants play. These are related to organisational structures, and sometimes individual mental structures, which are represented in the members' and the staff's internal worlds. A member's and a consultant's place in a conference can be determined by their subjective sense of their roles as affected by fantasy and can be distorted in particular by narcissistic illusion, projective identification, and sadistic attacks on the task. In groups, fantasies tend to be variations on the classical pattern, where a member might feel encouraged by his co-members to adopt the role of rebel, joker, or casualty and, in this way, to oust the staff from role. This is the archetypal structure represented in Sophocles' play, in which Jocasta encourages Oedipus to adopt the position of King and husband (Steiner, 1985, p. 164, 2011, p. 99). Inevitably, this type of fantasy leads to the struggle over dominance as the father/king attempts to reclaim his place in the family/dominion. In the infantile version of this fantasy, the struggle is also one between illusion and reality, since the child's immaturity makes the role he has chosen to adopt unrealisable. This, in my view, describes the primitive anxiety states present in the LSG, which is that members tend to rely on illusion as a means of survival.

In the context of group relations, confrontation with consultants is often confused with confrontation with reality. The member may attribute various motives to consultants and management, some of which are projections of the members' own situations. Typically, the fantasy is one where the consultant admires the member and other members are thought of as envious of the successful member and try to gain his position. This leads to a struggle over dominance, which I believe is similar to Freud's primal horde (1921c, pp. 122–128) or Turquet's engulfment/isolation dilemma (1972, 1994).

Steiner (2011, p. 102) argues that the classical resolution to the Oedipus complex, as described by Freud (1924d), is a paranoid solution that gives rise to resentment and wish for revenge. Steiner suggests that, alongside this, a depressive outcome also exists. In this version, the child is initially dominant in phantasy. At first, this leads to a triumph over the father with the phantasied blessing of the mother, but, as the child recognises that he has in phantasy destroyed both parents, feelings of triumph turn into despair and guilt. If the child in his development—and the members in the large group in theirs—can obtain support to enable them to tolerate this guilt, it can be used to initiate a move towards remorse and reparation and, therefore, a greater grasp of Sphinx—the scientific approach to learning.

We need to be clear that guilt cannot be processed adequately if shame and humiliation intervene excessively. The conflict over power and dominance invariably ends with a winner and a loser. Generally, the outcome is commonly the child's defeat and humiliation. In group relations, we are mindful of group process that singles out vulnerable individuals to carry shame and humiliation and we avoid that by refraining from naming individuals or singling them out in our interventions. Perhaps this is inevitable in our work, where we attach such importance to aggression and destructiveness and less to power and dominance. Yet, struggles over power and dominance seem often to lie at the source of destructive violence in many areas of human inter-action, so it seems to me urgent that they become the subject of group relations study. It is not difficult to find the roots of such struggles in early infantile development, particularly in the Oedipus situation. I suggest that these struggles are based on the individual's attempts to emerge from primitive persecutory states, seen so clearly in the large group, in which people can feel themselves to be, and sometimes are, victims of cruelty and injustice.

A member says,

> "Individuals have no value in this group; we're always defined as part of something else—nation, gender, race or faith. My individuality is being killed off. I'm looking for my small study group; I can't find it here and the consultants do nothing to help with my fears."

The wish for revenge arises in the large study group when members feel injured and wronged. Often, what begins as a demand for fairness (protection) becomes inflamed into a hatred, as other motives, such as envy, cannot be restrained and everything feels liable to be destroyed. Such unopposed destructiveness is terrifying and, in most cases, restraining forces are mobilised to protect the group from the devastating effects of its violence. Consequently, wishful revenge could be denied or bottled up and expressed as grievance.

A member of the large study group says he is surprised that a member asks the group's permission to go to the toilet. He says he cannot understand how the authority of the group is used to cow its members! This is followed by a suggestion that the members feel the group has nothing to offer them and its business can be ignored: "What does all this matter, after all is said and done?" Complaints are made about the dismissive behaviour of the administration, the management's apparent indifference to members needs, the tatty state of the bedrooms, and the breakdown of the central heating.

The feelings of hatred in the group are bound in a complex patho-logical organisation, and the sense of hurt and wrong form the focus of grievance. Sometimes, revenge is repeatedly thought about in fantasy. Nevertheless, the chronic disguised hatred, which is often suffused with sadism, is extremely destructive and is often felt to arouse retaliatory vengeance by the consultant. Because the violence is restrained, the object is hurt, but not destroyed, and retaliatory acts are provoked, keeping the cycle of hurt and revenge alive.

An important source of grievance is the sense of unfairness connected with helplessness in a context of unequal power, where the staff are experienced as strong and exerting authority and members are perceived as weak and having to submit. Such inequalities are typically confronted in the Oedipus situation, which introduces the member to new realities that are experienced as profoundly shocking and can lead to a deep sense of hurt, injustice, and betrayal. Such inequalities are not felt to be a natural consequence of the member in need of others but, rather, as a cruel exercise of power, as in the following example.

> In this session, the membership appears restless and offers a series of non-sequiturs. A member says: I have an image of a worm that is cut in pieces and regenerates, like the events in the conference. Another member responds: I had a dream in which I am naked and a consultant walks in and says that he does not have time to stay. This is followed by members complaining that there is no soap and shampoo in the bedrooms; management keeps a distance from us and appears uninterested in our welfare. A discussion follows on the failures of capitalism that rejects people's dependency in the name of cost reduction and austerity measures. The implication is that the membership is burdensome for the consultants, who move away exhausted, leaving the membership to organise themselves like street gangs.

In this vignette, I am suggesting that the tone of apparent non-co-operation by the group membership through hazy formless discussions, followed by a dream involving a consultant who cannot stay or understand nakedness, points to a defence against narcissistic injury that results from the group's lack of power to retain the consultants' interest and their unconscious wish to overturn them. The result excludes the consultants as possible helpers in learning and leaves the membership to find its own way, increasing its sense of weakness and prompting a paranoid–schizoid position.

There are parallels here in the link between organisational imperatives to survive that appear to be accompanied by an indifference towards the fate of individuals. This generates an almost inevitable tension between the social responsibilities of social and communal life and the dualism of the expectation of care and attention and deep fears of neglect and abandonment. These tensions are the focus of group relations endeavours and its work with enterprises outside its network.

The Oedipus situation, deriving from the ideas of Klein (1945) and Freud (1924d), includes primal scene phantasies that are traumatic and provoke revenge because they shatter the illusion of exclusive relationships which so often form the basis of narcissistic object relationships. We understand that a good part of the hurt is connected with an awareness that the relationship of consultant and member is based on an inequality of power that the individual, in his narcissism, has previously denied. The individual discovers the facts of life in the group, in particular that differences exist between the consultant and the member. He resents these discoveries, feeling he is being subjected to unfettered expressions of power rather than acknowledging reality. It is not only the fantasy of the consultants' exploitation of their power that causes resentment, it is their possession of that power which is felt to be unfair. The greater power of the consultants exposes the vulnerable and dependent membership to the possibility of exploitation and abuse. No matter how well-intentioned and benevolent the consultant actually is, the sense of unfairness is inevitable. In the early stages of development of the LSG, paranoid–schizoid phantasies will dominate and are reinforced by the consultants' claim to hold and to work with the group-as-a-whole, thus excluding (castrating) the individual as individual.

An LSG member says,

"This LSG is like a constructed theatre and I feel I have been 'scripted' to annoy the consultants and get under their skin. But if I have been 'scripted', why do I feel guilty? The fact is that I do feel hatred towards the consultants, their elevated status over us, when it is clear they lack knowledge about us and yet still believe they can do the job. What is management up to in appointing them as consultants? Why don't they appoint me? I'd like to be a consultant."

The individual is obliged to submit, and the Oedipus complex is "dissolved" when he gives up his claim to be a consultant and forms an identification with him instead, seeking learning from the consultants and other members. In this situation, the member's identification with himself as the persecuted object protects him by preventing open

confrontation with the consultants. In my view, this type of identification leads not to a resolution of oedipal conflicts, but in the group
relations context, to a compromise that fails to deal with the underlying resentment and wish for revenge. Indeed, in the classical version
of the Oedipus complex, the father with whom the child identifies is
himself full of grievance and exercises a terrible control. If the member
solves the problem of his hatred through identification with a cruel
authority, he will, in turn, become afraid of being overthrown by his
co-members and will treat them with the same form of power to
which he himself was subjected (Steiner, 1990a,b, 1993).

We see here an authority based on strength and power. Even
though grievance is perpetuated in session after session, a pattern is
developed, which might be preferable to unrestrained destructiveness. In this version of the oedipal narrative, the members attempt to
overthrow the consultants by ignoring them, but do not free themselves from their influence, because they are possessed by thoughts of
replacing them. The members hate the consultants, who present an
obstacle to their craving for power, but they also love and admire
them. After they get rid of them, satisfy their hatred, and put into
effect their wish to identify themselves with the consultants, the affection that had been pushed underground during the early LSGs makes
itself felt in the form of remorse and a sense of guilt, which suggests
a move towards the depressive position. This seems to make a depressive solution to the oedipal conflict in the group and a move towards
Sphinx possible. Here, guilt reinforces the prohibitions of the repudi-
ated staff, who have now been introjected. However, when the structure has been acquired through the exercise of power, a sense of
injustice remains unrelieved. Resentment and the wish for revenge
dominates, whatever the outcome of the power struggle. If the consultants are stronger, the members submit with resentment, while if the
consultants are overthrown, the members are persecuted by guilt, and
the consultants, having been internalised, control the members from
within.

A power struggle remains an important organising principle central to our understanding of group dynamics of both small and large
groups. I think of this as the persecutory version of the Oedipus
complex, which is resolved in a variety of ways, but in which resentment plays a central part and Sphinx—the desire to learn—is undermined.

The large study group starts with grievance—the central heating is complained about and it is raining. A member says, "It is cold and uncomfortable. It is not rocket science to fix the central heating. Why doesn't the management see to it? I've asked several times and nothing happens." Another member says, "I am tired of hearing the repeated dichotomies of male/female, gay/straight, black/white, good management/bad management. Can't we move on to something else? We, the membership, keep looking to the management to provide more leadership and more help. We are behaving like a group of adolescents who want to kill daddy because we're not understood, but we also do not want to kill them because we need them; the group would cease without them. I wish it were different, but it isn't. I wish I knew everything, so that I would not have to rely on them for knowledge about the group". A member replies, "This envy seems to be everywhere—destructive envy, towards the consultants because they appear to have knowledge of the experience of the group mind and we do not. The consultants know, but they are not telling."

For the membership, the consultants provoke that painful mixture of love and hatred that characterises the depressive position. The membership's recognition that it is mature and has an adult learning relationship with the consultants can stir feelings of despair. The hatred that in the persecutory version was directed at the "tyrannical consultants" is also directed at the relationship between the consultants. Envy and jealousy justify grievance and accentuate the membership's hatred so that its destructiveness is then felt to attack everything good. When this is acted out, it leads to a conviction of "bad" consultants and the potential for learning (Sphinx) is thwarted. When the membership comes to recognise its need of the consultants it has "lost", it is confronted with feelings of remorse, guilt, and despair. Now the guilt is depressive and can lead to remorse and a wish to make reparation. It arises from the coexistence of loving and murderous impulses and leads to what Melanie Klein meant by the "loss of the loved object" (Klein, 1952, p. 253), which is the situation where the membership becomes aware that it needs and values its good objects but is also "aware of its own incapacity to protect and preserve them . . ." (Riviere, 1952, p. 51). This realisation leads to despair and depression that have to be surmounted if reality is to be faced and development of learning is to proceed. If the membership retreats and withdraws and now wishes to emerge, it has to face a psychic reality that it has been evading. When depressive anxiety dominates, the membership has to acknowledge that, in the group fantasy, it has attacked and destroyed its good objects in acts of vengeance that leave it devastated. Only then can it face the task of reconstructing the group's desire for learning and begin the long and painful effort to make reparation and find forgiveness. When the membership finds the pain and cost of this move to be too high, or when humiliation is extreme, the membership will retreat to the protection of an omnipotent organisation (Steiner, 1990a, p. 87)

Sometimes the rivalry between membership and consultants emerges as clever sparring or a scoring of points, and, at the same time, it has a serious fight-to-the-death quality when both feel the foundations of their identities are being attacked.

A member says,

"I find it hard to think of the group as a system like the body is the system—the intake of food and air, digestion and evacuation. I'm a small part of that system and I am preoccupied with myself and my survival in the group."

I have come to see this process as part of a power struggle arising in the Oedipus situation in which the group members believe that either the consultants would triumph over them or they would over the consultants. Neither outcome leads to development, but only to the maintenance of the status quo. The result is not a working through of oedipal rivalries, but is a transformation of these into a chronic aggrieved state, which interferes with development and smothers moves towards liveliness, curiosity, and learning—Sphinx.

Despite differences in age, gender, race, size, or inequality, elements of rivalry are ubiquitous and are felt, not as painful and natural aspects of reality, but as giving rise to feelings of exploitation and injustice. It is, in fact, very difficult to make this judgment, since exploitation and abuse of the real experiences do occur, but they are not integral to the existence of difference. A tolerance of difference is necessary for development and for creativity, but difference can also provoke envy, and it is often when this is attached to injustice that destructiveness becomes so magnified.

To be needy and helpless is one of the most dreaded experiences we are subjected to. If no one is available to hear our cries and to recognise and respond to our needs, we face the anxiety of abandonment and persecution. This fear relates to the helplessness and prolonged dependence of early infancy and is directly expressed through the need to find and get through to an available object. In the LSG, the individual needs to reach, and to make an impression on, an object who is able to contain his anxieties—that is, one who is able to be emotionally responsive and able to understand rather than enact. When anxieties are high, the individual member communicates his needs through projective identification at a concrete level, and in the LSG these concrete projections could make containment difficult, since they provoke action rather than understanding.

Containment is, therefore, only ever partial. When it fails, powerful defences are mounted. The most common defensive pattern is one in which neediness is denied and replaced by a narcissistic type of object relationship. The needy, helpless, and deprived self is projected and disowned and identification occurs with an authority object that is expected to provide.

The narcissistic group cannot tolerate a view of itself as immature or weak and unorganised because it is convinced that being in this state would mean that it would be helpless. It is unable to elicit the right attention because it lacks any confidence in the means of drawing the consultants' attention to its emotional needs. The capacity to do this depends, on the one hand, on the group's ability to use projective identification to enter the mind of the consultant in order to draw attention to its needs and, on the other, the consultants' capacity to receive and respond adequately to its projections.

In considering the application of group relations thinking to institutions outside the group relations network, I offer the following example. In 2010–2011, I conducted a research project (Gill & Sher, 2012) examining the views of key players in the financial crisis of 2007–2010. This research revealed patterns of cultural, political, and institutional behaviour that, looked at from the perspective of group relations, had the hallmarks of a huge, unmanaged inter-group event in which panic, ignorance of, or concern for, every other part of the system other than your own, and b/a fight/flight characterised our inter-institutional and international relationships that continue to this day and have dire consequences for millions of people. Here is a quote from the research:

> Our respondents seemed unable to consider the invisible forces at work; everyone to a greater or lesser extent was involved—the

borrowing public, corporate customers, investors, shareholders, regulators, the media, politicians. Seemingly, everyone was persuaded that
growth was indefinite, ignoring their own often-quoted advice that
whatever goes up, must come down. Together with our interviewees,
we struggled to understand the imponderables of culture; the atmosphere and climate of the sector that had engulfed everyone and forced
upon them a way of thinking and acting that no one single agency
caused or had the power to stop. After many very good years, the
"bubble" had been pricked by mysterious forces that were beyond
control of even the "masters of the universe". Even as the crisis
unfolded, the competitive forces and denial continued.

The industry was in "silent complicity"; we were engaged in a "feat
of levitation" that could not go on and on. But it went on and we all
believed in it. People knew that eventually the house of cards would
fall down. Many CEOs felt "we're OK; we will benefit from the catastrophe of others". Many allowed themselves to feel reassured
because the regulator approved of the model of banks not needing
much capital. How many said it was about to explode? Why were
institutions under pressure to increase their leverage? There was enormous pressure from the institutions. Owners, media, shareholders . . .
everyone . . . none of them said "stop!" (p. 66)

On the whole, our research demonstrates that bankers, regulators,
shareholders, politicians, and civil servants have a good grasp of the
issues that led to good and bad behaviour in the financial crisis. They
clearly differentiate between fraudulent behaviour of individuals, but
they are unable to comprehend how the invisible forces of culture drove
a particular type of behaviour that underpinned the crisis. Behaviours
that are driven by culture present a paradox to them; on the one hand,
they recognise and associate competition, rivalry, and pace of business transactions as positive forces very much at the root of their suc-
cesses. On the other hand, they realise that these cultural norms might
have played a far greater role in the crisis than they are able to understand. It is hard for the finance masters to believe that there are forces
affecting them over which they have little or no knowledge or control.

Conclusion

In many respects, group relations work goes against the grain of contemporary social thinking. Its emphasis on envy and destructiveness

seems to run against the hopefulness, even utopianism, about human nature that characterises political thought. Its interest in the mutuality of learning and "caring relationships" seems rather out of sympathy with a much tougher-minded and more aggressive attitude of mind of contemporary ideas on political and social leadership. Group relations draws attention to the inevitable presence of both powerful positive and negative feelings in human beings. It defines development in terms of a process of differentiation and individuation; it is a rather powerful experience in how to separate one context and its feelings from another. The insistence in group relations work on a firm segregation of the different roles of staff and membership from one another and the avoidance of "democratic" and "egalitarian" looseness in these matters enforces strict attention to boundaries. This is very far from the ideal of a unified, holistic, non-specialised community in which people might find all their needs realised. Group relations commitments to understanding, choice, and responsibility take forward the liberal and rationalistic ethos of Freud's and Klein's work, while its stress on containment and dependency points towards a more "social" conception of people's relation to society.

These are un-utopian assertions that are needed if group relations is to face up to its responsibility to respond to the conditions of global, virtual, and post-industrial life. But there is a utopian content also in object relations theory: a commitment to the values of life, of relationship, of membership in a social community from birth, of creative development, and of normal care for others, which properly form part of a group relations' conception of people and society.

References

Bion, W. R. (1961). *Experiences in Groups*. London: Tavistock.

Bollas, C. (1987). *The Shadow of the Object: Psychoanalysis of the Unthought Known*. London: Free Association.

Britton, R. (1989). The missing link: parental sexuality in the Oedipus situation. In: R. Britton, M. Feldman & E. O'Shaughnessy (Eds.), *The Oedipus Complex Today* (pp. 83–102). London: Karnac.

Freud, S. (1921c). *Group Psychology and the Analysis of the Ego. S. E.*, 18: 67–143. London: Hogarth.

Freud, S. (1924d). The dissolution of the Oedipus complex. *S. E.*, 19: 173–179. London: Hogarth.

Gill, A., & Sher, M. (2012). Inside the minds of the money minders: deciphering reflections on money, behaviour and leadership in the financial crisis of 2008. In: S. Long & B. Sievers (Eds.), *Beneath the Surface of the Financial Industry: Towards a Socio-Analysis of Money, Finance and Capital* (pp. 58–73). London: Taylor & Francis.

Guntrip, H. (1961). *Personality Structure and Human Interaction*. New York: International Universities Press.

Klein, M. (1945). The Oedipus complex in the light of early anxieties. In: *The Writings of Melanie Klein, I* (pp. 370–419). Reprinted in: R. Britton (Ed.), *The Oedipus Complex Today: Clinical Implications*. London: Karnac, 1989.

Klein, M. (1952). On observing the behaviour of young infants. In: M. Klein, P. Heimann, S. Isaacs, & J. Riviere (Eds.), *Developments in Psychoanalysis* (pp. 237–270). London: Hogarth Press. Reprinted in: *The Writings of Melanie Klein, III* (pp. 94–121). London: Hogarth Press.

Lawrence, W. G. (1997). Centring of the Sphinx for the psychoanalytic study of organisations. Lecture given at the ISPSO Annual Meeting, Philadelphia, 27 June.

Lear, J. (1999). *Open Minded: Working out the Logic of the Soul*. Cambridge, MA: Harvard University Press.

Meltzer, D. (1975). *Explorations in Autism: A Psychoanalytical Study*. London: Karnac.

Parsons, M. (2000). *The Dove that Returns, The Dove that Vanishes: Paradox and Creativity in Psychoanalysis*. London: Routledge.

Phillips, A. (1994). *On Flirtation*. London: Faber & Faber.

Riviere, J. (1952). On the genesis of psychical conflict in earliest infancy. In: M. Klein, P. Heimann, S. Isaacs, & J. Riviere (Eds.), *Developments in Psychoanalysis* (pp. 37–66). London: Hogarth Press.

Rosenfeld, H. (1965). *Psychotic States: A Psychoanalytic Approach*. London: Hogarth Press.

Rustin, M. (1981). A socialist consideration of Kleinian psychoanalysis. Paper presented to a seminar of the New Imago Group, January, 71–96.

Steiner, J. (1985). Turning a blind eye: the cover up for Oedipus. *International Journal of Psychoanalysis*, 12: 161–172.

Steiner, J. (1990a). Pathological organisations as obstacles to mourning: The role of unbearable guilt. *International Journal of Psychoanalysis*, 71: 87–94.

Steiner, J. (1990b). The retreat from truth to omnipotence in Oedipus at Colonus. *International Review of Psychoanalysis*, 17: 227–237.

Steiner, J. (1993). *Psychic Retreats: Pathological Organisations of the Personality in Psychotic, Neurotic and Borderline Patients*. London: Routledge.

Steiner, J. (2011). *Seeing and Being Seen: Emerging from a Psychic Retreat*. London: Routledge.

Turquet, P. M. (1974). Leadership: the individual and the group. In: G. S. Gibbard, J. J. Hartman, & R. D. Mann (Eds.), *Analysis of Groups* (pp. 349–371). San Francisco, CA: Jossey-Bass.

Turquet, P. M. (1994). Threats to identity in the large group. In: L. Kreeger (Ed.), *The Large Group: Dynamics and Therapy* (pp. 87–144). London: Karnac.

CHAPTER TWO

Virtual teams and group relations in the WEB 2.0 era: insights from an MBA experiential distance-learning course

Oren Kaplan and Keren Lipinsky-Kella

Management in the WEB 2.0 era

We live in a world where interactions between individuals and organisations often take place by virtual means, particularly the Internet. The average worker in the USA receives approximately one hundred email communications a day and spends about two hours of the working day dealing with them. The Internet's WEB 1.0 version initially enabled limited personal interaction. However, the next generation of Internet services, WEB 2.0, included platforms that enabled active interaction on websites such as blogs, talkbacks and social media. These created the foundation for wide-ranging and revolutionary social phenomena that we are only now beginning to assimilate and understand.

Today, organisations are using social media and online communications to carry out tasks that are crucial to their functioning. Traditional organisational branches have changed beyond recognition, both in the way they conduct business and in the identity of the players who are active in the field today. The role of the new learning in the organisational world and beyond inevitably requires investigation into how its practice alters personal, interpersonal, and systemic processes.

The current MBA experiential distance-learning course was planned and executed on the assumption that changes brought about by the virtual digital era could have far-reaching implications for the building blocks of the organisational system, for better or for worse, and could even influence their very survival.

Any change in the primary task means a corresponding change in the role of the manager. What, then, should we teach today in schools of business administration and how should we train the managers of the future? Previously, the learning goals for a student in social and managerial sciences could be defined quite accurately and they would change at a moderate, controllable, linear pace. However, today's rate of information growth is exponential. The Internet doubles in volume every six months, and, in the space of just twenty-four hours, the equivalent of eight years' viewing time of video clips is uploaded to YouTube.

When information and interaction, that is, the content and the process, change so rapidly and dramatically, the premises and paradigms of traditional models of work and learning must be reviewed. It becomes imperative to question not only *what* we are teaching the managers of the future, but also *how* we are teaching them. Assisted by this case study of the present course, the writers will address two related central issues. The first issue focuses on the conditions that either enabled or inhibited learning within the framework of the course. The second deals with the definition of the primary task in different learning cultures, as expressed in the course. This leads to an exploration of how the case study could deepen the understanding of learning from experience in the wider sense.

As lecturers at the School of Business Administration, who are exposed to the rapid penetration of social networks into the daily lives of individuals and organisations, we have to confront the question of whether and how these developments are likely to influence, or should influence, teaching and learning within academic frameworks.

Excited by the new possibilities, we initiated a plan for an experiential course that would deal precisely with these issues. While academic learning traditionally focuses on content and knowledge, we believed that, to research issues like these, they would have to relate to the process. In other words, learning from experience, the familiar processes in the GR model, would be an exceptionally effective way of researching the subject.

The course included a blog system, which served as an academic environment for the fifty MBA students, who were asked to operate throughout the semester in various types of tasks and virtual teams. The setting, boundaries, and primary task were defined and managed by faculty, but, as in group relation settings, the content and events were created by the course participants. Clearly, this is not a traditional academic model and the challenge was two-fold: presenting the course in the spirit of GR in the "here and now", and, at the same time, adhering to the rules of academic culture, which requires clear structure, content, and authority.

Reverie about memory and desire

> I am. Therefore I question. It is the answer – the "yes, I know" – that is the disease which kills. It is the Tree of Knowledge which kills. Conversely, it is not the successful building of the Tower of Babel, but the failure that gives life, initiates and nourishes the energy to live, to grow, to flourish. (Bion, 1985, p. 52)

If we were on a NASDAQ Investor Road-Show, the pitch would sound something like this: *The current course is a ground-breaking, distance-learning Internet venture in which a class of students work in virtual teams in a pilot programme which is innovative on both the pedagogical and technological fronts.*

The sales pitch would have to be provocative, almost grandiloquent, if a high level of expectation was to be set, although the chances of actually living up to those expectations would be low. Risk-loving, opportunity-seeking investors would otherwise not take the bait.

Perhaps it was this kind of promise or desire that initiated the lecturers' involvement in the adventure described here. Perhaps this influenced the decision by the conference organisers to invite the team to present their findings to an audience and publish them in the current book. And perhaps this audience (you, the reader) would be captivated by the entrepreneurial fantasy about the virtual course presented in this chapter.

> "Our disappointment at the end of the course was probably not justified. We were not disappointed because the course did not succeed, or

because it received negative reactions from the students. The course was "good enough" [Winnicott, 1953], but the fact is that entrepreneurial promises create expectations that are difficult to fulfil, and the innovative rapidly becomes the obvious."

As early as 1895, Josef Breuer described the very same process with great modesty in his introduction to the theoretical section of *Studies on Hysteria*, which was probably the most astonishingly innovative start-up of the twentieth century, the beginning of psychoanalysis and free association. It was, thus, about 120 years ago that Breuer stated:

> When a science is making rapid advances, thoughts which were first expressed by single individuals quickly become common property ... there is always a danger of regarding as a product of one's own what has already been said by someone else. (Freud (with Breuer), 1895d)

The latter could probably represent the deep meaning of Bion's famous expression of "no memory and no desire".

Memory and desire: "If you will it, it is no dream" (Herzl, 1960)

Expressions like "Internet venture" or "start-up" bring certain associations to mind. In the current era, the Internet is a source of "desire" and inspiration for entrepreneurship and innovation. It arouses feelings of curiosity and enthusiasm for "something new", something "beyond". It might even be of a mythic or spiritual nature, as if a virtual image of the late Steve Jobs could be whispering to somebody personally, "If you will it, it is no dream".

This "whisper" was, of course, contained in the famous statement by Theodor Herzl, the founder of Zionism, made in his 1902 book *Altneuland* ("Old New Land"). Today, more than 100 years after Herzl published his Zionist vision, there is only one narrative that unites Israeli society from right to left, from Jews to Palestinians, from the secular to the ultra-religious, and, ironically, it has nothing to do with the land of Zion. It is instead the desire to be touched by the stardust of a new enterprise start-up. As if in fulfilment of this desire, the technology industry has been acknowledged as the engine of the Israeli economy and a source of sustainability.

Dan Senor and Saul Singer's 2009 bestseller, *Start-up Nation*, has become integral to the Israeli cultural discourse, especially in schools of business administration. The label "Start-up Nation" has become a source of admiration and national pride at both social and individual levels. Israeli children and students dream of a career as a start-up entrepreneur and of scoring an "exit"—the enormous wealth that follows when their brilliant, innovative idea conquers the world. A hundred years ago, the Zionist entrepreneur might have been a Jewish farmer on a kibbutz, but today the unconscious embodiment of the Zionist entrepreneurial spirit is a start-up that will conquer the NASDAQ, where more Israeli companies, according to the above book, are listed today than those of any other country outside of North America. Herzl's slogan, "If you will it, it is no dream", in its 2.0 version, is, therefore, a mantra for lovers of technology who are focused on the vision of the Internet.

Reverie about the Internet, Google, and the Tower of Babel

The Internet in its current configuration started in the 1970s as an American Ministry of Defense project designed to create communication networks that could operate in emergencies. In GR terms, one could describe the Internet as a "group without a leader" system, whereby the data are transferred between computers (the group) without depending on any specific computer (the leader) to protect the network from paralysis during a strike against it.

The first recorded group to be without a leader is to be found in the biblical story of the Tower of Babel, on which Bion is quoted above. Both Babel and Google originated from anxiety, both have a grandiose nature which guards against such anxiety, and both use reaction formation to deny individual differences. For example, the Internet website Facebook is a yearbook type template in which each page and face look almost identical in their appearance; Google is an authoritative traffic officer endlessly patrolling cyberspace.

When it comes to the Tower of Babel, Genesis 11: 4 recounts its origin: "Let us build a city and a tower, whose top may reach unto heaven; and let us make us a name, lest we be scattered abroad upon the face of the whole earth".

The similarity between the words "Babel" and "Google" makes one pause and think. In Hebrew, the two words almost rhyme and are built on the same rhythm: Babel with its repetition of the second letter of the Hebrew alphabet, and Google, with its alliterative repetition of the third letter of the Hebrew alphabet. The suffix "el", with which both words end in Hebrew, means God (Figure 2.1).

The English term Google stems from word play on the mathematical term Googol, which is represented as 1 followed by 100 zeros (Figure 2.2). Moreover, the double zero is a mathematical symbol for infinity. Google is a project no less ambitious than the Tower of Babel. It translates languages and texts from any language and culture into any other language and culture. The vision of a world that speaks one language is coming ever closer to fulfilment. It is for good reason that Michio Kaku, in his book *Physics of the Future*, claimed that, by the end of the twenty-first century, humanity would possess the powers of the mythological gods whom it had once worshipped. In Hebrew, Babel is "Bab" "El", meaning the "Gate of God", expressing the human desire to cross forbidden boundaries, to touch the sky.

If you will it, it is no dream (Herzl, 1902)

Incidentally, God's interpretation of the attack on authority was also connected with Babel, but this time there is a different meaning in the Hebrew: bavel=balal=confound: "Therefore is the name of it called Babel; because the Lord did there confound the language of all the

Figure 2.1. The similarity between the words Babel and Google in Hebrew.

Figure 2.2 Googol:
10000000000000000000000000000000000000000000000000000000000000000000000000000000
000000000000000000000000000000.

earth: and from thence did the Lord scatter them abroad upon the face of all the earth" (Genesis 1:9).

There is always a thin line between breakthrough visions ("If you will it, it is no dream") to grandiose aspirations (e.g., the myth of the "Tree of the Knowledge"). Internet projects and the Internet as a whole are connected to knowledge (e.g., "Distance Learning", "School of the Future") and are loaded with aspirations and expectations. Therefore, they might carry such tensions constantly.

The current case study about a distance-learning course may demonstrate how an academic course, one of many in the students' curriculum, came into a ground fertile for expectations, projections, disappointments, and others that were not necessarily connected inherently to its individual core and nature.

Methodology

The "primary task" of the course as defined by the team and presented to the students in the course syllabus was: to research, via experiential learning processes, at the personal, group and organisational levels, contemporary issues in management with an emphasis on the world of WEB 2.0.

The course took place over a fifteen-week academic semester with the participation of approximately fifty students in the MBA programme at the School of Business Administration at the College of Management Academic Studies (COMAS) in Rishon LeZion, Israel. With some 5,000 students, a third of whom are at the graduate level, the COMAS School of Business Administration is the largest in Israel.

The course in its entirety was taught by means of a-synchronous distance learning on a website open to the public through a system of purpose-built blogs. The staff and students did not meet face-to-face at all during the course and all interaction connected with the course took place on its website.

The website was constructed in such a way that each student had his or her own personal blog through which the course could take place. At first, the blogs were empty; not even the students' names appeared. Over time, a blog could be populated with content such as photographs and biographical information about the blog's author, and, of course, posts and comments on posts by other course participants. The course faculty also had a personal blog in which they posted information about the duration of the semester in relation to the frameworks and boundaries of the course, but primarily about responses to processes occurring during the course. Photographs of all the course participants were displayed on the website's home page and clicking on the photographs gave access to each individual blog. The students' weekly task appeared on the task page. For the most part, the tasks combined experience, theoretical analysis, and personal replication. All the written tasks were published openly as posts on the students' blogs. The students were allowed to use the system freely to write posts and other comments not pertaining to course tasks. In total, about 1,500 posts were written during the course, 300 of which were "root-posts", while 1,200 were "comment-posts".

The course was divided into a number of stages, which included various levels of orientation: personal, group, organisational, and social. In the first stage, the students primarily defined their "blog identity" and got to know each other, the technology, and the structure of the course. In the second stage, much as in the opening plenary of the Organisational Event in GRCs, students conducted a dialogue on points of mutual interest while trying to influence fellow students and recruit them to interest groups. In the third stage, the established groups promoted the projects they had chosen. The groups were asked to choose a social entrepreneurship project that could be completed during the time frame of the semester. This was the implementation stage in which the students worked as virtual teams within the temporary learning organisation.

Using the blogging format enabled faculty and participants to continually document manifest activities during and after the course. During the course, emotions and thoughts that came up in connection with the course were documented, and these served also as research tools. The staff used field-notes, writing qualitative observations on what was taking place during the study, combining participant observations and analysis. This, of course, is an important aspect of case study research (Eisenhardt, 1989).

Research questions

A delineation of the method followed and the background to the course process led to a deeper examination of the two central research questions that arose, and these were identified and selected from a range of fields. As stated above, the first relates to the issue of the conditions that enable or delay learning. The second relates to learning cultures that enable or delay the learning process.

Conditions for learning: creating a "good enough" container

Planning the course required the effort to preserve the design principles for GRCs in which the boundaries of space, time, and task were defined and set in order to enable free space and potential within those boundaries.

The students were given a timetable for their tasks at the beginning of the course. The course website served as the operating space, while each student's blog constituted their personal private space. An Internet site was chosen which was open to the general public, enabling observation and participation by external users, as in any other Internet space.

The course staff containment function required far more operational intervention than is usual for GRC frameworks or regular academic courses, even when it came to the technical support level. The students and the course system itself all needed extensive technical and non-technical support. The participants, staff and students alike, were required to read and process an enormous amount of information, which necessitated far more time than had been estimated and planned for at the outset of the course. Positive student feedback questionnaires at the end of the course regarding staff support for the students gave the impression that a "good enough" container had been created. However, it must be acknowledged that this achievement came about only with great effort and it is doubtful whether such a commitment would have been undertaken had the cost been realised in advance.

The staff sometimes wished they could revert to the safe role of "lecturer", to teach, to impart knowledge, to direct, to suggest solutions, and, particularly in view of the complaints and demands they received from the students, to provide concrete guidance. This is a survivalist compulsion, an immediate gratification of desire, as there is no certainty that any kind of result would be achieved by the end of the course. Resolution of the conflict was connected to certain "mantras" that the staff transmitted to the students. These mantras were aimed at calming the anxieties of both students and staff, and at creating trust in the process. For example, a message that appeared on the staff blog post read as follows:

> "Apparently there will be no classroom lectures in the second half of the course, so there will not be anybody to help us make sense of things. The basic assumption of the course is that the responsibility for learning is first and foremost up to the individual and, of course, the wider learning community. Knowledge is not in the hands of the course staff, but in the hands of 50 members of the community who know how to work. We all lead teams every day. We manage projects and learn new things, whether in a large organisation or just organising lunch or bath time for the kids. All these activities demand motivation, as well as a certain amount of learning, operating and motivating people. Of course, at the end of every task we could ask ourselves: Was it enjoyable? Did I benefit from it? Did I learn something new? Is there any point in doing it again? Do I have the enthusiasm? Or, perhaps: Is there something I should change? In short, here as well, just as in the outside world, it is all up to us."

It should be noted that, in this context, the relationship between faculty and students during this virtual course, which did not include a single face-to-face meeting, was a great deal more personal and intimate than is usual in regular academic courses.

The unique situation presented by the course, and the fact that the set tasks did not correspond to the framework and resources of a regular academic course, undermined the clear boundaries that characterise a lecturer's conventional work. Thus, it would appear that, even while the staff managed to create a satisfactory container for the students, as lecturers they lacked the wherewithal to deal with the physical and emotional needs arising from the course. The staff members were exhausted by the end of the course. They realised that they had undergone a powerful and unique experience. They also felt that significant events had taken place during the process, but, at the same time, they found it difficult to formulate what they had learnt, or even exactly what the students themselves had learnt. The systemic conclusion was that, without a fundamental change in the managerial infrastructure and behaviour of educational institutions, and a fundamental change in their ability to provide a "good enough" container for their employees in the changing process, the educational system would remain far behind the Internet revolution because of the inability or unwillingness of personnel to become a part of the revolutionary change in working habits.

Different cultures:
different interpretations of the primary task

"Learning from experience and the experience of learning—can these two co-exist in an academic setting?" This headline was the title of a paper presented at the previous Belgirate conference by another team from the same college (Kaplan et al., 2012). It elaborated on the complexity of operating an experiential learning process in the context of two different sub-cultures of learning, which traditionally suggest a different interpretation of the primary task.

The current distance-learning course also found itself facing such complexities. As in the previous case, the complexity was evident in the meeting between the learning culture of "business administration students" with the "systemic-psychoanalytic" learning culture of group relations. Without a doubt, the first is less tolerant of the vague; the culture of "business administration students" tends to clarify and measure tasks. It encourages and values analytic and rational processes, expects a high measure of certainty, and expects that the academic conversion process will render each academic course a work tool for its participants, preferably "tomorrow morning at the office".

In the current climate, an academic degree has become a major prerequisite for securing a job and gaining promotion, despite the fact that there is no direct connection between the content of studies and its contribution to a student's internal development in daily tasks that the graduate experiences in the workplace. It would appear that many students project their yearnings and disappointments on to their studies and the institution at which they studied. Thus, they display regressive tendencies characterised by what Bion called basic assumption dependency (Bion, 1961). The ability of the members of the group to move away from such a regressive position is, in itself, an important experiential learning process. One student expressed this movement well:

"To tell the truth, after sitting on this for a while and thinking about what I wanted to write in order to complete the assignment, I finally understood that any criticism should be first and foremost criticism of myself! It's me who is stuck in the paradigm! Since when was the academy an institution that digested educational content for me, expecting me to simply learn it by rote? Do we influence our own studies or, like so many before us, do we listen a lot but say little? Can one learn only from the lecturer, or can we learn from all the members of the class?"

The difficulty in adapting to a different style of learning, in which knowledge is not imparted by the lecturer to the students, but has to be created by the students themselves, contradicted the known learning patterns of students in academia and, thus, engendered questions and resistance. At the outset of the course, the staff identified, among almost all members of the team, enthusiasm and the desire to try out a new style of learning, but, as the course progressed, particularly towards the middle, frustrations increased and the voices of discontent were increasingly audible. The connections fell into place only towards the end of the course:

"At first I didn't understand why the course was called 'Issues in Management' and how this was connected to Facebook . . . But today, at the end of the course, after I have spent so long trying to understand my position in a virtual task team and how each person on his own and all the members of the team together achieve one goal, the connection between the title of the course and the things I have learned during the semester is clear."

Parallel to the tension and synergy that existed throughout the course between academic learning culture and the experiential learning culture of the GR, there was also tension and synergy between the "academic learning culture" and the "Internet culture". Traditional academic learning is based on the passive transfer of knowledge from the lecturer to the student, mostly in frontal lectures. The Internet culture, on the other hand, is pluralistic and based on knowledge created by its users that is democratically open and available to all. Dohn (2009) maintains that the two cultures have different perceptions of the essence of knowledge and ability. Academic instruction is built on the metaphor of "acquisition of knowledge" and competition to do with "who knows more", while Web 2.0 is built on metaphors of sharing knowledge, links, and experience. The element of competition exists on the Internet as well, but it focuses on the question of who will be read and copied by more people. In other words, jealousy, rather than envy, is at play.

In the two comparisons noted above, the "academic learning culture" was positioned against other cultures such as the "experiential learning culture" of GR or the "Internet culture". It seems that both of the latter two cultures are based on a potential space located between concrete reality and imagination. That space is characterised by vagueness and has a chaotic, dreamlike structure where the wider picture appears for an instant and disappears as quickly. It is based on the GR approach to the unconscious at the individual, group, and societal levels, and in the Internet world in the infinite dimensions of cyberspace.

Traditional pedagogic–educational practice favours an individualistic, objectivist approach in which learning is viewed as the student's "acquisition" of ownership of knowledge and capabilities, which will serve him or her in some external situation. Even in a team learning framework in the education system, such as preparing for examinations in a team, the final goal focuses on the individual and his or her individual achievements. Web 2.0 learning, on the other hand, is characterised by co-operation. The personal motivation is naturally prominent here as well, but its products contain the element of the "sum being greater than its parts". This trait is, incidentally, similar to the organisational reality in which the actions of individuals create an organisational product, whose success depends on the synergy between individuals and teams. For example, the creation of 300 root-posts by students was equivalent to traditional individual assignments submitted by students in academic courses, but the additional 1,200 comment-posts were a unique contribution of the social learning system based on Web 2.0 culture, which contributed to the "sum".

The course faculty's initial assumption, which turned out to be mistaken, was that most college students live the Internet culture and would, therefore, be connected to the staff practice and its spirit. In retrospect, it turned out that only a minority of students at that particular time were active in the participatory Internet culture, and that even those who were participating found it difficult to see it as a learning tool. There were two reasons for this. First, it appears that far fewer people than is assumed, including young people, are in fact active and involved in interactive cyberspace. For example, despite the fact that Israel was recently ranked highest in the world in the number of smartphones per capita, only a minority make full use of their capabilities. Thus, it quickly became clear to the staff that many of the students were not at all familiar with web culture. The second cause was the competition between cultures and the context of the academic learning culture, as, from the moment digital media became part of the context of an academic course, it was the academic learning culture that took over. Academic learning culture is individualistic in nature and it was this that dictated the definition of the learning task and blocked the creation of authentic participation. Representation of the conflict between the cultures can be illustrated by the repeated arguments of one student who complained throughout the course that no learning process was taking place. The student expressed bitterness and anger and demanded answers from the staff. His complaints are a prominent expression of standard academic perceptions of the meaning of learning, which characterised the frequent claims of GRC participants:

"I didn't learn anything or acquire any knowledge beyond what I already knew and I didn't have to contend with unfamiliar new material. . . . During the course I found myself presenting examples and using knowledge from other courses and displaying writing skills and tolerance for other opinions. But is the purpose of the course to test knowledge acquired in the past or is it to enrich me with new knowledge? . . . The stated aims of the course include 'learning about issues arising from experience' and 'active learning, through personal and group experience, about contemporary issues in management, especially in the Internet era'. However, there is room for academic instruction and direction of the experiential process through increased academic engagement with the course advisers, not just through words of encouragement and general statements, but by their providing references – as an academic course should be taught . . ."

The student's statements represent the perception of learning as "acquisition of knowledge". The word "acquisition", which stems from the world of consumption, is not coincidental in this context. It relates to the perception of many of today's students that payment for studies buys them the right to receive knowledge passively, almost without their investing any effort. The student's reaction suggests that he expected the lecturer to bear full responsibility for his learning and insight.

In several of their posts, the lecturers chose to express their perceptions of the meaning of learning. For example, the following message they wrote related to academic learning culture and aimed to create an understanding among the students that elements of the course could be found in all their studies and in their lives in general:

> "We must recognise, with a certain degree of embarrassment, that we forget close to 100% of the content of what we have studied over all our years in school and university. If the goal of academic learning is the acquisition of knowledge, this would suggest the complete failure of the system. However, if we recognise that the content of learning is a motivational factor for experiential learning, and not necessarily the aim itself, we can then perhaps claim, somewhat provocatively, that it would be better if most of the content were wiped from our memory to make way for further experiential learning in the future. Managers make many decisions based on their reservoir of experience. They do this spontaneously, with no time to go back to their books. In any event, they would be unlikely to find the correct answers there, as every issue is specific to its particular context. Acquisition of knowledge without engaged learning is futile, so during our business administration studies we must experience both theory and practice. We must also recognise that we all need a structured and rational anchor for learning to occur. "Content" is therefore a good excuse for experiential learning. But, without experience and practice, it has no intrinsic value."

Is this about "right or wrong" information transmitted to the students? Not necessarily. These are the lecturers' associations and beliefs about their philosophy of teaching and learning. It is a transparent statement on their subjective perceptions, much like the interpretations or interventions by staff in GR workshops.

The academic course discussed here, and the lecturers as its managers, lie on the boundary between these different learning cultures:

1. The academic learning culture of acquisition of knowledge;
2. The GR culture of learning from experience;
3. The capitalist market culture of business administration that examines the value of learning;
4. The participatory Web 2.0 learning culture.

The "Catch 22" of the "Learning from Experience"

> There was only one catch and that was Catch-22, which specified that
> a concern for one's safety in the face of dangers that were real and
> immediate was the process of a rational mind. Orr was crazy and
> could be grounded. All he had to do was ask; and as soon as he did,
> he would no longer be crazy and would have to fly more missions. Orr
> would be crazy to fly more missions and sane if he didn't, but if he
> were sane he had to fly them . . . (Heller, 1961)

Throughout the course, the complaining student mentioned above
was a prominent voice. One of the examples he used in making his
point objecting to the course was Hans Christian Andersen's fable *The
Emperor's New Clothes*. The familiar tale tells of two swindlers who
promised the emperor, who was exceedingly fond of new clothes, that
they could weave him a royal cloth that was invisible to fools and
could be seen only by wise men. A cynic could say that, in terms of
GR, this is the primary task: "You will acquire skills enabling you to
see unconscious processes that simple folk won't be able to see, and if
they say the Emperor is naked they will simply be revealed as fools
living in the darkness of their unconscious". In the tale, the people all
praised the emperor's magnificent new clothes until a small child
shouted out that the Emperor "hasn't got anything on" and the
charade collapsed.

Throughout the course, the lecturers looked at themselves in the
mirror over and over again to see whether "they still had their clothes
on". In frontal courses, lecturers have the confidence, supposedly, that
they are teaching the students "something", but in this special course,
their confidence was often undermined. It is important to note that, in
contrast to the protesting voice of that particular student, there were
many students who defended this new form of learning, and without
a doubt, traditional learning methods are today also the subject of
severe criticism. So where is the catch? Why do so many find the GR
learning from experience approach so difficult to digest? Perhaps the
answer lies in the theory itself. The GR approach, which encourages
the design of processes with no content, no memory, and no desire,
creates a vagueness and uncertainty that engenders anxiety. A strong
group with strong faith is required in order to survive in such conditions of anxiety, because anxiety causes regression in group behaviour
and leads to work being executed under basic assumptions that

reduce openness, associativity, creativity, and freedom of thought. This is a classic "Catch 22": structure without content may encourage learning from experience, but the anxiety that results from such a structure creates a regression that damages the group's willingness to devote itself to an experiential process. The introduction of structured content into the process reduces anxiety and increases certainty, but doing so harms opportunities for experiential learning . . .

The Internet WEB 2.0 world could also be examined in the light of the terminology of *Catch 22*, in the tension between "virtual distance" and "human touch". It was felt that this could be further investigated in future research.

References

Bion, W. R. (1961). *Experiences in Groups and Other Papers*. New York: Basic Books.

Bion, W. R. (1985). *All My Sins Remembered: Another Part of a Life*. Abingdon: Fleetwood Press.

Dohn, N. B. (2009). Web 2.0: inherent tensions and evident challenges for education. *Computer-Supported Collaborative Learning, 4*: 343–363.

Eisenhardt, K. M. (1989). Building theories from case study research. *Academy of Management Review, 14*(4): 532–550.

Freud, S. (with Breuer, J.) (1895d). *Studies on Hysteria. S. E., 2*. London: Hogarth.

Heller, J. (1961). *Catch 22*. New York: Simon & Schuster.

Herzl, T. (1960). *Old New Land (Altneuland)*. New York: M. Wiener-Herzl Press, 1987.

Kaku, M. (2011). *Physics of the Future: How Science Will Shape Human Destiny and Our Daily Lives by the Year 2100*. New York: Anchor Books.

Kaplan, O., Levy, J., Nutkevitch, A., & Tsadok, M. (2012). Learning from experience and the experience of learning in an academic setting. In: E. Aram & A. Nutkevitch (Eds.), *Group Relations Conferences: Tradition, Creativity, and Succession in the Global Group Relations Network* (pp. 113–132). London: Karnac.

Senor, D., & Singer, S. (2009). *Start-up Nation: The Story of Israel's Economic Miracle*. New York: Twelve.

Winnicott, D. W. (1953). Transitional objects and transitional phenomena. *International Journal of Psychoanalysis, 34*: 89–97.

CHAPTER THREE

Group relations work in contexts of complexity and transition

*Joan Roma i Vergés, David Sierra Lozano,
Jaume Benavent i Guardia, and Sandra Carrau Pascual*

Purpose of this chapter

The purpose of this chapter is to describe the effects we believe group relations (GR) work, including experiential conferences and consultancy interventions, has had on an organisation in Catalonia in transition that was established to care for the mentally ill. Although this chapter refers to one organisation, we consider this work paradigmatic of the transition work that can be carried out from a GR perspective and of the approach that the Innova Institute undertakes with other organisations. We describe additional methodologies based on systemic approaches that we used that can be complementary to, and coherent with, the more traditional GR methodologies. These have proved effective in achieving the purpose that the members of the organisation set for themselves.

Although the account might seem a continuous process of consultancy on a regular basis, what is presented in this chapter reflects a series of discrete events over eight years, including the participation of key managers in open events organised by the Innova Institute, as well as timely consultation interventions within the organisation and the combined use of different systemic perspectives. We refer to this as "a middle type of consultation" process built upon what we call Organisational Transnovation®. We begin by describing the organisation itself, explore the four dimensions of our "organisational transnovation approach", the GR and related activities, and what we believe were some of their impacts. We conclude with our reflections on GR methodology and applications and our own transition and learning during the time of our involvement.

The organisation

Since 2004, we have worked with an organisation (referred to in this chapter as the Association), founded at the end of the 1970s by the mother of two children who suffered from mental illness in order to ensure that they were properly cared for. At that time in Catalonia, before the end of Franco's dictatorship, there were no residential care services of the kind developed by the Association.

At that time, the mother assumed the presidency of the board and became the managing director. The Association began life with a bare-bones structure of care professionals, mainly psychologists, who operated under the management of the founder; in line with the criteria established by a family group, they provided ongoing residential care for both young people and adults. Initially, the only staff were the founder and a psychiatrist. After several months, they incorporated other professional staff (mainly psychologists) with the core philosophy that those receiving care could also be trained and supported to provide care.

In the forty years since its inception, the Association has grown dramatically. It currently employs eighty-eight workers. According to its care philosophy, thirty-five of the staff (almost 40%) self-identify as having a mental illness. The Association provides services to approximately 100–125 users per year and now boasts three residential centres, eleven therapeutic apartments, and a special work centre (SWC). It also provides a diverse range of services including: pre-employment, family assistance, a social activities club, community rehabilitation, voluntary work, psychological counselling, and social work. In its current configuration and purpose, the Association not only works to improve the living conditions of users, integrating them into society and systems of production, but also to fight the stereotypes and prejudices that isolate people with mental illnesses from their communities.

The Association began its work with Innova Institute after the new CEO attended one of our international GR conferences. He was engaged in a transition in which the founder had left, leaving the Association to face significant financial and strategic challenges. We worked with the new director, provided GR learning for senior managers, and included managers in open Innova conferences. During those eight years, the Association underwent a significant transformation.

The Organisational Transnovation® framework

The Organisational Transnovation® methodology integrates Innova's research and experience in accompanying many organisations and professionals in their transitions and transformations. Our interpretation of the "GR perspective and practice" involves four dimensions of Organisational Transnovation®, each carrying important weight. We believe that organisations are complex realities that should be addressed through four interrelated dimensions in order to support the transformation process. By addressing these four dimensions, we can support the organisation to continue to carry out services and products during its transition. These dimensions include the psycho-social, the techno-structural, the political, and the existential.

In other words, we analyse the relationship between organisational and management forms and the unconscious dynamics, their influence on each other, and the results that are generated. We also incorporate the political dimension, which we understand as the distribution of power and mechanisms of influence, together with the existential dimension that deals with the meaning of the organisation and the work of its members now and in the future—the intangibles that enable members to overcome temporary difficulties and persevere beyond the present realities.

We understand these dimensions as "prisms" that enable and enrich perception and comprehension and make available new repertoires of behaviour. In this way, the same phenomenon can be understood in complementary and dialectical ways from these diverse dimensions.

Our experience, from sharing seminars with other consultants from all over the world, shows us that there are different conceptions and practices regarding what we have called the "GR perspective and practice". For many consultants, there is a greater weight given to the psychic component, while, for others, more focus is placed on the technical facet. On occasion, the political and the existential dimensions are present but tend to receive less attention. Using these four dimensions equally to inform our own observations and data from the management team and family members of the Association, we have seen important changes over the time of the transition process in which we were engaged.

Psychosocial dimension

The psychosocial dimension encompasses relationships, social needs, group dynamics, emotions, and image-affective representations, as well as the exercising of roles, both consciously and unconsciously. In sole founder-run organisations, we have observed a natural tendency over time to adopt a centripetal approach that is a more inward view, especially when they are originally family-owned. It would be the equivalent in the individual to shutting oneself within the intrapsychic world. The Association, in its initial phases, was no exception. This lack of openness to external influence was described by some of its managers as a "closed plot", a "building with barred windows", or an "ancient castle with very high towers where nobody came out".

Consistent with Miller and Gwyne (1972, p. 73), we, too, have noted that in mental health residential care institutions the service-users receive projective identifications of rejection as "non-participants or non-contributors in society". In other words, they are considered "defective", "a shame in their career", or "objects of contempt" (in Honneth's terms, 2011). This barrage of negative projective identifications by members of society who consider themselves 'free' from mental illness contributes even further to inwardness, to dependent behaviour and, quite easily, to internal conflict between service users and staff.

Added to this, the founding director and mother was seen as a caring but terrible mother who, in exchange for security, demanded the strict fulfilment of her wishes and orders. None the less, when she left, this was experienced as very difficult. As one manager remarked, her leaving was experienced with "real terror, faced with the search for autonomy; although we knew where we were headed, as a group, we felt like abandoned children". During the period immediately following her departure, interdepartmental criticism increased and working together became increasingly complicated and fraught.

Since her departure, the Association has demonstrated greater openness towards outside influences. Within the Association, there has been greater fluidity of communication and an increase in the number of interdepartmental projects. The "castle" has now become a "more welcoming space with town houses". The boys and girls (as the previous director referred to the users, as if it were a school) have gone on to assume different roles according to the resource or service that they use. Likewise, the professionals have assumed greater autonomy and can receive training outside the institution.

The new director had a dream halfway through our consulting work, which we deemed significant: "I dreamt that the Association building is on fire but that we manage to get everybody out unharmed, with just the structure of the building remaining but then rebuilding everything inside in a different way". In other words, maintaining the boundaries but altering all the interior contents.

Techno-structural dimension

The techno-structural dimension refers to those elements that support the process of transformation as inputs and outputs, technology, knowledge, organisational structure, management models, ways of working, resources, the boundaries of space and time, and how their interactions effect the execution of the primary task.

The initial primary task of the Association was care orientated, aimed at maintaining the stability and protection of users, who were seen as patients or disabled persons to be protected or controlled. In more recent years, the task has shifted from a care orientation to one that promotes autonomy. "We moved on from an inward-looking mental hospital model to rehabilitation and assisting patients to develop a life itinerary", remarked one of the managers.

In the earlier years, the prevailing mode of treatment was primarily individual psychotherapy. However, by failing to incorporate the systemic environment of users, this treatment tended to further isolate already isolated residents or users from their families. Family members were seen as a hindrance in the rehabilitation process. Over the course of the transition, more group work and more systemic interventions were regularly used to enhance social networks and involve family members.

During the time of transition, users became "members" who could make use of a range of services. Also in the transition, the workshop went from being a point of shelter to an SWC where members were also treated as workers. The SWC increased its commercial services and now includes converted paper products, printing and binding services, painting, the sale of office material, and a courier service. The selection criteria for participation in the workshop has shifted from demonstrating the need for shelter to being able to show a sufficient degree of capacity to carry out the work.

There has also been an increase in the number of programmes adapted to different users and families, with access to resources becoming considerably more integrated and interconnected. Before, users could only be assigned to one specific resource.

Political dimension

The political dimension refers to aspects of power, its distribution and exercise, mechanisms of influence, relations with authority, both formal and informal, alliances and agendas, both manifest and hidden.

The new director explained that in the past "the members of the board of directors were all appointed directly by the director so that management would do as she wanted". Furthermore, the participation of parents as political subjects in the governing bodies of the Association was low. Now, the board has a more powerful political and appropriate governance role, both internally and externally (in respect of other associations and the federation), and is separate from the technical management.

By virtue of their expert status, the psychologists were, initially, unconsciously attributed a position of power by users' relatives, which meant that the latter did not participate in the rehabilitation plan of their relatives or siblings. The families gradually began to assume more of a leading role, including siblings, who had initially been criticised for their scarce participation. Relatives are now more involved in the therapeutic process, where meetings are no longer individual but, rather, held in groups, with an exchange of impressions on the rehabilitation plan to be followed.

In the initial phase of the organisation, the founding director did make some initial contact with the community and the environment around the Association, but the pervasive institutional isolation resulted in increased dependence on external authorities with very few opportunities for influence or interdependence.

The process of diversifying resource mobilisation and services over time has enabled the Association to achieve greater external recognition and obtain more resources. It has proved possible to interconnect the Association and society through programmes now open to the community.

The creation of co-ordinators was a step that generated considerable uncertainty. From the perspective of some co-ordinators, the professional staff members overstep their boundaries in terms of initiative, which obliges the co-ordinators to be very clear about their own role and distinct contribution. These new roles and discussions about them were, at times, difficult, but these have been helpful to the co-ordinators and psychologists in further clarifying their different and important roles and contributions.

Existential dimension

The existential dimension includes those aspects that touch upon the sense of the organisation's existence, its reason to be in society and the world. It is connected further to the sense that individuals are given and have in terms of their belonging to the organisation.

The transition involved a complex process of redefining the organisational purpose and *raison d'être* of the Association. If this process had followed its own course, as one of the managers remarked, "the disappearance of the institution was on the cards". The degree of deconstruction involved in altering the identity model meant that it was necessary to create a set of favourable conditions that were much more sophisticated and complex, with a broader time horizon.

The transition, as a member of the organisation said, meant the organisation went from the "school model" where "mathematics, natural sciences, physical education, and crafts were taught" to a "purpose geared towards rehabilitation and integration in daily and community life". This changed the role of the various stakeholders and the meaning of their participation in the institution. Generally speaking, they were able to tackle more consciously the tension between two models or visions of the world: freedom and autonomy on the one side, and the care, maintenance, and dependence of the patient on the other.

Specifically, the families were also able to innovate in the sense of contributing to the organisation in a more participative manner and enhancing their role as relatives of a person with a mental illness.

Meanwhile, for the professional team, the transition involved reorientating their engagement towards patients as users and towards their relatives instead of primarily working to obey or please the figure of authority (the former director).

These changes during the transition have boosted enthusiasm and commitment in respect to organisational projects and how they are carried out. An example of this is the growing number of projects arising from the collaboration between professionals from a variety of areas. As one of the managers stated, "Now everybody knows what task they have to perform. There is a greater workload, but at the same time more awareness and commitment. For instance, the turnover of users and colleagues has decreased since the initial phase."

GR methods and complementary systemic methodologies in transitional processes

Members of the Association staff participated in the following GR and complementary activities from 2004 to 2012.

More traditional GR events

1   The new CEO attended Innova's International experiential conference "Leadership, Innovation and Management—Experiences in Transformation" in 2004. Then all of the eight senior managers from the different service areas also attended over that eight-year period.
2.   Most of the managers were involved in the open "Leadership In Action" events (our method for role analysis and application) in small groups once a month, from 2006 to 2012.

3. Many staff—psychologists, educators, social workers, and managers of the organisation—participated in 2007 in "State of the System Events" to explore the conscious and unconscious dynamics aroused by the transition.

4. Many staff participated in open "U-Turn events" (our version of the Listening Post, developed with Erika Stern) in order to explore and analyse the broader environment from 2008 to 2012.

Complementary systemic methodologies

For organisations that require a more concerted effort for building a shared vision and strategy for change, as was the case in the Association, or those that require a new organisational design, we develop what we call generative methodologies (ones that do not foreclose the meaning that might be discovered) and that share the main values of a GR approach. We used the following with the Association.

1. In 2009, fifty members participated in a "Prospective Conference" and "Multiple Dialogues" meeting.

2. In 2011, forty technician professionals from various departments of the Association attended a two-day work session together with twelve workers from the SWC, conceived as customers in a session called "Systemic Contributions Methodology" process.

We believe, further, that these other methodologies could be used effectively with the Association because of the GR work that had been done previously with many members, which then permeated the institution, particularly through the work of its managers. Leadership and containment were key for the success of the applications.

Potential impacts of the work

As we know, it is not easy to establish a direct causal relationship between GR activities, other systemic approaches, and what results in individuals and the organisation. This is, in part, related to our recognition of the complex systemic factors that effect change. Second, individual and organisational change is deeply effected by the ways in which authority is taken up by leaders and staff. Third, it is also quite difficult to attribute a positive organisational transition over time to specific consultants' interventions.

We also believe that the search to understand "our influence" on the Association and our desire for positive outcomes could arise from a potentially narcissistic and omnipotent position. Hence, we might be inclined to attribute organisational improvement to our interventions and activities when, in fact, we have most probably contributed only partially, together with other stakeholders of the organisation. It is with these provisos that we describe how we think GR interventions and those from other systemic perspectives contributed to a positive transition for the Association.

Enhanced capacity to lead

The CEO recalled his first conference experience:

> "Personally I have made a change. If I had not done internal work with myself, I would still be blaming everybody for everything that is happening. Suddenly I discovered the systemic organisational dimension. Having unenthusiastically accepted the position of director, I discovered the meaning of my work and the reason why I wanted to carry on doing what I was doing. I discovered the difference between knowing about something and what it was to know through experience. Now I am more aware of my own processes and projections towards others and those of others towards me. I discovered the management of the role and the use of boundaries. Now I have a clearer and wider vision. It was also a difficult time since my internal wardrobe became disorganised and it took me some time to get it reorganised."

This declaration sums up rather well the individual process that the CEO experienced in his first GR Conference, both as a person and in terms of his role. It encompasses some of the main themes that GR offers in the experiential conferences. Having gained this understanding, the CEO was more able to assume his authority and work with the unconscious institutional dimension.

Enhanced role autonomy

We identified the paralysis and collective terror caused by the loss of the authority figure which prompted the transition. At the same time, this guiding figure still remained influential from a distance, instilling even more terror and the feeling of vulnerability.

This dynamic manifested itself clearly during the exploration of the "state of the system" sessions that took place over the course of a year in different groups. In sessions of great tension, the groups, and with them the institution, gradually assumed the capacity for more role differentiation and autonomy among themselves and between themselves and the past director. This further created the conditions for differentiating the roles between co-ordinators, service providers, and users.

From this point onward, the co-ordinators or managers had the opportunity to participate in successive experiential conferences and in the leadership in action sessions. The organisation became more professional, as demonstrated in the acquisition of specialised professional training, the use of managerial staff to oversee economic matters, and more structured work meetings. These changes occurred gradually, as permitted by the internal process of the Association, in such a way as to safeguard against any possible destabilisation to its users.

The staff members of the Association were invited to "U-Turn sessions" where they analysed the experience of the broader external environment together with other participants from other organisations. Members of the Association stopped regarding the environment as something threatening or contemptuous. The professional members of staff began to participate in open forums, in fund-raising activities, and in collective projects with other institutions.

Strengthened management functions

Over this time, a managerial team was progressively consolidated. As it discovered its identity and task within the Association, it also incorporated in its sessions the "analysis of the state of the system" in order to identify how the unconscious dynamics of the institution were represented.

During this period, a new organisation began to take shape and a new vision and organisational identity were gradually formed. This generated notable tensions with the members who were most attached to the previous dynamics and roles. The awareness that the Association was altering the initial psychic contract led a few members to leave the organisation on their own; others discovered that they could remain in the organisation but now wished to be in less demanding posts.

Clearer role differentiation and alignment

The prospective conference methodology is based on different approaches coming from Emery and Trist, Rainman and Lippit, Ackoff, Weisbord, and others. The two-day conference occurred in 2009 with approximately fifty participants representing a range of stakeholders (managers, technicians, users, external agents, partner institutions, suppliers, and municipal institutions). This group, coming from different perspectives, analysed together the "shared vision of the desired future of the institution" through images of the past, present, and future in order to obtain a common foundation and to develop strategic plans.

One week before the prospective conference, following the methodology, we conducted an activity that we call "multiple dialogues", to which representatives of the various stakeholders of the Association were invited. While the conference itself focused on a single question, the convergence of shared meaning, along with a set of strategic lines of action, the "multiple dialogues" promoted divergence regarding important issues for the institution. This event is designed to stimulate the exchange of different visions, the acceptance of rejection, trial and error, the possibility of chaos and disorder, before putting things in order again through the creation of a new shared meaning in the prospective conference.

Both events brought about, for the first time, the visualisation in one room for the stakeholders of the Association—the users, family, professionals, other staff members, and managers. Seeing these important stakeholders and engaging with them, they were able to collectively envision their future direction. Acknowledging each other through dialogue, they took the first step in the process of multilateral influence and experienced the synergistic action that cumulative energy can produce, in which the whole is greater than the sum of parts.

They were able to explore what differentiated them from each other and could begin to legitimately assume their own role in relation to these differences while strengthening the elements that give meaning to what they shared together. These dialogues facilitated the emergence of new projects and lines of action. In short, it was possible to connect the political dimension to the existential one. From the psychosocial dimension, this represented the stimulation of a basic assumption of pairing in the sense that it created a climate of collaboration and hope for the future and renewed enthusiasm and commitment for the organisational project as a whole.

In particular, the family members of users strengthened their role as influential agents in the rehabilitation work, while the care professionals were able to incorporate the family members into this process, narrowing the traditional gap between the two groups. The clarity and differentiation of roles facilitated the reintrojection of the negative projections in such a way that everyone could begin to assume their own authority. Meanwhile, the users were also able to assume their authority and contribute to the process, taking into account the limits that their illness imposed.

Improved organisational functioning

The systemic contributions methodology is an organisational perspective-in-action and is directed towards the improvement of organisational functioning as a whole. It is specifically directed towards efficiency in work interactions between the various parts of the organisation or network of roles interconnected by mutual contributions and in a continuous process of accommodation. It incorporates several systemic approaches such as the socio-technical approach (Emery, Trist), the soft systems methodology (Checkland), the human work systems (Hoebeke) approach and the model of viable systems (Beer), along with perspectives developed through the science of complexity.

This event made it possible for those present to visualise the organisational network and enabled the emergence of techno-structural points of friction that posed an obstacle to the interdependence of linked processes and functions. One of the main benefits of this intervention was better linking and co-ordination between the various organisational areas. The members were able to gain awareness of the complexity of their daily activities and connect the meaning of their own task to the meaning of the tasks of others. More clarity made for more understanding regarding task completion for themselves as well as others. As a result of this event, temporary and self-regulating work groups were created that continued to meet with a view to reaching agreements and putting improvement plans in place.

Learning and applicability for participants and organisations

From the perspective of institutions, managers and members, and participants, promoters of GR activities, and from our own view, we know, applicability of GR learning is of concern. Applicability (transfer of capacities) and its perceived usefulness does not depend only on those who attend an event or activity, but also rests with the members of the system who might benefit directly or indirectly and, importantly, on what organisational conditions are required to make applications possible.

What participants learn and the excitement this generates in them might be similar to the dynamic of "catastrophic change" promoted by a leader (Messiah figure). Former participants of experiential activities sometimes enact the excitement of their discoveries by trying to transfer them immediately into their organisations. However, many acknowledge the difficulties of this task because of the initial rejection by other members of the organisation. Undoubtedly, the new perspectives and behaviours arising from a different conception of the role do alter unconscious homoeostasis for the individual and the group or organisation. The transfer of these learnings then can become quite difficult, particularly if the figure of authority in a person's organisation does not use his or her power to create favourable conditions to enable the emergence of new perspectives. In other words, conditions for a "potential space" of learning and experimentation remains only a potential, but not actual, space. In the case of the Association, change was promoted by the CEO.

Even if leaders do create these conditions, the possibility of a new–old split (with all its unconscious dilemmas) might lead to a scenario of "fight", with those who support the new elements being then identified with a new environment that is perceived as threatening or adverse. This was not the case with the Association.

The nature and richness of an individual's or shared experiential learning is often difficult to express in ways that others can understand. The inexplicable nature of this type of learning is often seen as profound, strange, mysterious, or magical, or, conversely, as completely useless and one that does not contribute to organisational efficiency. It is important to help participants to reflect on these aspects and put words to these learning experiences. This contributes to a better incorporation of learning within themselves and their systems and to work on the projections or feelings of love, idealisation, envy, or hatred.

If learning is seen as mysterious or magical, the consulting institution promoting this kind of learning may be branded as a sect, or administrator of hidden powers that seduces managers. The institution could be projected as a powerful or hidden enemy, or a church, on which one must depend, as was the case for the Innova Institute at some points during our consultations and events.

We believe that helping organisational actors deal with and work through the introjection of heroically acquired knowledge, to which few have access, will help remove this mysterious halo that occasionally surrounds GR activities and make them more down to earth and potentially more useful for the day-to-day working organisations.

Learning and application for Innova

From the perspective of Innova, after accompanying the Association and other organisations, we developed new ways to apply our own learnings to the GR conference itself, in particular the application event and the institutional event, as well as in other post-conference activities.

From our experience, GR activities and approaches do help to develop in participants the analytical and critical capacities for understanding the context and for taking up their role. These capacities enable individuals and organisations to create new ways of talking and thinking together, new repertoires of possible actions and recognition of potential obstacles. We made this learning more explicit in the application event in the GR conference itself. Working with the Association, we saw the importance (for/with participants) of analysing and anticipating the psychic-political and techno-structural conditions of their system of origin in order to contribute more effectively to the transitions of roles and systems they sought. In the role innovation event in the GR conference, we work to assist members to anticipate and create the conditions for applying the learning obtained during the conference.

Working with the Association, we learnt within the institutional event to stress the importance and interconnection of the four different dimensions (as noted earlier in this chapter) and, specifically, to stress the importance of the techno-structural dimension of boundaries and organisational arrangements that groups created to carry out this purpose and relate them to the psychic and political dimensions they were experiencing. For us, the institutional event in the LIM conference is the place to clarify and increase the understanding of the links between the different dimensions: politic, techno-structural, existential, and psychosocial. The role of the consultant during this event is key for that purpose, which is to help participants to make these links between the dimensions.

Taking as central the unconscious role of the management team in the Association and other organisations, we learnt to ensure that the management role was visible in the institutional event. The institutional event in the GR conference is the place where participants are enabled to recognise their fantasy of management and the "institution in the mind".

The capacity to be organised—the techno-structural dimension— to confront management as such and the capacity to reflect on the relations in the group and/or with the help of a consultant in this institutional event are key in creating a representative system that could then contribute to managing the institutional system.

On the other hand, although we know, theoretically, that the meta-system is important from a systemic perspective, our experience as staff of the GR conference is that we often feel trapped by the institutional dynamics in the here and now and tend to forget about the wider context.

The experience in working with this Association made us alert to this centripetal move or tendency. This awareness, together with the U-Turn open events that we regularly organise in Innova, enabled us to create an entirely new event in the GR conference, called the 'state of the system event'. The primary task of this event is to reflect on the relation between the conference itself and its context. Participants are invited to share images, dreams, and associations that reflect "where" the conference is before considering the issues they feel pertinent to the conference process and aim.

For many participants, the significant learning from the conference, in relation to their role and situation in the organisation, tends to diminish as time goes by. By continuing to discuss the application of the role on a regular basis, participants can continue the practice of reflection and application. We developed and now promote a post-conference continuous learning activiy called the ;eadership in action programme. In the Association in particular, the fact that they could participate regularly in small role analysis groups in this programme with external members proved very useful for the managers, as they could focus on current work situations and projects. Since we know that the homeostasis of the unconscious system would invite them to role repetition, this opportunity provided a means to disrupt that homeostatis.

Further learnings for our institution

Innova Institute has become a referent for transformative organisational work through the years. We have grown through our contribution to the networks of which we are a part and the client organisations with whom we have worked. What seems important to us is the sense of continuity that our network and client organisations project into, or attribute to, our institution, specifically for our GR work. They tell us this continuity reminds us all that GR work can continue, either with us or with similar institutions or other GR institutions in other countries. This reflection has helped us to see the usefulness of mixed teams for shared projects for the benefit of our clients and members.

We wonder if our institution could be identified by client organisations as a good enough mother providing conditions of potential spaces. At other times, we understand the opposite, sometimes as a perverse mother who, in fact, produces perverse spaces (Fischer, 2012), especially in those organisational moments of intense turbulence. Our relationship and way of working with this Association points out a non-traditional consulting contact in the sense of sharing different pespectives between two institutions, Innova and the Association, in which we combine open GR activities and complementary systemic interventions. We call this "a middle type of consultation process". This leaves the tempo and continuity of the process almost completely in the hands of the organisation and the members, who have a wider perspective and a longer time horizon.

This type of relationship follows the path and rhythm of the transition process of the organisation itself. One of the signs of a healthy development relationship for us is the capacity in the organisation to identify the moment in which it would recommend speeding up a process and/or, from the view of Innova, to identify the conditions where we would recommend specific interventions for the sake of the organisation's purpose or the pressures and demands of its stakeholders. We believe the Association helped us learn to share the tempo of work together.

In the work with the Association, Innova itself underwent transitions. As the Association learnt to become more outward looking, we became more committed to social justice and democratic concerns, offering public spaces for reflection on becoming active citizens, questioning the political leadership and institutions, and challenging the dismantling of public services in the time of the current crises. We lent our expertise to organisations working toward the creation of a new constitution with citizen engagement in a context of political autonomy.

We thank the participants of Belgirate IV for their contributions in helping us further clarify our thoughts and a special mention to Barbara Williams, who chaired our presentation and helped us edit this version, structure the contents, and make the paper more comprehensible.

References

Fischer, M. D. (2012). Organisational turbulence, trouble and trauma: theorizing the collapse of a mental health setting. *Organisation Studies*, 33(9): 1153–1173.

Honneth, A. (2011). *La sociedad del desprecio*. Madrid: Trotta.

Miller, E. J., & Gwynne, G. V. (1972). *A Life Apart*. London: Tavistock Publications.

CHAPTER FOUR

Embedding diversity in local government: experiences of establishing an ethnic advisory panel, Auckland, New Zealand

Rina Tagore

He aha te mea nui o te ao
He tangata, he tangata, he tangata
What is the most important thing in the world?
It is the people, it is the people, it is the people

(A Maori proverb)

Introduction

This paper illustrates the relevance and value of the group relations (GR) model in understanding and working with groups in the context of a local government and civic engagement. The narrative is personal and based on my experiences during the establishment phase of the first Ethnic Peoples Advisory Panel to Auckland Council, a local government, in New Zealand.

The four topics of the paper are:

- migration and re-discovering self;
- the New Zealand context: the Maori people, and later immigration patterns and increasing ethno-cultural diversity of the most ethnically diverse city; context of local government;

- in lieu of a small or large study group: observations and reflections drawn from regular Panel meetings—the group finding and making a place for itself, in the external world and for itself;
- negotiating space, finding voice—what does it mean for the process of inclusion, supporting diversity, and the challenges therein.

My primary work is as a community and social development professional and my first experience of group relations work was when I joined a group relations conference in India in 1999. Subsequently, I took up opportunities to consult and work in conferences. The insights and learning have since become an integral part of my being as a useful lens to understand and work with systems, groups and their transactions.

Locating myself

I grew up in India and migrated to New Zealand in 2003. Migration and relocating brought to the fore a feeling of becoming an "Indian". I found that, as a migrant, my so-called "Indian" identity took precedence over my other identities as a professional, a colleague, a daughter and a wife, a sister and an aunt, a commuter, a job seeker. I had to rediscover myself. The meaning of social capital became very real now that I was devoid of it in my new home. I had to re-establish my social position, professional identity, and all that I took for granted back home in India. I also had to unravel what it meant to be an Indian. An acute awareness of being the "other" evoked in me greater interest in understanding intergroup relations, peoples, cultural differences and similarities.

I took up work in the local government, the primary task of which is to serve the common good of its communities. Intergroup interactions in a city with rapidly changing ethnic demography became personally and professionally relevant.

When legislation set in motion processes to set up an ethnic advisory group to the council, I found the group relations methodology of significant value and relevance. It helped me to understand the journey of the Ethnic Peoples Advisory Panel, the intra- and intergroup dynamics within the terrain of politics of identity in a young nation such as New Zealand. The method gave me a framework, or an internal point of reference, in engaging, connecting, and "consulting" with the ethnic advisory group.

The experiences of group relations work invariably are ingrained in the mind and heart. The imprint is not stagnant, but is a lens that challenges internal assumptions and those in the surrounding environment. It helps with "sense-making", to understand surrounding phenomena. Life, in all its parts and as a whole, is in a constant state of flux. Applying the here-and-now perspective lends a powerful tool to check on patterns, assumptions, and movements of collective thought and action. For me, GR gives an internal lens in managing and keeping in role and holding boundaries. By boundaries, I refer to a conscious effort to be aware of responsibilities, delineating the purpose and task of respective roles, and respecting these at all costs. Challenging as it might be, it allows both a process of "letting go" and enabling the group identity to unfold. The purpose of this chapter is to illustrate, through a personal narrative, the working of a group, set up by a local government, in its establishment phase. The chapter highlights the relevance of insights and use of GR in working through the challenges of providing advice to the group outside of a standard group relations conference.

Over time, I am more comfortable with my identity as a migrant. The sense of coming to ease was by gaining clarity that my identity could not be compartmentalised in a meaning constructed by others. I, too, had a responsibility in breaking down what I believe to be superficial understanding of "culture and expression of identity". While symbolic expressions of celebrating festivals are important, I believe that diversity needs to be an everyday affair and not just a symbol that remains a token. Interactions between individuals and groups need to permeate beyond the surface. Where there is scope to talk about difference, where "difference" adds value, it leads to creativity and broadened thinking as much as a capacity to work through differences.

Auckland, another home

New Zealand is a relatively young nation. It is a land of settlers. The first people of the nation, the Maori, are said to have first settled in the thirteenth century AD. There are myths surrounding the discovery of New Zealand, or Aotearoa. Popular mythology has it that the great Polynesian voyager, Kupe, discovered New Zealand, a story elaborated by early European settlers. The myth that New Zealand was discovered by a Dutch voyager, Abel Tasman, was, none the less, placed relative to the arrival of the indigenous people of the land, the Tangata Whenua.[1]

Shared mythology is more persuasive and often more powerful than history:

> It was an inspirational account of the discovery on New Zealand. . . . Its telling was part of a process that fitted Maori tradition into the cultural patterns of late nineteenth and early twentieth century Pakeha[2] New Zealand, which was looking for stories of resonance and nobility to make the human occupation of the country seem more deeply rooted and worthy of pride than it might be by virtue of its (at that time) rather thin European heritage.
>
> The same account (Kupe's discovery of the land) became a source of pride for Maori and an antidote to the concurrent and widespread view that Tasman and Cook "discovered" New Zealand. (King, 2003)

The Treaty of Waitangi

This chapter is not a historical chronicle of New Zealand. However, between history, myths, colonisation, and migration are people negotiating spaces, defining and shaping their identities and that of a nation. It is in this context that the waves of migration followed and that the "ethnic peoples" of New Zealand discover and locate themselves.

One may wonder what factors propel people from one location to another as voyagers, explorers, conquerers, to spread the message of God, trade, and/or colonise. There are consequences of such movement, and, for the Maori people, the loss of land, language, and identity has been a significant reality. In the history of colonisation, the Treaty of Waitangi (or Tiriti o Waitangi) is unique in New Zealand. It was a political pact, in writing, between people of the land and the coloniser ("Crown") that was to be the basis of forming a nation state. However, shared understanding was a myth, as the two versions, an English and a Maori one, carried significant differences.[3]

"The other"

As a land of settlers, the different waves of migration created in their wake opportunities for people in New Zealand to revisit their idea of identity time and again. Invariably, there is politicisation of immigration (where presence or arrival of a particular group or category is perceived to be problematic) causing loss of the nation's distinctive social and cultural characteristics and fear of economic threat, assuming that potentially there will be job losses, and the like.

I find the following lines by Chattopadhyay (2003) relevant in understanding the phenomena of attribution of blame.

> The need then arises to rid oneself of those inner attributes that one cannot accept, i.e. cannot admit into one's conscious, one's memory. Through the attempt at ridding to buy the rather temporary feeling of goodness, to temporarily rid oneself of inner tension, one splits those unacceptable attributes and the associated feelings from the wholeness of one's being and projects those on to one or more persons, who are the "others". This process becomes easier as the other is perceived as different, distant and alien. As a person becomes psychologically more and more mature, the intensity of this need goes down.
>
> However, once this unconscious process starts in infancy, it continues, like most other unconscious processes, in one's adult life as well. The nature and intensity changes contextually and varies from individual to individual, largely depending on their degree of psychic maturity. (p. 1)

In the 1960s and 1970s, the immigration policy sought to meet demand for labour from the neighbouring Pacific island nations. A few decades later, there was a growth in people from China and East Asia moving to New Zealand and, with that, a perceived threat related to "Asian influx".

That is the general context in which over the years people from all over the world have sought to migrate to New Zealand or have, as refugees[4] been located to this small country.

Contemporary factors that drive the movement of people are different to what obtained earlier. Today, we have global markets defining trade and business and countries competing for migrants' skills and labour. Wars and conflicts are another reason for many to move on. At the core of people's movements are aspirations to build better futures and to explore and expand choices for the next generation. Inherent to that, there are the problems of settling in, of finding meaning and purpose. People seek connection and relatedness as they establish new identities.

Changes in local governance in Auckland

The work of local government authorities is within the legislative framework established by parliament. Local councils in New Zealand[5] are critical in public decision-making. Auckland is the largest region in the country, with two-thirds of the country's population that is very diverse. In 2009, the Parliament made legislative changes for governance reforms in Auckland. The intent was for the city to be a leading metropolitan region and a global player in the south Pacific region.

The legislation[6] that dismantled the local governments in Auckland (seven local and one regional) set up instead a single governing body with twenty-one local boards. There is one mayor, twenty councillors for the region, and 149 local board members .

To honour the Treaty principles of partnership, an Independent Maori Statutory Board (IMSB) was established.[7] The legislation also required the mayor to appoint two advisory panels to act as conduits for communicating the interests and concerns of Pacific and ethnic peoples, respectively.

At this point, it would be useful to unpack the term "ethnic" in the context of New Zealand.

Diversity, ethnicity, and identity

People differ from one another in all manner of ways: ethnicity, gender, skin colour, physical, mental, and physical ability, culture, language, accent, social class, family structure, sexuality, religion, interests, lifestyle, and so on (Bromell, 2008).

The word diversity is frequently used to refer to the ethno-cultural diversity in the population. Statistics New Zealand defines ethnicity as

> ... the ethnic group or groups that people identify with or feel they belong to. Ethnicity is a measure of cultural affiliation, as opposed to

race, ancestry, nationality or citizenship. Ethnicity is self perceived and people can belong to more than one ethnic group.[8]

Enumerating ethnicity and categorising identities into neat boxes is challenging. I found the following lines helpful in understanding culture and ethnicity in the context of people negotiating space and identity:

> Culture is defined as "the ways that people in all societies draw upon a vast repertoire of knowledge to perform innumerable tasks, most of them so mundane that they take them for granted" and ethnicity as, "a specific form of cultural distinctiveness and boundary formation grounded in beliefs about social connectedness and descent that often shapes political discourse and action". Everyone has a culture and these "cultures" are highly permeable, exhibiting borrowings and exchanges with other cultures. Ethnic group identity is not, on the other hand, a universal condition, but rather, a possibly ephemeral, political instrument used to shape relations of "them" and "us". (Bromell, 2008)

The Treaty of Waitangi allows continued action for indigenous people to receive due recognition on their land. As a result, by default, there is, in the formal arena, a space for expression of identities and cultures. The discourse is closely linked to a nation coming to terms with rapidly changing demographics. The 180-odd ethnicities of people in Auckland is an indisputable fact about the city.[9]

Periodically, there are outcries about incidents of discrimination and racism. There are expressions of distrust and division as much as there is evidence of an understanding across communities and cultures. The general adage in New Zealand is "a fair go for all", and Auckland aspires to be an inclusive city.

The institutional design within the public sector to represent the varied interests of stakeholders and distinct population groups is, in part, through population-based ministries and departments: Te Pune Kokiri for Maori, Ministry of Pacific Island Affairs for Pacific Peoples, Ministry of Women's Affairs for women, and Office of Ethnic Affairs for ethnic people[10] (Barrowman, 2006).

A new category—New Zealander—was introduced in the census in 2006. Research shows that the term "New Zealander" was generally viewed as distinct from ethnicity and linked to tenure in New

Zealand, affinity with New Zealand, being born in New Zealand, nationality, and, for a few, ancestry. There is, however, a view that a sense of national identity cannot be fostered if people focus on cultural differences. Naming a single category to hold all identities could be an indication of resistance to exploring the challenges of working with diversity. The call to identify with a single category perhaps denotes an authority that demands loyalty and allegiance.

Auckland Council's Ethnic Peoples Advisory Panel

The city mayor appointed twelve individuals with an interest in voicing issues of concern to ethnic people in Auckland's local government. Their appointment was based on public consultation, open recruitment, and selection.

The legislation[11] states the purpose of the Panel, as follows:

to identify and communicate to the Council the interests and preferences of the ethnic peoples of Auckland in relation to—

- the content of the strategies, policies, plans, and bylaws of the Council; and

- matter that the Panel considers to be of particular interest or concern to the ethnic peoples of Auckland; and

- to advise the mayor, and the Council's governing body and local boards, of the Council processes and mechanisms for engagement with ethnic peoples and communities in Auckland.

Role and authority

The twelve members were long-term settlers in the country, on an average of at least two decades. The seven women and five men came from different ethno-cultural heritage with networks in local communities. They held nine different ethnic traditions and spoke that many languages; between them, they held three distinct religious categories. These were the obvious markers of diversity. To begin with, for a period of up to three months, one member was appointed by the mayor to be the Interim Chair. This allowed members time to acquaint themselves with each other and the purpose before electing a chair.

Locating my role

Alongside the change in governance structure, the dismantling of eight councils led to a restructuring of eight organisations into one. I was catapulted into the role of Principal Policy Analyst, responsible for advice and support to the panel.

My role involved interpreting tasks on both sides of the table, to deliver strategic advice to the panel and its membership, and to interface with various council departments that engaged with the panel.

It was an establishment phase on all fronts: for the panel as a group, for the panel in its role in relation to a new governance structure, and for the organisation in its new structure. With GR as an internal anchor, I could navigate subjective experiences and perceptions in engaging with the panel and its membership in the here-and-now.

I was able to

- Recognise and hold my role boundaries.
- Be reflective and cope with what could be projections and introjections.
- Focus on task and purpose.
- Recognise patterns and provide advice to the panel.
- Support the panel membership in holding their role and establishing their own work mechanism.

My role gave me a unique vantage point as an observer, a facilitator, and a receiver of myriad projections. I suspect many of my subjective experiences were, from time to time, magnified. At one level, I was an insider:

- being of "ethnic" category;
- as a person of Indian and South Asian background;
- as a migrant settler to New Zealand.

At another level, I was an outsider, as I did not hold similar levels of "ethnic proximity" to the group members and, as a member of the council's staff, I was at a further distance.

The panel negotiated its purpose, role, and task through a Terms of Reference and Relationship Agreement and Work Program. In addition, their monthly meeting agendas also had to be negotiated to make the panel relevant for its purpose. As the single point of contact for all purposes for the panel, I was frequently pushed to be a super administrator for the group.

Vignettes of observations and reflections

Business meetings or study groups

In preparing for the panel's first business meeting in the city's Town Hall, I had to ensure correct seating arrangements with the right number of chairs. The need to invest time in creating the physical containers is an integral part of group processes so that the physical boundaries are fit for purpose. I experienced the meetings as being small study groups, relative to all that might be occurring in the larger system.

Plenipotentiary, an issue of representation

The matter of representation posed a challenge in the early days. Members held a view that each individual represented their respective ethnic communities living in Auckland. Officers, on the other hand, were of the view that the Panel, as an appointed advisory body, did not fully represent the twelve ethnic groups to which they belonged. The members did not come through an election process and were not representatives in a classical sense. The ethnic community sector had many more leaders. Further, there was a risk that the organisation could use the Panel as a proxy for the substantive effort of engaging with diverse population groups. The source of authority for members was a singular idea of identity; there was some difficulty working with plurality within multiple identities held in individuals.

> According to embedded intergroup relations theory, the group is an entity representing various groups. An individual reflects a uniquely related set of roles representative of an intergroup. Each individual belongs to multiple identity groups including the ones they were born into such as race and gender, as well as to other groups that they choose to belong to such as professional, work and social group.
>
> . . .
>
> Individuals who represent identity groups meet at the boundary that separates them from other groups. These boundaries can be impermeable or permeable, depending on historical relationships,

hidden agendas, stereotypes, belief systems, values, etc. Intolerance of difference, ambiguity, paradox, and multiple realities locks groups in paranoid–schizoid relations and make it difficult to work across boundaries.

. . . Holding and expressing multiple (salient) identities and working within "multiple realities" carries risk and political implications for the exercise of authority (Skolnick & Green, 1998). They warn of the temptation to focus on one side of the contradiction and lose perspective of a natural and central aspect of group existence. (McRae & Green, 2009, pp. 113–114)

During the initial three-month period, there was some jostling for position and power. There appeared to be a coup in the making as members sought informal meetings, and exchanged emails. Most members were silent spectators, and the situation was brought to the attention of the membership. A challenge for me was to help to bring to the surface the underlying tensions without being caught up in interpersonal exchanges.

The mayor met the panel and conveyed core messages on inclusion and working with differences. His message stressed the role of the panel in demonstrating collaborative and inclusive practice. A key task was for the panel to work with differences—of opinions, ideas, and perspectives—and make Auckland an exemplar of an inclusive city.

Visible markers of diversity

The Interim Chair was appointed for three months; however, some of the members demanded that there be an election sooner. Competition surfaced early on, with moves to discredit the Interim Chair on grounds of gender and age discrimination. The group identity appeared to have anchored its starting point on visible markers of diversity, such as gender and age. This move prevented exploring difference at a deeper level, possibly a defence against the task of embarking on the journey of inclusion. It would mean having "to unmask the familiar narratives that explained things in terms of gender, race, orientation, and nationality" (McRae & Green, 2009, p. 116).

To continue to use visible markers of diversity as a primary basis of discourse allows parties to remain in their comfort zone without a deeper exploration. Such exploration demands a shift in thinking and requires members to work with the unfamiliar and unknown.

Establishing territories—informal or formal

Members became busy in organising informal meetings, with a purpose of formulating agenda items. Teetering on the edge of formal and informal territory, the group was establishing and testing boundaries. I drew their attention to the nature of the group, which was formal and had a mandate to deliver. Setting agendas was a formal requirement. Perhaps the idea of informal was an expression of the uncertainty in the minds of "ethnic peoples" in gaining legitimacy of existence in the shared territory of institutional structures and systems. Could, after all, an ethnic panel have legitimate space within the local governance system?

Capturing identity on cards

It was early days of the panel when the tsunami struck Japan in March 2011, causing substantial destruction and loss. The disaster was a starting point for the membership to find its *raison d'être*. A first formal action was to express condolence to the Japanese people in Auckland through a card. The panel made its identity known to part of the larger system through a visible marker.

The panel members spent a significant amount of time discussing business card requirements with great urgency and priority. This visible marker item seemed critical for the existence of membership. Individual identity took precedence over getting to know each other or the task of the group.

Gender dynamics

In the early meetings, I experienced what could well be projections of weakness, many of which were, in my view, gender based. Three officers, all women, received disconcerting comments about their appearance and clothing. Subjectively, the feeling induced was that professional advice from officers was secondary and fell by the wayside when the point of focus or interest was appearance.

At one meeting, members were vocal in conveying their anger and dissatisfaction with the leadership within the group, with accusations about slips, delays, and an inability to steer the group. At the end of the meeting, the designated leader approached me, making physical contact by touching my back and enquiring about me with comments that I appeared tired. The gesture felt out of place, the tone condescending, and, in that single moment, it felt as though helplessness and impotency had been physically transferred on to me. It took me a few days to sort out my thoughts and feelings since, for the first time in many years of my work life, I felt gendered and trapped in my identity as a woman. Other senior officers present at the meeting corroborated my view that the leader's behaviour was out of place.

No memory, no desire

In working with the panel, I frequently stepped back to reflect on my experiences. I will make mention of meditation in this context. The process of meditation is said to have three aspects to it:

- the object being observed (visual, sensations, attitudes, etc.);
- the process or act of observing (using sensory and mental instruments);
- the observer, who is observing.

The "here-and-now" experience, and being fully in the moment in relation to groups, is the awareness and experience of the three aspects listed above. Allowing for a reflective process meant a capacity and focus to observe the members, the group, and myself and my emotive states.

In "Notes on memory and desire" (Bion, 1967), Bion says,

Memory is always misleading as a record of fact since it is distorted by the influence of unconscious forces. Desires interfere, by absence of mind when observation is essential, with the operation of judgment. Desires distort judgment by selection and suppression of material to be judged.

Memory and Desire exercise and intensify those aspects of the mind that derive from sensuous experience. They thus promote capacity derived from sense impressions and designed to serve impressions of sense. They deal, respectively, with sense impressions of what is supposed to have happened and sense impressions of what has not yet happened.

Psychoanalytic "observation" is concerned neither with what has happened nor with what is going to happen, but with what is happening. (Bion, 1967)

The work context with the panel was not psychoanalytical intervention. However, I realised that it was important that I strive for calm and focus on purpose in my interactions. To do so meant that I did not allow myself to prejudge transactions and the members. It was about engaging with purpose and disengaging at other levels in order to avoid the risk of internalising projections.

The awareness and distinction between myself as an observer, the act of observing, and the object of observation—the membership and the transactions—was a way of being fully present. As a result, members, over time, took charge of their dialogue and group deliberations matured without officers leading or directing discussions.

Stage of infancy

In nearly all the meetings in the first year, one member in particular was constantly mobilised to be the child on behalf of the group. He would seek explanations repeatedly, particularly after lengthy discussions on a point were completed, and he would ask a question well after the group had discussed the same point at length. In some ways, he held the identity of an infant on behalf of the group. At one meeting, the expression of a child-like state came through as he complained of feeling cold due to the temperature in the room. This remark led to an almost dramatic moment when a council officer, sitting on the side, got up and enveloped the member in her large shawl. The pattern had been that of one member constantly taking up the role of the baby who needed constant attention, throwing tantrums if not given attention, refusing to grow up, take charge, and be responsible. The process reflected, to me, the struggles of the panel to establish its identity. As an entity established by the council, it was dependent, and yet the group had to slowly establish itself to find an independent voice.

A common preoccupation for some members was about obtaining vouchers for parking their cars free of charge. Their repeated demands led me to feeling that my core task was providing parking vouchers to the panel. The issue gained further visibility as it escalated as a concern, and was mentioned as a resource gap in the Chair's first report to the council's governing body. The only interpretation that I could link to this need was the panel's struggle to find a parking lot for itself in the governance system. Even though there was a clear, designated space as an advisory body in the structure, if the panel was a vehicle, it was going around in circles, reluctant and struggling to find a place. The reluctance was a defence against addressing the primary task of providing strategic advice to the council. Instead, that was verbalised was a complaint about insufficient parking vouchers.

Dinner-dance and dress syndrome

A significant challenge in embedding diversity is to take the journey from the exotic to the ordinary, where diversity is an everyday affair. There is a need to shift the discourse from "dinner-dance and dress"[12] as the only platform where difference is acceptable, to that of a deeper engagement, one that helps build a capacity to talk to each other and critique ourselves in understanding what the daily "walking along" means for all of us. I would think that we, in Auckland, have begun to play with waves of diversity, dipping in and out. The changing demographic contours create their own push factors, and the public arena is sometimes compelled to respond. The establishment of the Ethnic Advisory Panel is one example of making structural changes to influence the local governance system.

Catering requirements at meetings was another issue that would surface frequently: beef or no beef, Halal or not, vegetarian options, desserts, celebratory meals for festivals such as Eid and Christmas. While I would channel requirements and requests to caterers, the issue was a point of consternation for the panel. On reflection, I thought that clearly the journey from the phase of "dinner-dance and dress" to discourse was yet to mature.

Food was a significant concern for a few members, though most were comfortable. The issue of Halal food and Halal certified caterers came up, too. As an officer, I was an interlocutor of sorts to the organisation. I would regret hearing adverse and unjustified comments about the Ethnic Panel (their "demands for Halal food"). It upset me, as there were officers ready to stereotype the panel. It was somewhat disturbing that one member was stirring up a non-existent issue. The Chair's remark that people of Islamic faith brought more to the table for discussion, not limited to the need to provide Halal food, helped to counteract the flurry of email exchanges and emotions on this subject.

On another occasion, a leader from the Jewish community was to present to the panel on the topic of mediation training. Catering arrangements for the meeting took into account the different food required. What came as a surprise to me was when a member, with knowledge of the Judeo-Christian tradition, questioned me in bewilderment as to why different types of food had been arranged. I was led to provide a somewhat defensive explanation about diverse food requirements derived from religious faith.

Perhaps this panel member was unconsciously motivated to express disbelief on the demonstration of an inclusive practice. On the surface, the task had been to talk about mediation and conflict management in the community. At a deeper level, the challenge for organisations and groups is in the capacity to leverage difference as a resource. A more common approach is that which focuses on difference as a source of conflict. Perhaps, in that moment, there was an opportunity to experience oneness with the Other.[13]

The panel expressed dissatisfaction, frustration, and blame in the regular dialogue and discussion. There was an expectation of instant answers that were not always available from the organisation. The predominant preoccupations were to do with administrative system and process requirements. Over time, these pressures eased as the panel and the organisational systems fell into place.

I suspect that in many ways the blame was a means to gain a sense of togetherness in the group, and council served as the common enemy.

> One of the things that a group needs in order to preserve this sense of togetherness is a common enemy. The existence of such a group helps the process of splitting, supports the feeling of self-righteousness and aids the group in submerging its internal tensions. The common enemy acts as internal glue and the process of rallying towards a common goal operates, whether that goal is healthy for the group or otherwise. (Chattopadhyay, 2003)

Relationships with the larger system

The panel discussed at length how they might communicate with the wider communities, groups and organisations. Many ideas and options were tabled. Eventually, even though they were on the verge of going ahead with the idea of embedding the panel's messages in existing communication channels, they changed tack and arrived at a decision to produce their own newsletter. This debate could well be a metaphor for the journey of integration and the challenge of embedding diversity in the mainstream. At this juncture, the Panel's group identity took precedence to make ethnic people visible in the wider system.

On completion of one year of its existence, the Chair signalled that the panel would host an Annual General Meeting (AGM). The term AGM stood at odds with the fact that the panel was an appointed advisory group. The panel, however, did have as part of its Terms of Reference a commitment to hold a community forum. The confusion of terminology might well have been reflecting a desire for accountability towards the larger system. It was, perhaps, the panel's unconscious desire to gain legitimacy and endorsement from wider ethnic communities.

Looking ahead

At the time of writing this chapter, the Ethnic Peoples Advisory Panel has existed for about eighteen months. Over this period, they have signalled to the council the following:

- that the officers and departments need to engage with the panel in a substantive manner. That they are not a proxy for engaging meaningfully with wider ethnic communities;
- that there is a regular channel of conversation with the mayor and the governing body through periodic reporting
- that the panel needs to engage with wider ethnic communities in order to deliver on its task of providing advice to council.

In its short life, it has established a voice in the governance system, albeit not as a direct decision maker. Officers from council departments regularly engage with the panel on the basis that it is a sounding board for ethnic issues and concerns.

For his part, the current mayor has assured the panel that he values its role and significance. The panel's legislated tenure is for three years, parallel to the term of local government. However, in a year from now, the decision about its continuity in either the current or a different format will rest with the mayor-elect. For a more dispassionate view and assessment, an external evaluation is under way. It will provide analysis and advice to inform future directions. The panel seeks permanency and a decision-making role in the governance structure.

What might be the purpose of negotiating these spaces and construction of identities? Expanded and multi-layered identities broaden boundaries and the capacities to navigate with ease, moving from one territory to another. Ethnicity is both grounded and constructed, both material and symbolic. Ethnic differences are organised and mobilised within contexts of political and economic structure. I would think that, over time, the Ethnic Panel, too, will locate itself accordingly.

The challenge is gaining authority and giving new meaning to representation in the context of local government and civic participation. No group could represent the diversity of views and perspectives held within the 180 ethnic identities of Auckland's population. The unstated task for the panel is related to embedding ideas and perspectives and institutionalising inclusive action.

My experience of group relations work was particularly helpful and relevant in the past two years as a council officer responsible for supporting the Ethnic Panel. My narrative illustrates that the relevance and use of the methodology is not limited to group relations conferences, HR practice, and organisational development alone. The value of group relations comes to the fore at unexpected moments, both in life and in work situations.

Notes

1. Indigenous people of the land—people born of the whenua, that is, of the placenta and of the land where the people's ancestors have lived and where their placenta are buried. In the pre-European era, Maori had no name for the country as a whole. In the Maori world (of many tribes with

territorial authority in different areas of the land), there were different names that persisted until the middle of the nineteenth century.

2. Pākehā: a Māori term for New Zealanders who are not of Māori blood lines, largely referring to those descended from British and Irish settlers. The etymology is unclear, but essentially refers to mythical human-like creatures, with fair skin and hair, sometimes described as having come from the sea. Nowadays, the word is used as a collective noun referring to Caucasian people, and sometimes even as means of describing a "western world-view".

3. The Treaty in brief: The Treaty is a broad statement of principles on which the British and Māori made a political compact to found a nation state and build a government in New Zealand. The document has three articles. In the English version, Māori cede the sovereignty of New Zealand to Britain; Māori give the Crown an exclusive right to buy lands they wish to sell, and, in return, are guaranteed full rights of ownership of their lands, forests, fisheries, and other possessions; and Māori are given the rights and privileges of British subjects.

   The Treaty in Māori was deemed to convey the meaning of the English version, but there are important differences. Most significantly, the word 'sovereignty' was translated as "kawanatanga" (governance). Some Māori believed they were giving up government over their lands but retaining the right to manage their own affairs. The English version guaranteed "undisturbed possession" of all their "properties", but the Māori version guaranteed "tino rangatiratanga" (full authority) over "taonga" (treasures, which may be tangible). Māori understanding was at odds with the understanding of those negotiating the Treaty for the Crown, and, as Māori society valued the spoken word, explanations given at the time were probably as important as the wording of the document.

   It is common now to refer to the intention, spirit, or principles of the Treaty. The Treaty of Waitangi is not considered part of New Zealand domestic law, except where its principles are referred to in Acts of Parliament. The exclusive right to determine the meaning of the Treaty rests with the Waitangi Tribunal, a commission of inquiry created in 1975 to investigate alleged breaches of the Treaty by the Crown. More than 2,000 claims have been lodged with the tribunal, and a number of major settlements have been reached.

4. New Zealand is a signatory to the UN Refugee Convention (1951) and can accept a quota of up to 750 refugees every year.

5. There are eleven Regional Councils and sixty-seven territorial authorities (city/district councils). Auckland Council came about as a result of

amalgamating eight former councils on 1 November 2010. Local councils are collectively referred to as "territorial authorities".

6. Local Government (Auckland Council) Act 2009 and Local Government (Auckland Council) Amendment Act 2010.

7. The task of the Independent Maori Statutory Board is to promote issues of significance for the Mana Whenua and Māori of Auckland and to assist the Auckland Council in its decision making. A member of the Board has a seat alongside the elected leaders on the council governing body. The board and the council are required to meet at least four times each year to discuss the council's performance of its duties.

8. An ethnic group is made up of people who have some or all of the following characteristics:

    • a common proper name
    • one or more elements of common culture which need not be specified, but may include religion, customs, or language
    • unique community of interests, feelings and actions
    • a shared sense of common origins or ancestry, and
    • a common geographic origin. (Source: Statistics New Zealand)

9. Auckland is the most ethnically diverse region in New Zealand, with more than 180 different ethnicities, and almost 40% of Aucklanders were not born in New Zealand. In the 2006 Census*, the largest proportion of Auckland's population (56%) identified themselves as New Zealand European. This is significantly lower than for New Zealand as a whole (67%). (The Auckland Plan, Auckland Council, New Zealand, 2012)

10. The Government definition of ethnic groups covers those who share fundamental cultural values, customs, traditions, and characteristics that differ from the larger society (CAB Min (04) 42/5A). This includes people from New Zealand-born and established communities, recent migrants, and refugees. It also includes people with multiple ethnic identities. While this definition includes Māori and Pacific groups, Te Puni Kōkiri (TPK) and the Ministry of Pacific Island Affairs (MPIA) usually serve these groups. (Source: Office of Ethnic Affairs, Dept. of Internal Affairs)

11. Local Government Act 2010, Section 86 (Auckland Transitional Provisions).

12. An expression used by Ms Liu Shueng, a consultant who has worked with the Human Rights Commission and the Office of Ethnic Affairs.

13.   Thinking inclusively can involve intense experiences, with a powerful impact on how one views oneself in relation to the world. Under these conditions, differences can be thought of as

resources rather than threats. This is the experience of Oneness with the Other, which includes other persons while going wider and wider as we permit ourselves to meditate in it (According to Bion, 1970, cited by Bazalgette, 2009)

Internet sources

www.legislation.govt.nz/act/public/2010/0036/latest/DLM3016017.html. Accessed on 16 September 2012.

www.stats.govt.nz/surveys_and_methods/methods/classifications-and-standards/classification-related-stats-standards/ethnicity/definition. aspx. Accessed on 15 September 2012.

www.ethnicaffairs.govt.nz/oeawebsite.nsf/wpg_URL/Resources-Research-Section-1-The-Concept-and-Usefulness-of-Ethnicity-Information?OpenDocument. Accessed on 17 September 2012.

www.nzhistory.net.nz/politics/treaty/the-treaty-in-brief. Accessed on 23 September 2012.

www.maoridictionary.co.nz/index.cfm?dictionaryKeywords=Tangata+Whenua&search.x=0&search.y=0&search=search&n=1&idiom=&phrase=&proverb=&loan=. Accessed on 6 October 2012.

http://en.wikipedia.org/wiki/P%C4%81keh%C4%81. Accessed on 1 October 2012.

www.mpia.govt.nz/demographic-fact-sheet/. Accessed on 3 October 2012.

http://braungardt.trialectics.com/sciences/psychoanalysis/wilfred-bion/wilfred-bion-notes-on-memory-and-desire/. Accessed on 4 October 2012.

References

Barrowman, R. (Ed.) (2006). *Policy Implications of Diversity*. Wellington, NZ: Institute of Policy Studies, Victoria University Press.

Bazalgette, J. (2009). Leadership: the impact of the full human being in role. In: E. Aram, R. Baxter, & A. Nutkevitch (Eds.), *Adaptation and Innovation: Theory, Design and Role-Taking in Group Relations Conferences and their Applications, Volume II* (pp. 31–50). London: Karnac.

Bion, W. R. (1967). Notes on memory and desire. *Psychoanalytic Forum*, 2(3). Available at: http://braungardt.trialectics.com/sciences/psycho-analysis/bion/bion-memory-desire/

Bromell, D. (2008). *Ethnicity, Identity and Public Policy – Critical Perspectives on Multiculturalism.* Wellington, NZ: Institute of Policy Studies, Victoria University of Wellington Press.

Chattopadhyay, G. P. (2003). "The Other" in the politics of relatedness between developing and developed nations. *Socio-Analysis, 5:* 14–35.

King, M. (2003). *The Penguin History of New Zealand.* Penguin.

McRae, M. B., & Green, Z. (2009). A world of difference: lessons and innovations on the study of race, authority, and identity. In: E. Aram, R. Baxter, & A. Nutkevitch (Eds.), *Adaptation and Innovation: Theory, Design and Role-Taking in Group Relations Conferences and their Applications, Volume II* (pp. 109–122). London: Karnac.

CHAPTER FIVE

The Rothschild 117 Project: dreaming in the boulevard

Josef Triest, Judith Levy, Ilana Mishael, Yael Shenhav Sharoni, and Simi Talmi

The riots and protest movements which have been erupting, one after the other, like subterranean geysers bursting up on to the surface, in different city squares around the globe—in Egypt, Yemen, Libya, Syria, Manchester, Wall Street, Rothschild Boulevard, and elsewhere—have created the impression that we are witnessing an encompassing, systemic phenomenon, a kind of social tsunami sweeping over the world, taking its unique shape according to the social "geology", culture, and context of the place it strikes. As group relations professionals, living and working in Israel, we became interested in researching it when the protest movement hit the heart of Tel Aviv, taking the form of a tent-town, which sprouted up in Israel's most lucrative avenue—Rothschild Boulevard. In the attempt to fathom the social processes, both conscious and unconscious, behind this extraordinary occurrence, we found ourselves initiating a kind of "action research" by offering a daily "social dreaming" meeting—in the middle of the street. We invited passers-by, together with consultants, and mental health professionals alike, to share their dreams and try, as much as possible, to get to the bottom of the social motifs, explicit and implicit, that were revealed. This chapter tells the story of this unique project (which, to the best of our knowledge, has been the only one of its kind at that point of time) as it took place during the first wave of the Israeli protest, in the summer of 2011 (5 August, to be exact).

Besides depicting the course of this intervention and the way it developed, we discuss some of the motifs arising from collected dream sequences. We also elaborate on the relations between those active in the project and the "establishment", in this case, OFEK (Organisation Person Group) association, whose members made up the majority of the professionals involved (and to which all the authors of this chapter belong). We thought of it as a kind of parallel process that would allow us to formulate some working hypotheses about the structure and dynamic of the social protest movement as it unfolded in Israel. Our closing discussion indicates a possible paradigm shift in leader-led relations on a wider scale. We begin, however, with a brief portrayal of the circumstances which led to the social protest in Israel, and of its cultural context.

The place—Rothschild Boulevard

Rothschild Boulevard is named after a renowned philanthropist who played a major role in the history of Zionism—Edmond de Rothschild. He was born in 1845 into a well-known family of bankers in a small town near Paris, and died in 1934. The chronicles of the settlement of Israel have designated him as one of the major donors, providing funds for buying lands during the first Aliyot (waves of immigration). Among other things, his contributions funded the training of professional agronomists. In fact, he might also be depicted as responsible for establishing the first instances of an administration for the budding "Yishuv", by appointing an elaborate network of officials to manage his investments in Palestine. Corrupt administration and indifferent establishments were among the main targets marked out by the current protest movement.

The protest movement

The local protest movement was (and perhaps still is) an uncommon, highly intriguing phenomenon in Israel's social landscape. It was led mainly by young people in their late twenties and early thirties. At one time, it brought hundreds of thousands[1] of people out of their homes and into the streets, most of them employed and middle-class: students and their parents (and grandparents), whose economic burden had become too great to bear. They were protesting against a large variety of wrongdoings under the aegis of the somewhat general slogan: "The people demand social justice" (or, as one amused, flamboyant, and quite cheerful group of teenagers repeatedly shouted in one of those demonstrations, "the people want all kinds of things!", while a short-legged teenager chimed in with her megaphone, in the same rhythm and in the same breath, "and other things as well"). Many other slogans were also heard, such as: "the economy is free—we are slaves"; "we want justice, not charity"; "children are not luxuries", etc.

Despite the fact that many of the social dilemmas and financial problems were represented, it was striking that political issues, which usually occupy public attention and threaten to tear Israeli society apart, like that of the "occupied territories", were completely absent. This enabled a collective illusion that "there is place for everyone". Actually, it seemed that the boulevard turned, for a while, into a space where differences were not really relevant, where young and old, poor and rich, were almost the same. The world seemed gentle, emotional, non-hierarchal, and without barriers.

As a social phenomenon, this profoundly (until now) non-violent protest movement[2] succeeded in generating an unexplained wave of public sympathy, even from those parts of the public that it criticised most harshly. Office-holding politicians vied for the new movement's favours and high-ranking professionals put themselves at the service of its leaders, although the demands made by the protesters were rather vague, and despite their disdainful rejection of the government's attempts to come up with some practical solution to the issues they raised. It seemed as if the purpose of the new movement's leadership (mainly women) was not to attain clear and palpable material achievements, but, rather, to protest by simply expressing an emotional state of mind, that is, by giving voice to certain feelings of frustration, anger, and discontent.

The initiative for creating a public dreaming space in the middle of the boulevard

The story of the initiative to sustain a daily space of "social dreaming" at the heart of the boulevard is told from several personal perspectives, using our notes as sources. That, we hope, will convey some of its original vividness and spontaneity.

Yossi Triest writes,

> For me it started with a phone call from a friend (Simi Talmi), made just before she went abroad. We can't stay out of this, she said. Her words acted on me like a spark, igniting a great flame of initiative (which is usually quite unlike me). Within a short period of time I was joined by additional enthusiastic partners (Ilana Mishael, Yael Shenhav-Sharoni, Judy Levy—in her unique role as chairperson of OFEK—and others) and alongside them, more and more volunteers answered my call to hold a daily meeting in a small, fenced playground we found (and actually occupied) in the middle of the boulevard. The consultants, most of whom had no previous experience, were recruited as volunteers (with no regard for skill or training) from among the members of OFEK and other organisations or circles; some were colleagues or friends with whom I was involved directly. Later on, professionals from broader circles joined in after hearing about our activities. I insisted on inviting the consultants as private individuals and not as official representatives of OFEK or any other organisation whatsoever, since I had a strong feeling that that would be the only way to join the protest movement without being rejected. I took up, as a metaphor, the "open-code" paradigm, utilised by developers of applications for computer operating systems, in contrast with the closed systems of Microsoft and Apple, for instance. That is to say, I declared that we are free to do whatever we thought would be useful—without asking anybody's permission.

The logistics of the project were arranged in the following way: every day, we divided ourselves into teams of three, with one of the three consulting consecutively, trying to maintain some measure of continuity. Reports of our meetings were diligently, fervently written down and distributed by email among members of OFEK as well as other circles (this included a Facebook page, the first to be opened by OFEK, following our activities—nevertheless, it remained somewhat derelict). The only consistent element was the time and the place—117 Rothschild Boulevard, every night for an hour between 7.30 and 8.30, out of which fifteen minutes were devoted to reviewing the entire meeting. On Thursdays, we held public meetings with all the consultants of the past week, in a far-from-successful attempt to address the various themes that came up throughout the week.

We soon discovered that dreams cannot be heard in the noisy carnival that was the boulevard: a jazz band to our left, a speaker on our right, and a film screening in front drowned out the stories of those who gathered in the strange space we carved out for ourselves. Yossi Triest:

> I decided to buy an electronic amplifier (which was retrospectively funded by OFEK), and the dreams began being heard. I must admit— I was astounded to witness the impressive "political force" a dream can wield, if it is only heard.

This is what it looked like, then: some hand-written signs declaring that we are collecting "Boulevard Dreams"; a small group, between seven and twenty-five people (changing daily): half professionals and half passers-by, men, women, children, young and old sitting scattered about (we learnt not to sit in a circle, which turned out to be uninviting for passers-by, but scattered here and there), some curious onlookers leaning on the short fence which surrounded us, candles on the floor (a characteristic which will be mentioned further on), and people sharing their dreams and associations.

> The dream narrations were inevitably combined with political and social statements, calls for self-assertion, wishes for a better future, hopes that such a better future will indeed come true, heart-breaking stories of homeless people who were the "regular" tenants of the boulevards and occasionally joined in, excited by the chance to hold a microphone in their hands, and children, some of them very young (4–6 years old), who not only narrated their dreams but also offered interpretations.

> We operated in this manner for four weeks. Autumn winds and the dwindling of the protest brought our efforts to an end.

Goals

The chief goal of our activity, as we saw it, was to establish a kind of "action research". Both the method—that is, the strategy of blending into the current of activities which overwhelmed the boulevard, as if we were a piece of wood floating down a river—and the "social dreaming matrix", were chosen as means of research in the hope of forming some initial understanding of the psychological forces, especially the unconscious ones, which were generating the social dynamics that bred the protest movement. (This trend was not always clear to those active in the project, as we were all more or less "infected" in one way or another by the exuberant spirit blowing through the boulevard, sweeping away with it so many layers of Israeli society in the optimism of one "magical" summer, until the rain began.)

Initial strategy and modus operandi

The organising principal guiding our activity in its initial stages was joining up with the social movement without setting off its "antibodies". The main idea was this: in our work, we are not operating or acting through organisations or institutions, but we are not averse to putting their interests and resources to our good use. We are not establishing any kind of structured institution. Our daily activity is the sole "container" for our work-groups, and not the other way around. As far as the "organisation in the mind" is concerned, we pictured the space in which we were operating as a system whose waves are expanding towards infinity, without swelling in any familiar or preconceived place—unlike the "classical" pyramid structure of organisations, where information trickles toward the top and then is pumped to its periphery *ad infinitum*. For this reason, we also refrained from initiating any formal selection of consultants and consistently avoided the use of narrow, sectorial, professional jargon—the kind we would ordinarily employ in our work. As expected, at this point our success was partial at best.

The social dreaming matrix was chosen as our instrument mainly because we believed it could pave a "high road to the [social] unconscious" as it was expressed in the boulevard.

The interrelations between the "dreamers" and the "establishment" (OFEK): a parallel process

One of the most prominent features of the protest movement, as we gathered, was its suspicion of establishments, although these (mainly municipal authorities) strangely refrained from evicting the protest activists, letting them utilise city facilities for quite a long time. Apparently, the endeavour was based on "the spirit (and power) of the masses", rather than on elected or institutional representatives. A parallel process surprisingly emerged between those active in the social dreaming project and OFEK, the organisation whose resources supported the project, and which neither identified itself with it (for reasons of principle) nor led it.

This is reported by Judy Levy, then chairperson of OFEK, who personally took part in the project early on. She was also drawn in by Simi Talmi's spontaneous suggestion that OFEK should be actively involved in studying the social and organisational processes fuelling the protest. Her emotional response, as reported by her, differs dramatically from the one described by Yossi Triest at the outset, and might serve as an impressive testimony to the influence of one's role on one's experience. Judy Levy writes,

> Looking back on it now, I realise that I felt an initial resistance—on both a personal and an organisational level. First, while I was as excited as anyone by the scope and tenor of the protest, I did not feel personally connected to it during the first weeks. While I ideologically abhor the excesses of capitalism, I could not help feeling that my financial and personal status in life did not entitle me to be part of that protest. As far as OFEK was concerned, as the Chairperson of the organisation, I instinctively felt, and still do, that we should avoid any political involvement or statements.

This starting position led to the development of intricate relations between OFEK and those active in the project. Following the collective agreement of OFEK's management to take part in the protest as a data-collecting agent, a considerable amount of the organisation's resources were put at the project's disposal: consultants were recruited and teamed up through OFEK's communication network (normally reserved for messages from OFEK's management to its members). The megaphone, purchased privately to allow the project to take place, was eventually funded by the organisation. Detailed daily reports, summing up the meetings, were distributed through OFEK's mailing list. Still, as Judy Levy reports, the honeymoon was short-lived, and, as the project grew longer, more and more members began complaining about "heavy email traffic", feeling as if OFEK was being hijacked by project activists: "In fact, as the social dreaming event continued, I became more and more uneasy about using the mailing list and tried to find ways to encourage the group to set up its own mailing list, though unsuccessfully."

In retrospect, the two organisational cultures, that of the project activists and that of OFEK, collided on at least two fronts: while co-ordinators of group relations conferences choose the consultants they wish to work with, the dreaming project invited consultants to volunteer, accepting anyone who wished to participate. While OFEK gained its reputation through the high professional level of its members, project consultants were not required to prove their previous experience and most, in fact, were altogether inexperienced in working with social dreaming matrices. This matter gave rise to some harsh criticism; for example, it was suggested that the Rothschild Boulevard activity was, in more ways than one, a protest against what is often perceived as OFEK's elitism. While it is not easy to prove such an argument, it attests to the foul mood that emerged. The ever-growing split between the project and OFEK management reached its climax when, days before the activity came to an end, the management decided to bar its use of the OFEK mailing list.

As Judy Levy writes,

> The climax was an explosion of anger directed at me, as the OFEK Chair, by an OFEK member who objected to the use of organisational email for this activity. This led me to discontinue the project's use of our mailing list a day or two short of the actual ending of the activity. That decision attracted a lot of anger towards me from the side of the project's participants. It seemed to them that I had acted just like the Tel Aviv municipality—in an arbitrary and high-handed manner. This was the worst conflict of roles I had experienced since I became Chairperson . . .

All in all, however, it seems that, despite all the difficulties involved, this unusual activity unsettled the organisation in a way which proved eventually beneficent. Judy Levy concludes that "the creation of a parallel process with the OFEK establishment suggests that the researching body can be a fruitful object of study in itself, in the context of the research", and she adds,

> The social dreaming event, in my view, set out (unconsciously) to prove that things can be different, that freedom of choice is good for

both the event and the organisation and that, in general, breaking down some of the rigid traditional structures in the organisation is vital for its existence. And there is no question that the effects of the social dreaming were good for OFEK: the organisation got more exposure, it "mingled" with society in an unprecedented way,[3] and the positive energy that permeated it brought a sense of inner revitalisation.

Social dreaming on the boulevard: the white protest

In this part we—Yael Shenhav Sharoni, Ilana Mishael, and Simi Talmi—present a few samples of the dreams we collected and the recurring themes we could identify.

The noisy nature of the event did not allow for a deep process of working through during the sessions. Some of the ideas were brought up afterwards, in our weekly meetings, where those of us who acted as consultants discussed our thoughts in public. We believe that the unconscious motifs that came up in the matrix can shed some light on the dynamics and self-perception of the movement we were trying to explore.

Dreams in white: seeking to belong

One of the first dreams to enter the matrix was recounted by a seventy-year-old man:

> "... I dreamed I was a white butterfly that didn't want to be white ... I moved closer and stole colours from people ... I became a colourful butterfly ... something extravagant ... I thought this was the prettiest butterfly in the field ... the white butterflies said: who got you all dirty? ... I told them I made myself dirty, and they drove me away ... I went to the colourful butterflies and they drove me away too ..."

One of the central themes in the dreams and associations in the matrix was the colour white. Lawrence (2010), the "father" of the social dreaming method, suggests that the dream that enters into the matrix first represents the story of the matrix itself. If this is indeed true, the dream of the white butterfly could be considered as representing the "collective unconscious" of the social dreaming matrix.

The prominent association arising from this dream is the fact that the protest was dubbed in Israel "the white protest", as it mostly involved the middle class, and its activists were mostly European or western in origin (Ashkenazi Jews, referred to as "whites"). This nickname was an ironic reference to a previous wave of protest that took Israeli society by surprise some fifty years earlier, when a militant group of "Eastern Jews" violently protested against ethnic discrimination in Israel. This group, known as "The Black Panthers", entered national consciousness when Golda Meir, then prime minister, called them "not nice". The current protest was no doubt that of the "nice", who objected to their having been "too well behaved", in their ongoing effort to bear the burden of the Israeli economy, which privileges and supports various sectors such as the orthodox Jews and the settler population. While the former take no part in the labour market, the latter receive considerable economic subsidies, in the form of state-sponsored infrastructure and tax benefits. In this sense, the butterfly becoming "dirty" might be perceived as an expression of self-irony, facing the accusations depicting protesters as "goody two-shoes", afraid to "get dirty" in their struggle.[4]

The reference to blacks and whites has another connotation: it no doubt ties Israel to the claim that the ongoing occupation leads to apartheid. This theme, which normally divides the Israeli public (to such an extent that it might lead to civil war) was, as mentioned, utterly absent from the current protest, which seemingly clung to a purely social agenda. No wonder, therefore, that it returned through "white" dreams.

The inclusion–exclusion theme

The rejection of the non-white butterfly as "dirty" was interpreted as reflecting the segmented and divided nature of contemporary Israeli society, which is based more on the rejection of otherness than on any positive identity. The difficulty in containing difference and complexity (the unity of the "whole object", both good and bad, white and dirty) might have found its way into the dream.[5]

The tension between society and individual

Another aspect of the rejection of the butterfly, with all the personal pain it entails, might have been related to the tension between society and the individual in Israel, whose culture exhibits quite a few streaks of Me-ness (Lawrence et al., 1996). It is possible that the white butterfly represents the individual, seeking the freedom to find its own unique voice in a situation where thoughts float unrestricted, as if "owned" by no one and by everyone. Nevertheless, it could, just as well, represent the individual's sense that the need to acknowledge others makes one "dirty" or stained.

The gender motif: feminine vs. masculine leadership

The theme of the colour white came up in two more dreams about white brides.

> "... I dreamed I was standing at the top of a hill, and a parade of brides wearing white was coming down. I was excited and came down after them ... someone asks: who invited you? ... lots of people and large signs ... I don't feel like I belong ..."

> "I'm sitting in a bridal salon ... I am not the bride ... this was towards the end ... I went over all the stages ... I am served an elegant tray with dental floss ..."

While the image of "brides wearing white" is hard to ignore, one should also read these themes against the background of an intensifying struggle between genders, manifest, on the one hand, through an increase in sexual harassment lawsuits and, on the other, through the exclusion of women in the orthodox community (according to the orthodox interpretation of rabbinical law, women are not supposed to intermingle with men) which resulted in a heated public debate. Perhaps the wish these dreams express is that of renewing the possibility for living together—highlighting the absence of a bridegroom. Could this mean that a suitable match is yet to be found? That "marriage" is a metaphor for putting an end to rivalries?

Another dream expressed the conflict between men and women more explicitly. A woman related,

> "I dreamed that I was meeting an old friend, one I haven't seen for many years. We embrace ardently and my husband steps in and tries to separate us. I can't understand why he won't mind his own business."

This dream could be read as calling out for feminine leadership, expressing disappointment in the masculine leaders of Israel who brought the country to what it is.

The dreams about the brides led the group to discuss the colour white also as a symbol of purity: that was immediately criticised: an excess of "whiteness" or purity has always had an exclusionary effect of what is not pure or white. Those who supported this interpretation claimed that Israel is suffering from too much self-hate and self-criticism—that seeing only "the empty half of the glass" weakens the struggle for change. They quoted the following dream.

> ". . . I was in a group . . . responsible for a child . . . I needed to fill the back-pack with toothpaste . . . it was full of white fluid . . ."

In this sense, the different means for cleaning and whitening teeth might perhaps express a serious wish for healing and health, representing the search for means to "whiten" and clean social "rot and decay".

The tension between parents and children: the pain of the missing parent, the Israeli leadership crisis

The "white" thread led our dreams further afield, to the intergenerational relationship between parents and children. The predominant feeling in this area was that of the absence of parenthood (dead parents) and of disappointment due to the collapse of existing leadership.

> ". . . In my dream, I come to visit my mother . . . who died . . . but in order to visit her, I must go through a very large pool of water . . ."

And another:

> ". . . I am swimming with my father in the sea . . . high waves, and I almost drown, I'm screaming . . . dad . . . and my dad doesn't come back . . ."

A child of five took the microphone with great confidence and shared an interesting dream:

> "I was in a great blue sea . . . there are a lot of filters, filtering out the plankton . . . I tried to get out . . . through the plankton . . . later, there was

a dolphin who brought me to shore . . . I'm lucky it was just a dream . . . if it was real . . . I don't know if I would have got to him . . . to shore . . . when I got back to the pool, I saw that it was just a toy . . ."

Instead of parents, who should have been taking care of him, he has, at least, a dolphin to show him the way. Not all is lost, then, there is still hope, yet the task is a little too much for a child. He should be playing in the swimming pool, not out in the ocean (which probably represented the stormy water in which Israeli society lives).

Quite a few dreams dealt with the same sense of having lost one's way and the absence of guidance or leadership.

"In my dream there was a rhinoceros . . . who was trying to surf the waves and lost control . . . and he laughed. . ."";

"I dreamt I was driving a new car . . . on a bad road . . . I feel something's not right . . . I got out and see the car has no wheels . . ."

". . . I dreamt last night that Benjamin Netanyahu ended his term of office . . . he succeeded during his term to deal with the protest and with the Palestinians . . . too bad later his life he ended . . . like Sharon[6] . . . a sort of vegetable . . . I don't know, all this stuff he had to deal with . . . the Arabs . . . later on he just stops functioning . . ."

"I'm at a nursing home . . . visiting my aunt . . . she's a holocaust survivor . . . and when the visit is over . . . I find my way out";

". . . I dreamt about my father, he started cooking something and stopped because he was out of chicken soup and black pepper . . ."

In contrast with these weak parents/fathers, various alternatives of young, somewhat "lost" parents arose, probably representing the confusion of the middle generation that is now in leadership positions in Israel.

"I'm travelling . . . my mother is young . . . on this trip . . . I'm with her . . . and my son is walking behind us . . . we are in front . . . I don't know whether to walk with my mother or with my son . . ."

". . . I took a car . . . I was driving . . . there were three roads, and I didn't know which way to turn . . . I needed to go north . . . and I couldn't find which way north is . . . someone told me to get out of the car and walk with her . . . she couldn't find the north either . . . an elegant man came along . . . with a nice car, and said he would take me . . . we walk and walk . . . I missed the place and had to go on walking . . ."

The motifs of seeking or losing one's way as a result of the failures of parents/leaders were some of the most prominent themes to arise in the matrix. While we cannot elaborate any further in this context, we must direct the reader's attention to the fact that in all the dream narratives we have quoted, the protagonists are persistently presented as victims of others (whether failing parents or harsh circumstance), not even once expressing guilt feelings or taking responsibility for the injuries, abandonments, and damage they have caused themselves. Such dream stories simply never came up. The absence of violence in most dreams led us to reflect on what we felt was strikingly missing— Israel's national trauma, the Rabin assassination.

Non-violent street circles – possible connections to the Rabin assassination

The circle of those participating in social dreaming, sitting around candles on the playground, like other circles engaged in other activities throughout the boulevard, was strangely reminiscent of the murder of Yitzhak Rabin in 1995. Thousands of teenagers took to the streets then, too, gathering around candles, staring at the flames with tears in their eyes, as if wishing to weld a torn people back together. The desire to merge seemed to replace guilt feelings and fear related to patricide (Erlich, 1988).

As mentioned before, the 2011 summer protest stood out in its utter non-violence. It even shunned outspoken criticism of the current leadership. Protesters did not address leaders directly—it seemed as if they looked right through them. One could wonder about the meaning of this and the source of this quiet power. The youths who took to the streets in 1995, gathering in street circles in an anti-war and anti-violence spirit, were the same generation that led this protest, with the similar motives of searching for wholeness. Are we now witnessing another link in the chain of national post-trauma reactions to the extremely violent internal act of assassinating a prime minister?

Nevertheless, our candle flame did not always remain so innocent and nostalgic. On the last day of the matrix, dreams and associations relating to natural selection came up—only the strong win; violence is a must. Our associations turned to Jan Palach, the Czech student who set himself on fire, committing suicide in protest at the Soviet invasion into Czechoslovakia in 1968 and causing a wave of self-immolations and suicides. This was connected to the beginning of the Tunisian revolution in December 2010, when a young man named Muhammad Boaziz set himself on fire and died, driven by frustration and angst at his efforts to earn a living.

One year later, during a demonstration marking the one year anniversary of the Rothschild protest, Moshe Sillman, an Israeli citizen, set himself on fire in rage and despair.

Some closing remarks

The phenomenon: first working hypothesis

As we mentioned in the beginning, we see the tent protest in Israel as part of a global phenomenon, breaking out on to the surface in all manner of squares around the world, everywhere embracing the local language and taking shape according to prevalent social circumstances and political structures. While this current framework allows little room to elaborate on the causes of this phenomenon, our conjecture is that it is a kind of side effect, brought about by the process of globalisation and technological innovation, which has been exposing growing numbers of people to alternative, more promising, possibilities of being. In Israel, it seemed like a kind of wishful dream to live in a non-violent environment, so different from our day-to-day reality.

The matrix: second working hypothesis

The synchronisation of centres of social activity spread across the world could be related, among other things, to the new socio-technology of social networks supported by cellular and computer hardware (Smartphones, laptops, Wi-Fi) and internet applications, which have opened new possibilities, paving new roads for human consciousness, including what almost seems to be a real-life manifestation of Foulkes' idea of the "Matrix"—the network of the social unconscious (Foulkes & Anthony, 1965).

Masses (see Freud, 1921c) were always considered instruments for the effacement of personal identity. The new technology has enabled the realisation, as it were, of the fantasy of having the voice of the individual heard "all over the world", merely by publishing a "status", a "tweet", or a picture on Facebook, Twitter, Instagram, etc., from one's own mobile phone to the whole world. As we said before, the mass, which was perceived as a "faceless mother" (by Turquet, 1975) that robs individuals of their personal identity, has obtained "a face" and became a "Facebook".

The status of leadership: third working hypothesis

The characteristics of leadership in the protest system reveal a fascinating phenomenon: this local, contemporary revolution (unlike previous ones) is usually named after the square in which it takes place, rather than after the local leader who instigated it. (For example, "Tahrir revolution"—who can recall the name of the Facebook user whose words incited it?). It almost seems as if the very square had "opened its mouth" and begun to talk. The protagonist–background relations between the masses and their leaders, which have already been overturned several times throughout the history of ideas governing the work of group relations (consider, for instance, Freud's (1921c) view, which sees the leader as the cause for mass regression, in contrast to Bion (1964), who sees the leader as an anointed representative of the group's unconscious) have this time reversed the roles of background and protagonist so dramatically that one can get the impression that the masses are leading the movement, without any apparent leadership initiating this process. This is, no doubt, a change in the culture of leadership and especially in its perception.

However, has the representation of leadership really changed in the *unconscious* as well? Could it be that the "primal father figure" has been usurped by a "great mother-figure", that a representation of feminine leadership (in contrast to female leaders), whose image is the matrix as a cosmic womb, a container, a life-giving ground lacking any directionality, is replacing the figure of the phallic general, whose leadership is supposedly based on the ability to point out the "right" direction? We shall leave this intricate issue for further discussions.

The characteristics of the system: fourth working hypothesis

The protest movement constitutes a system whose stability (in contrast with traditional organisational logic) is undermined the more organised it becomes. That is, it is unified by feeling, first and foremost.

In retrospect, it seems that the Israeli movement's main objective was to give rise, in the face of a turbid wave of hatred, to a vicious cycle of wars and existential anxieties, and an interminable sectorial struggle in which, time and again, narrow interests of powerful minorities (such as the settlers) blatantly and shamelessly outweigh the public interest, to a different wave, one of unity and affection, a social embrace, a sweeping—and inevitably illusory—feeling of "togetherness", which restored to the so-far muted middle class not only its voice, but also its freedom of speech and solidarity.

As the stability of the system is based, under these conditions, on the extent of emotional sharing, the arising situation is emblematic of chaotic systems: the less defined and distinct the system is, the more stable it is. Once a plan of action is needed (that is, to specify the movement's demands, whom it is addressing, and what means it is offering for fulfilling these demands), once the massive denial of power struggles and political conflict starts to fade, it is only natural that the sense of unity and cohesiveness crumbles, paradoxically leaving the system more and more chaotic.

*The role of the "social dreaming matrix"
in the protest: a closing remark*

This chapter attempted to pass on our experience of an unusual activity that applied group relations knowledge and tools in the "market" conditions of a spontaneous protest movement. It was an enlightening and enriching experience for all of us. Still, more than allowing us to fathom the nature of dreams, the social dreaming matrix provided us with a means for action research. In retrospect, we believe that this choice was not incidental.

Observing the events on the boulevard as a kind of "organisational event" *in vivo* raises structural and systemic questions with regard to the actual existence and role of the dream matrix on the boulevard.

One could ask "Why would the protest system create such a sub-system, placing it in a defined structure—the playground?" It is our assumption that the role of the dream matrix in the protest was to serve as a kind of "potential space", namely, a playground. It served as a tent, restricting and containing within it, in a floating, creative atmosphere, the various contents and contradictions, so that the protest system could deal with the social order. It somehow brought back the belief in the importance of dreams, once they gained the political power to be heard in public.

Notes

1. More than ten per cent of the adult population took to the streets.
2. The chapter refers only to the part of the protest movement that took place in August 2011.
3. For the first time in its history, OFEK opened a Facebook page.
4. While this may be purely coincidental, it is still interesting to note that, at the time, the Panthers' protest became famous through the act of stealing milk bottles, which were then delivered to the doorstep by the milkman, and handing them out in poor neighbourhoods. The current protest was instigated by a Facebook group crying out against the rising prices of cottage cheese—the very symbol of Israeli domesticity. The traditional cottage cheese container bears the image of a country house (a cottage), which marks an Israeli bourgeois fantasy. Black and white are contrasted in this historical association as well.
5. In this context, it came to us that the colour white contains, on a physical level, all existing colours. It is an emblem of multiplicity, gathering a multitude into one whole.
6. Ariel Sharon's time in office suddenly came to an end when he had a stroke. For several years he has been in a comatose condition in hospital.

References

Bion, W. R. (1964). *Experiences in Groups*. London: Tavistock.
Erlich, S. (1988). Adolescence reaction to Rabin's assassination: patricide, is that so? *Sichot*, 13(1): 81–85.
Foulkes, S. H., & Anthony, E. J. (1965). *Group Psychotherapy* (2nd edn). London: Karnac Classics.

Freud, S. (1921c). *Group Psychology and the Analysis of the Ego. S. E., 18*: 65–143. London: Hogarth.

Lawrence, W. G. (2010). *The Creativity of Social Dreaming.* London: Karnac.

Lawrence, W. G., Bain, A., & Gould, L. (1996). The fifth basic assumption. *Free Associations, 6/1*(37): 28–55.

Turquet, P. (1975). Threats to identity in the large group. In: L. Kreeger (Ed.), *The Large Group* (pp. 87–158). London: Karnac.

PART II

STUDYING THE RELATIONSHIP BETWEEN GROUP RELATIONS WORK AND ITS IMPACT IN ITS CULTURAL AND GEOGRAPHICAL SETTING

CHAPTER SIX

Exploring group relations work in China: challenges, risks, and impact

Hüseyin Özdemir

Introduction

This chapter is written from the perspective of a director and organiser of three group relations (GR) conferences in China. The conferences took place in 2010, 2011, and 2012. I try to focus the GR-work from two perspectives. One is what it is like to introduce GR work into a foreign, as well as very complex, country and culture (Özdemir, 2013). The second challenge was to conduct the conference in context with the sponsoring company. These three GR conferences were part of a wider organisational development (OD) process of the sponsoring company. What we tried from the very beginning of the OD process in 2004 was to bring socio-technical system thinking into place.

The GR conferences were designed for members who wanted to improve their understanding of their roles, their personal authority, and their responsibility in roles in order to manage them accordingly. In 2011 and in 2012, we conducted post-conference research. One of our Chinese staff members conducted interviews with twenty-two former members. Some of the original quotations are included in this chapter, with some light editing of the original English for clarity.

Another reason for the amount of original voices in this chapter is that the participants of Belgirate III in 2012 expressed interest in "hearing" some more voices of the Chinese members. So, these voices give the reader the opportunity of forming his or her personal view on GR work in China. For those who are planning to run GR Conferences in China, those comments also might provide some helpful insight.

The chapter first provides a brief overview of the Chinese culture. Then the facts of the three conferences are presented. Thereafter, the results are shown.

China

China is interesting not only as a low-wage country for the manufacturing sector. Given its high population, it has developed itself into a potentially vital and thriving market for international companies (Liefner, 2005, p. 1). Systematic organisation development is, in China, still a largely unknown field. Group Relations Conferences do not exist there. Companies focus, alongside technical trainings, on intercultural trainings for their expatriate leaders (Herbolzheimer, 2009, p. 48).

Cultural influences

Chinese society is strongly influenced by Confucianism, Buddhism, and Taoism (Mun Chin Kok, 2006). Values based on Confucianism are "respect", "responsibility", "group cohesion", "harmony", "potential as human beings", and "humans as part of a network". Learning is based on "copy and follow", instead of "study and learning from experience" (Kolb & Tianjian Jiang, 2005). Confucius believes that all human beings are born into a social class (Xiao Juan Ma, 2007, p. 129). "Jun-Zi" means educated person (the "noble character"), who has to be respected. "Xiao-Ren" means "little man", who has to be controlled. A Chinese proverb says, "All things belong to the little man but education to the noble".

Traditional Chinese values erode

Traditional values begin to change. Therefore, Chinese society is in a dilemma.

Confucianism has been torn apart. Maoism is largely gone. Western values and lifestyles keep creeping into China together with Hollywood movies, MTV, Coca-Cola, and McDonald's. The first question one needs to ask is: what morals do the Chinese need? Confucian virtues? Not really. Maoism? Almost impossible. Western values and moral standards? Well, they belong to the West.

Or a little bit of the positive from each of the three moral codes? Whatever the case, the Chinese need to create a new moral system to fit with the changed social environment, something with which the Chinese can identify and behave accordingly. (Yanan, 1996, p. 99, translated for this edition)

Yanan Yu and Godwin Chu conducted a study in China which looked at the change in cultural values. There were 2,000 participants asked to select from a list of eighteen traditional Chinese values, those were: "what they are proud of", "which they wish to unlearn", and "for what value they have no opinion". The responses of 2,000 participants showed the following results (Table 6.1).

The authors were shocked that the second strongest negative evaluation was the traditionally very important Chinese value of the "Way of the Golden Mean". The way of the golden mean should be seen as a Chinese philosophy of life. The Chinese are not looking for extremes in life. Rather, they seek to harmonise relationships and bring peace to the human soul (Yanan, 1996, pp. 127, 177).

Furthermore, it can be stated in terms of the interaction of various levels of hierarchy that Confucianism, as a value system, emphasises hierarchy, authority, compliance with regulations, status differences and the absolute respect for superiors (Selmer, 2002, p. 21).

In China, the elderly are traditionally respected, which the older people naturally demand. The younger people are socialised to obey their elders. This expectation of the young is so subtle that people in the west might not notice it (Selmer, 2006, p. 350).

"Saving face" in China is an important part of everyday interaction. In the Western world, morality is linked to the aspect of blame. In contrast, morality in China is linked to the issue of shame. Therefore, criticism means much more than the naming of a situational failure, and it is more likely to lead to evading or avoiding criticism (Busch & Sellmann, 2007; Fargel, 2011).

In conclusion, one may conclude that the community, the common good, and the culture occupy a very important role in Chinese society

Table 6.1.   Index* of responses to questions about eighteen traditional
Chinese values in a study of 2,000 participants (Source: Yanan, 1996).

No.	Value	Index
1	Long historical heritage	89.7
2	Diligence and frugality	86.2
3	Loyalty and devotion to state	67.5
4	Benevolent father, filial son	48.0
5	Generosity and virtues	39.8
6	Respect for traditions	38.5
7	Submission to authority	33.2
8	Harmony is precious	29.5
9	Tolerance, propriety, deference	25.3
10.	Chastity for women	−13.5
11	Glory to ancestors	−23.8
12	A house full of sons and daughters	−35.5
13	Farmers high, merchants low	−43.3
14	Pleasing superiors	−48.9
15	Discretion for self-preservation	−55.9
16	Differentiation between men and women	−59.2
17	Way of golden mean	−59.6
18	Three obediences and four virtues	−64.0

* Index: Percentage of those who are proud of these values minus percentage of those
who would like to eradicate those values.

(Xiao Juan Ma, 2007). Chinese education places particular emphasis
on the spirit of collectivism and the promotion of community
(Fthenakis & Oberhuemer, 2010, p. 277). An important and interesting
conclusion of this work is that in both cultures, the eastern and the
western world, "education and learning" are regarded as fundamental to the development of society (Kolb & Tianjian Jiang, 2005).

Chinese history and political system

In relation to the thousands of years of Chinese history, it is not that
long ago that the former president of China, Deng Xiaoping, opened
the country to international investors and entrepreneurs in December
1978. Since 1980, the Chinese people have had contact with foreigners.
Until then, the country was largely isolated from the outside world
and its influences. Since then, the country has changed rapidly from a

planned economy to a prosperous market economy (Kolb & Tianjian Jiang, 2005), but with a still very strong central government that continues to define the basic parameters of the economy. In 1979, the government opened the country, by means of the joint venture law, to foreign capital (Luo, 2000, p. 159). Therefore, the time period in which free market principles have been introduced is relatively short. Besides their enormous economic performance, the Chinese are also proud of their education system, since they have also won awards and gained international recognition (Xiao Juan Ma, 2007, p. 133). Employees value their corporations and identify with them, especially if their company has a good reputation and offers them security (Xiao Juan Ma, 2007, p. 74).

In addition to Shanghai and Suzhou, Wuxi is an industrially and technologically highly developed area in the region, with increased demand for labour (Hebel & Schucher, 1999, p. 123).

Collective and individual perceptions, such as decision-making behaviour, are determined by one's personal value system (Hofstede, 2001; Kluckhohn & Strodtbeck, 1961; Rokeach, 1979; Schwartz, 1996). Values help people to select, to filter, and to evaluate internal and external environments (Staehle, 1999, pp. 171–176). Values can be divided into either individual or collective values. The collective, societal values are dominant preference models in a given society and its culture. The west has different preference models than those of China (Jullien, 1999; Wittkop, 2006).

Confucianism is the basis of China's great cultural tradition, and the values that it has significantly shape interpersonal relationships today (Shenkar & Ronen, 1987). To understand the values of the Chinese, it is necessary to know the basic ideas of Confucianism and its particular importance in society. The Confucian ideals of "respect", "responsibility", and "cohesion in groups" have significant influence on the Far Eastern societies (Chamberlain, 1997). For example, the widespread paternalistic management style in China is attributed to Confucius.

> The paternalistic leadership style is rooted in three thousand years of imperial rule. Under Confucianism (551–479 BC), which became the official orthodoxy for China during the Han Dynasty, the family was the basic building block of society, and the father's authority over family members was absolute. Although a similar power structure

existed all over the world, in the West, the patriarch's authority was assumed to derive from God. (Jing et al., 2005)

The city of Wuxi

Wuxi is located 103 km from Shanghai.

> Wuxi is a city richly endowed by nature. Owing to its pleasantly warm and moist climate, it boasts a reputation of the 'Land of Fish and Rice'. Relying on the nearby Yangtze River and ancient Grand Canal, it had been a port city with the busiest rice and cloth market in China before 19th century. In modern times, with its rapidly developing industry, Wuxi became one of China's top 50 cities with broad strength and is thus called the 'Little Shanghai' for its prosperous economy. With a splendid history of over three thousand years, Wuxi claims to be 'the Pearl of Tai Lake'. Early in the Spring and Autumn Period (770 BC–476 BC), it had been the economic and politic centre south of Yangtze River. (www.travelchinaguide.com/cityguides/jiangsu/wuxi, accessed July 4th 2013)

Organisations as socio-technical systems

A socio-technical system (STS) (see Figure 6.1) is an organised number of people and technologies, which is structured in a particular way in order to produce a specific result (Cummings & Srivastva, 1977, p. 55; Sydow, 1985, p. 27). The production of typical outcomes of an organisation (e.g., manufacturing products or installation of production equipment) is the major task of a primary work system (Trist, 1981). Emery (1959) has adapted the terminology of socio-technical systems to apply to organisations. Therefore, organisations fulfil one or several primary tasks (Sydow, 1985). This understanding of organisations is one of the foundations for the implementation of Group Relations Conferences in China.

The conference as a whole also can be understood as an STS. The "technical" elements were the primary task, structures, roles, territories, and resources such as flip-charts, drawings, etc. Elements of the social subsystem are the feelings, the inner images, the unconscious, the relationships, the values, etc.

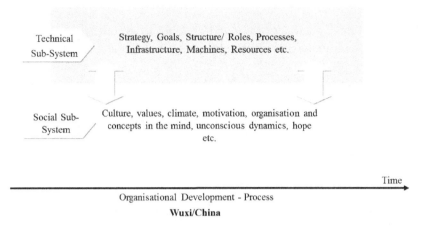

Figure 6.1.   Two sub-systems of an organisation.

The sponsoring institutions

All GR conferences were sponsored by an industrial joint venture, based in Wuxi with Headquarters in Germany and in China. Oezpa is the organising institution of the three GR conferences. The co-founder and co-director of Oezpa directed the three conferences and invited Chinese as well as international staff members.

The Tavistock Institute of Human Relations, directed by Dr Eliat Aram, supported the GR conferences in China. Dr Mannie Sher, Director of the GR Programmes of the Tavistock Institute, was invited by the director to take over the associate director's role in 2011 and 2012.

Membership

The participants of these three conferences all had leading and technical functions. In the third conference in 2012, the future general manager of the sponsoring company in Wuxi also participated. Thus, four to five levels of hierarchy were present in the conference.

Primary task

The conferences were designed as temporary learning organisations. The primary task of the conferences, in which staff worked to provide opportunities, was to experience, explore, and learn from development and management of roles and systems, to experience leadership, authority, self-management in roles, and psychodynamic processes in organisations.

This goal could be reached by allowing oneself and others to experience the conference, to communicate these experiences and to examine their meaning in order to learn from the conference. This primary task was not easy for the Chinese members, as they came mostly from the same company. The traditional Chinese concept of group cohesion, as well as the language challenge, made it difficult for the members to experience and initiate ideas by themselves. Acting autonomously was difficult for them.

First GR conference, 2010, Wuxi

The first GR conference was held in 2010 and lasted for four days. We had developed Chinese staff over the years in the OD Programme (Özdemir, 2010). In this conference, we also introduced the training group. In this first training group, we strengthened the Chinese staff members in their roles as GR staff. To this end, we presented psychodynamic concepts such as unconscious dynamics in organisations, transference, countertransference, the organisation in the mind, and organisational role analysis. In the first conference, we conducted seminars by using video conferencing. Topics of the seminar events were system, group and role thinking, psychodynamic concepts, personality, and learning. The staff comprised: Dr Hüseyin Özdemir (Director, Germany, Switzerland, Turkey), Lucia Shijin (Associate Director, China), Olya Khaleelee (online staff, UK), Michael Pavlovic (online staff, Germany), Qin yu (administration, China), and Rafael Sarim Özdemir (administration, Germany, Switzerland). The schedule for this conference is shown in Figure 6.2.

Second GR conference, 2011, Wuxi

A year later, in 2011, the second conference was held. Twenty-six members, consisting of directors, managers, and employees, participated. Three members joined from another international company in

2nd of August 2010		3rd of August 2010		4th of August 2010		5th of August 2010		6th of August 2010	
Time	Monday: preparation day	Time	Tuesday	Time	Wednesday	Time	Thursday	Time	Friday
9:00	On-the-Job Training (OTS)	09:00	OTS	09:00	OTS	09:00	OTS	09:00	OTS
10:30	OTS	10:00	OTS	10:00	Break	10:00	Break	10:00	Break
10:45	OTS	11:00	Break	10:15	Large System	10:15	Large System	10:15	Large System
12:15	Lunch OTS	11:30	Opening Plenary	11:15	Break	11:15	Break	11:15	Break
13:15	OTS	12:00	Lunch-Break	11:30	Departmental Event	11:30	Departmental Event	11:30	Application Groups
14:45	Break	13:00	Departmental Event (P)	12:30	Lunch-Break	12:30	Lunch-Break	12:30	Lunch-Break
15:00	OTS	14:30	Departmental Event	14:30	Departmental Event	14:00	Departmental Event (P)	13:30	Application Groups
16:15	Break	15:30	Departmental Event	15:30	Break	15:00	Break	14:30	Break
16:30	GM-Role Consulting	15:45	Break	16:00	Concept Call (international)	15:30	Concept Call (international)	14:45	Closing Plenary
18:00	End of the day	16:00	Concept Call (international)	17:30	Concept reflection	16:30	Break	15:45	Break
		17:30	Concept reflection	18:00	End of the day	16:45	Concept reflection	16:00	OTS post-conf-gather
		18:00	End of the day		OTS	17:15	End of the day	17:00	Closure
			OTS				OTS		

= New

Figure 6.2.   Schedule 2010, first GR conference.

Wuxi. Four international staff members from Germany, Switzerland, the UK, and Australia took part. This open residential conference was directed by Dr Hüseyin Özdemir from Germany/Turkey. Three Chinese also worked within the staff: the assistant to the general manager, an employee of the human resources department, and an external Chinese manager.

We decided to work with the future general manager and his Chinese deputy in one review and application group as a group of two. I took over the consultant's role for this group. The conference started with a welcome speech by the sponsoring general manager.

The staff comprised: Dr Hüseyin Özdemir (Director, Germany, Switzerland, Turkey), Dr Mannie Sher (Associate Director, UK, South Africa), Lucia Shijin (China), Barbara Lagler Özdermir (Switzerland, Germany), Dr Brigid Nossal (Australia), Qin yu (administration, China), and Jingjun Wang (administration, China). The schedule for this conference is shown in Figure 6.3.

Monday, 20th June,2011	Tuesday, 21st June,2011	Wednesday,22nd June,2011	Thursday,23rd June,2011	Friday, 24th June,2011
Directormeetg., 8.30 –9.00	Directormeetg., 8.15 – 8.45	Directormeetg., 7.30 – 7.55	Directormeetg., 7.30 – 7.55	Directormeetg., 7.30 – 7.55
Staff meeting, 9–5 p.m.	Staff meeting, 9–11 a.m.	Staff meeting, 8.00–8.45 a.m.	Staff meeting, 8.00–8.45 a.m.	Staff , meeting, 8.00–8.45 a.m.
	Welcome by Sponsor,1.30	Sys, 9–10 a.m.	Sys, 9–10 a.m.	LS, 9–10 a.m.
		Coffee/ Tea, 10–10.15 a.m.	Coffee/ Tea, 10–10.15 a.m.	Coffee/ Tea, 10–10.15 a.m.
	Lunch with members,12	LS, 10.15–11.15 a.m.	LS, 10.15–11.15 a.m.	Seminar-Event,10.15–11.15
Registration 1 p.m.	Coffee/ Tea 11.15–11.45 a.m.,(Admin)	Coffee/ Tea 11.15–11.45 a.m.,(Admin)	Coffee/ Tea 11.15–11.45 a.m.,(Admin)	Coffee/ Tea 11.15–11.30 a.m.,(Admin)
Opening Plenary 2-3 p.m.	SE-P 11.45–12.45 a.m.	SE-P 11.45–12.45 a.m.	SE 11.45–12.45 a.m.	Seminar-Event 11.30–12.30 a.m
Coffee/ Tea 3–3.15 p.m. (Admin)	Lunch 12.45–2.15 p.m.	Lunch 12.45–2.15 p.m.	Lunch 12.45–2.15 p.m.	Lunch 12.30 a.m.
Sys,3.15–4.15 p.m.	Staff lunch meeting 12.50–1.45 p.m.	Staff lunch meeting 12.50–1.45 p.m.	Staff lunch meeting 12.50–1.45 p.m.	AG 1.30-2.30 p.m.
Coffee/ Tea 4.15–4.30 p.m.	SE,2.15-3.15 p.m.	SE,2.15-3.15 p.m.	SE,2.15-3.15 p.m.	
Sys 4.30 5.30 p.m.	Coffee/ Tea 3.15–3.45 p.m.	Coffee/ Tea 3.15–3.45 p.m.	Coffee/ Tea 3.15–3.45 p.m.	Coffee/ Tea 2.30–2.45 p.m.
Coffee/ Tea, 5.30 – 5.35	SE 3.45–4.45 p.m.	SE 3.45–4.45 p.m.	SE-P 3.45–4.45 p.m.	Closing Plenary 2.45–3.45 a.m
LS, 5.35–6.35 p.m.	Coffee/ Tea, 4.45–5	Coffee/ Tea, 4.45–5	Coffee/ Tea, 4.45–5	Staff meeting , 4.15–5.15
	RG, 5–6 p.m.	RG, 5–6 p.m.	RG, 5–6 p.m.	
Staff Dinner, 6 p.m.	Staff Dinner, 7 p.m.	Staff Dinner, 6.30 p.m.	Staff Dinner, 7 p.m.	
	Staff meeting, 8.30–10pm	Staff meeting, 7.45–9.15pm	Staff meeting , 8.15–10,pm	

Figure 6.3.   Schedule 2011, second GR conference.

Third GR conference, 2012, Wuxi

The third conference, in 2012, was held, like the two others, in a five-star hotel in Wuxi. The sponsoring company invested in the venue as well the external staff from the west. Alongside these investments, making the leading staff available for the conference for five days was also a huge expenditure for the company. The participants honoured this by showing general interest and full attendance, although they maintained critical opinion towards the conference in all three cases. They feared it could have been an Assessment Centre organised by the General Manager of the major sponsoring company. In this conference, we offered seminars by the staff members. Topics were a case study on OD, action research, and their own OD process from 2004 to 2012.

The staff comprised: Dr Hüseyin Özdemir (Director, Germany, Switzerland, Turkey), Dr Mannie Sher (Associate Director, UK, South Africa), Mónica Velarde Lazarte (Peru, USA), Professor Dr Sandra Schruijer (the Netherlands), Lei Qingbao (China), Si Xianqi (China), Qin yu (administration, China), Jingjun Wang (admininistration, China), and Pearl Stegmann (administration, Germany, China). The schedule for the conference is shown in Figure 6.4.

Monday., 25th June 2012	Tuesday, 26th June 2012	Wednesday, 27th June 2012	Thursday, 28th June 2012	Friday, 29th June 2012
		Director meeting 7.30 – 7.55	Director meeting 7.30 – 7.55	Director meeting 7.30 – 7.55
Staff meeting 9.30 a.m.–5 p.m.	Staff meeting 9 a.m.–10.30 a.m.	Staff gathering 8.15–8.45 a.m.	Staff gathering 8.15–8.45 a.m.	Staff gathering, 8.15–8.45 a.m.,(8.40 – 8.55,Admin)
		LS, 9–10 a.m./ TG	LS, 9–10 a.m./ TG	LS, 9–10 a.m./ TG
		Short break, 10 a.m.	Short break, 10 a.m.	Short break, 10 a.m.
	Welcome by Sponsor 11.30 a.m	Seminar Event 10.15–11.15 a.m.	SE 10.15–11.15 a.m.	Seminar-Event 10.15–11.15 a.m.
	Lunch with members 12 p.m.	Coffee/ Tea, 11.15 a.m. (11.20 – 11.35 a.m. Admin)	Coffee/ Tea, 11.15 a.m. (11.20 – 11.35 a.m. Admin)	Short break 11.15 a.m.
	Registration, 1 p.m.	SE-P, 11.45–12.45	SE, 11.45–12.45	Seminar-Event, 11.30–12.30
	Opening Plenary, 2-3 p.m.	Lunch, 12.45–2.15 p.m.	Lunch, 12.45–2.15 p.m.	Lunch, 12.30 p.m.
	Short break, 3 p.m.			AG, 1.30-2.30 p.m. wth TG
	LS, 3.10–4.10 p.m./ TG	SE, 2.15–3.15 p.m.	SE-P, 2.15–3.15 p.m.	
Training Group (TG)	Coffee/ Tea, 4.10 p.m. (4.15 – 4.25 p.m. Admin)	Coffee/ Tea, 3.15 p.m.	Coffee/ Tea, 3.15 p.m.	Short break, 2.30 p.m.
Training Group	Seminar Event, 4.30-5.30	SE, 3.45–4.45 p.m.	Seminar Event, 3.45–4.45	Closing Plenary, 2.45–3.45 p.m.
	Short break, 5.30 p.m.	Short break, 4.45 p.m.	Short break, 4.45 p.m.	Post Conf. Staff gather., 4 p.m.
	RG, 5.45–6.45 p.m. wth TG	RG, 5–6 p.m. wth TG	AG, 5–6 p.m. wth TG	
Dinner, 6 p.m.	Dinner, 7 p.m.	Dinner, 6.30 p.m.	Dinner, 6.30 p.m.	
	Staff meeting, 8.15–9.45	Staff meeting, 7.45–9.15	Staff meeting, 7.45–9.15	

Figure 6.4.   Schedule 2012, third GR conference.

Training group (TG)

Within the first and the third conferences there was a special training group. The Chinese staff members had the chance to learn the underlying methods, concepts, and dynamics in the training group. The training group consisted of Chinese and newly appointed international staff members. The selection criteria to become a TG member were openness and interest in learning according to this model, a high level of social skills, counselling skills, and recognition within the organisation.

Conceptual inputs were given by the director of the training group. The first TG in 2010 was directed by the Conference Director. The learning as a TG member was experiential. TG members had to work fully as staff members with all the restrictions that had not been experienced yet. The second TG was directed by an international staff member, Mónica Velarde Lazarte, from Peru. Conceptual topics were around issues like: role and system thinking, consulting, organisation as a socio-technical system, Bion's basic assumptions in groups, and other psychodynamic concepts.

Summary and findings: development of GR in China from 2010 to 2012

In our work in China, we focused on issues of economy, management, organisation, and personal development. Questions relating to political and social problems in China were deliberately not mentioned by the international staff. In my role as the director, I tried not to put the participants and my staff at risk. For me, as director of the conferences, I was always aware there might be a chance to come into conflict with local authorities. Therefore, my behaviour was as neutral and cautious as possible.

During the third conference, there was an argument between the hotel management and the directorship of the conference regarding information walls that were put up in the hallway of the hotel.

They would not allow us to display these at first. They probably thought there was a connection to the "wall newspapers" found in communist countries. Later, our Chinese staff members convinced them, and we were allowed to put our walls in the hallway of our floor.

My aim as the director was to introduce the GR work as basically as possible. This meant I had to convey basic concepts, such as "here-and-now-events", small systems sitting in a circle face to face, large system sitting in a spiral, opening and closing plenaries set up like chairs in a lecture hall, with staff sitting in the front. Step by step, we increased the complexity of the GR work by, for instance, introducing "here and now events" in the second conference (Table 6.2). The table shows the key elements of the three conferences. The results of the interviews are listed below. Statements have been edited for clarity.

The foundation was set for the GR conferences by the long term OD process in one of the involved companies. The strong relationship between the sponsoring general manager, his managers, who were mostly the members of the conferences, and the director of the conferences created the basis for the conferences.

Chinese staff involved

Complexity also increased by getting Chinese staff involved. At the same time, the Chinese staff helped us international staff understand the cultural background of Chinese behaviour. This was the reason

Table 6.2. Key elements of conferences 2010–2012 (overview).

Year	Members	Format	Here & now events	Intersystem event	Description
2010	24, directors, managers, general manager (GM)	Staff training before and on-the-job Video seminars (time difference! Language! Offered text) Post-conference interviews	Large system	Departmental event (including GM)	On site Preparation staff one day before First departmental event Factory live issues/CEO visit 4 int. staff (2 via Skype), 5 Chinese In-house in factory Involvement GM in system events
2011	26, directors, managers	'Full orglab: small system, large system, system event Post-conference interviews	Small system Large system	System event (= "Institutional event")	Hotel, welcome by GM 4 int. exp. staff, 3 Chinese Open conference
2012	30, directors, managers, future general manager	SE, staff training on-the-job No small system Post-conference interviews	Large system	System event (= "Institutional event")	Hotel, welcome by GM 5 int. staff, 5 Chinese Open conference, 3 from other company (German) Cases/Summary OD process RAG with GM 5 management levels in conference

why the Chinese staff, although less experienced in GR work, became an important part of our work. The involvement of Chinese people on the staff was appreciated and seen by the members as a positive development.

> "Generally, the way of orglab is very special; it's different from ordinary training. The first time it's an experiment, the second time is an improvement, it tried to involve Chinese colleagues in the management team (HÖ: staff)." (Chinese member, 2012)

> "The third time orglab is better, and we felt better seeing our colleague join in the consultant's team." (Chinese member, 2012).

Working language

The working language of the conferences was English. In the systems event, members' subsystems, where members worked without a consultant, the Chinese spoke their own language. In the RAGs (Özdemir & Özdemir Lagler, 2013), we asked them from time to time to talk in Chinese and then to translate their summary to the consultant. Translations were offered by members and organised for seminar events (SE). The staff asked members to translate during the seminar event. External translators were not used. The struggle with the different languages was part of the learning.

> "No [HÖ: I didn't try out]. Because of the language problem, so I just followed one of my colleagues." (Chinese member, 2012)

> "The [HÖ: Chinese] consultant made a conclusion at the beginning, and then we discussed and drew pictures. We found that different people may have different opinions on the same issue." (Chinese member, 2012).

English as a language and the accent of the staff members, besides the "GR language", was difficult to follow and to accept. Beside the fact that the language issue is a defence against reflecting one's role and learning, etc., it seemed to be a fact that the understanding of each other was difficult. "Language, it's better to have Chinese consultants" (Chinese member, 2012).

> "Suggest using Chinese, because using the mother tongue is more freely [understood]." (Chinese member, 2012)

"Our English is not so good, and some of the consultants have strong accents, so we don't understand well. Maybe this type of learning is a good way in the western countries, but could be adjusted a bit when applied in China according to the real situation of our company. Because most of the Chinese are not so open, and dare not speak." (Chinese member, 2012)

Chinese members with their technical background

Chinese members, with their technical background, showed reactions similar to those of members in the west. At the same time, the Chinese cultural background had an impact on the learning. Besides being challenged as a member with a technical professional background, the Chinese cultural aspects were challenging, too.

"Do not know what exactly I learnt from it. Maybe I used something unconsciously, but couldn't tell exactly. I think the orglab is different from others; it's about 'understand by yourself'. We could improve relevant abilities by observation and communication." (Chinese member, 2012)

"At the beginning, the consultants sometimes act like the management, sometimes act like the consultants, we didn't know what their real roles are. Due to the influence of my education background (engineer), I thought the consultants should tell us how to do things; we expected consultants to tell us the goal and the process. But later I understood what they do is to let us to feel, to experience, but not tell us the result." (Chinese member, 2012)

"Not so much influence, maybe I could use something unconsciously. We Chinese prefer a detailed topic, then discuss it or study it together or separately." (Chinese member, 2012).

Wish for cognitive and "fast" learning

Members were interested in having presentations by staff members and learning on a cognitive level. Written texts helped them to understand the English sentences and the meaning behind them. Discussions among the Chinese, in their own language, helped in taking in the theory. There was a wish for fast learning and to be given "how to do" instruments.

"I feel better when the consultants give us [a] presentation about [the] case study." (Chinese member, 2012)

[HÖ: ("We got most out of) Seminar Event: when there's a consultant to show a presentation, and others listen to it . . ." (Chinese member and staff in 2012)].

"Two group relations psychology theories are introduced into the group relations workshop; when participants are able to link the theory to their daily life, they are more interested. Chinese people [who are] current[ly] under great pressure lack patience. They want to see very quickly the application of the theory or what the use of the theory is. Participants think Chinese people are born to understand relationships, only western people write it as a theory. Participants lack self-reflection." (Chinese staff member, 2010)

"It helped [us] to understand faster if there was [a] PPT [HÖ: Microsoft PowerPoint] presentation." (Chinese member, 2012)

"ᵃThey [HÖ: staff] made some changes, e.g., sharing some cases, and helped us to analyse them; this way is closer to the traditional Chinese one." (Chinese member, 2012)

More guided learning and curiosity

Members wished for more guided learning. They were curious and were interested in exploring the theme.

"I like the seminar event. But [it would be better] if the SE could be changed to: give a topic or suggestion at the beginning, and talk about it in the groups, then put the results together, discuss again, then draw a conclusion." (Chinese member, 2012)

"I think this kind of workshop is accepted more or less by us, but we still need guidance from consultants. I wonder if the consultant could recommend some books or materials for us to read." (Chinese member, 2012)

Wish for personal feedback, explanation and "results"

The members asked in all three Conferences for personal feedback. The staff role was appealing to them. Competition with Chinese staff members by higher ranked members was expressed.

". . . if it needs to continue, could we make some changes for the Orglab? Could the consultants give the participants an instant feedback after every event? Could give everyone a chance to recommend themselves to be a consultant, before we start the Orglab." (Chinese member, 2012)

"Hope the Orglab could have an exact goal or purpose, and let us know what we could get after taking that." (Chinese member, 2012)

"It's better to give us a clear explanation after the large system and system events." (Chinese member, 2012)

"Those types [HÖ: Here and now events] are all good, but I prefer the one which has a consultant, and [if we] could get feedbacks from consultants." (Chinese member, 2012)

"Orglab is designed to be a dynamic system, and to let participants to develop in it, but there are no comments on the results. But, as Chinese, we always want to know if our results are right or not, and [we] wanted to get some judgements." (Chinese member, 2012)

"It's better to add some one-to-one communication." (Chinese member, 2012)

Personal learning and transfer

The personal learning and the transfer of GR learning was seen. Some were still struggling and trying to find out what all those conferences were about.

"All of those areas, especially in daily work. When all the people are waiting, we should discover by ourselves, and break the silence, then [with regard] to [the] effect on [the] environment, we should not always wait for others' orders and changes. And it's good for personal development. When we [then] face a strange environment, or environment changes, we might know how to react." (Chinese member, 2012)

Different levels of learning

The members found that there are different levels of learning. Members could realise that not only the spoken word is important. They learnt that there are different levels of communication and understanding.

"I learnt when someone says something to you, you do not only listen to the words, but also need to listen to his/her feelings. In that way, you could communicate better and gain more [understanding]." (Chinese member, 2012)

"I could use one word to describe what I experienced: "understanding". We usually take everything for granted, thinking others would understand us, but the workshop helped us to know [that what] others think may be different from [what we think]. What I got from the workshop are: 1. Understand each other; 2. diversity may be managed." (Chinese member, 2012)

"It's not a technical training, it won't teach you exact things, but will allow you to feel, to experience. From that you could know the position of the organisation, how to communicate with others, and how to locate your position in the organisation, then to develop yourself. I think the workshop is good for leadership skills." (Chinese member, 2012)

Still not clear and accepted

Learning—after taking part in three conferences— is still not clear, and neither is it accepted. To transfer the learning to the organisation back home seems to be possible.

"I am not so clear about what I learnt from the Orglab, because the training doesn't have a very clear purpose. Different people may have different strengths in different areas, e.g., maybe one person is not so good in the punching position, but he could do well in injection, so I think we could find out different people's talents." (Chinese member, 2012)

"If [we were to] divide the level into 3, I think I'm on the lowest level. . . . so what I need is to get some information, so that I won't fall behind in my current working area." (Chinese member, 2012)

"Do not know what exactly I learnt from it. Maybe I used something unconsciously, but couldn't tell exactly." (Chinese member, 2012)

"Cannot remember something special; maybe the seat position was interesting (every time is different). Everyone has some blind points. There's something we didn't know, or didn't realise, or didn't want to admit, but we could challenge and change ourselves by role-play." (Chinese member, 2012).

Key topics of learning

Key topics of learning were mentioned in the interviews. One important aspect was seen in the self-management and the learning, both in the role in the conference and in the organisation back home.

"I think the orglab is different from others; it's about 'understand by yourself'. We could improve relevant abilities by observation and communication." (Chinese member, 2012)

"I think all the topics are the same [HÖ: interesting;, whatever question you propose, you do not get a clear-cut answer, just discussion, no true or false. I think it's about challenging us. For example, the first day I went there, I remained silent, because I didn't know anything about the Orglab at all, but the next day, I dared to propose questions. So I think Orglab is [a] process about breaking one's limits, about breaking through the mental boundaries." (Chinese ember, 2012).

"I couldn't say what I learnt; I [can] just tell what I feel and experience. Every group is an organisation, everyone takes different roles in different organisations, and this workshop also provided us [with] opportunities to try different roles." (Chinese member, 2012)

Staff members are seen as support

Although the staff behaved with distance, Chinese members saw us as a support. We were not seen as enemies. The members showed some disappointment that they did not get enough inputs from consultants. Our staff behaviour was experienced as being held from a distant perspective.

"They contributed a lot, especially in the first two Orglabs, because at those times we didn't know how to play, we needed others to guide us, but when we become familiar with these their contribution will be less." (Chinese member, 2012)

"Very important, because they could help us to sum up things we talked [about]." (Chinese member, 2012)

"I think the consultants contribute a lot to the designing part (design the workshop, but didn't do that much in the workshop time. They didn't give us many inputs; just asked us to experience by ourselves." (Chinese Member, 2012)

Differentiation between experienced and new staff was made. Chinese staff members were not only accepted, but were also seen as an opportunity for better understanding.

> "Maybe experienced consultants know what they want to share, but new consultants don't know exactly. So it's better if the consultant could detail the topic they should discuss, or guide them back when they are far away from the topic." (Chinese member, 2012)

Large systems diversity

The large system (large study group) was experienced as both diverse and depressing. The difficulty of being in a large system was also seen as a chance to listen to different voices. Members saw the possibility of staying in an observing role.

> "I found it was interesting in large system, because we were not limited by a certain topic; it was different from those trainings I took before." (Chinese member, 2012)

> "Large system is a bit depressed; maybe it's [intended to] simulate a real scenario. (Chinese member, 2012)

> "Large system, because we could hear more different voices and ideas in it." (Chinese member, 2012)

Freedom of being in the system event

The freedom that was experienced in the systems event (institutional event) encouraged members to try things out.

> "Systems event. Because we could discuss by ourselves, and went to other groups to observe, or asked consultants for consultancy." (Chinese member, 2012)

"One picture is worth a thousand words"

Drawings in the review and application group, as a mode of expression and understanding, were seen as helpful.

> "Use drawings to express ourselves. It did explain some problems we had met." (Chinese member, 2012)

Boundary management

Members were interested in the strict boundary management by the staff and questioned the meaning of it.

"I'm a conservative person, this conflicts with my profession. I am impressed with one sentence I heard in the workshop that is "we think there're boundaries, and we are unable to break them, but the truth is [that it is] not like that." (Chinese member, 2012)

Fear of losing face

The fear of losing face by making mistakes (see Chinese cultural influences, p. 104) silenced Chinese members. There was a wish to adapt the orglab more to the Chinese culture.

"But in the large systems, there are more people; pressure is greater, people are afraid to speak because they are scared to be wrong." (Chinese member, 2012)

"Could [we] adjust the type of workshop a bit according to Chinese culture and customs?" (Chinese member, 2012)

"I prefer small groups. We could speak [ab]out everything we want in seminar events, but in the review and application groups, we will think more before speaking when consultants are there." (Chinese member, 2012).

Language challenge

Speaking up publicly in English was seen as a challenge. At the same time, some saw it as a chance to find their voice in this unfamiliar setting.

"Speak[ing] English in public [HÖ: was a challenge]." (Chinese member, 2012)

"As a Chinese, I am always shy, so I tried to learn 'How to be open to express myself in public?' in this workshop." (Chinese member, 2012)

"A bit high, especially the challenge for myself. We need to overcome the fear of speaking, and the fear of having different ideas from consultants." (Chinese member, 2012)

"The last day. A lot of people spoke out how they felt at the last meeting, while I dared not speak, but the person sit[ting] next to me encouraged me, so I tried to speak. I think it's a good start for me." (Chinese member, 2012)

Most beneficial sessions

Besides seminar events and review and application groups, Chinese appreciated the systems event (institutional event) most.

"I prefer [the] systems event; it makes us feel free and comfortable. The issue we talked [about] in our group was the influence when the new boss comes, and our expectation of him." (Chinese member, 2012)

Four days of experiential learning: too long

Four days of experiential learning seemed to be too intense for a learning process. The new learning format was too exhausting.

"We think this time is better than the last one, ideas are more [plentiful], and [there is] more activity, but I feel is it too much to spend four days doing this?" (Chinese member, 2012)

"I think four days are too long. We felt confused on the first day, and then understood a bit on the second day, more on the third day, but [on the] fourth day [we] didn't get any more. So I think maybe 2.5–3 days are enough." (Chinese member, 2012)

References

Busch, M. W., & Sellmann, S. (2007). Expatriates der deutschen Automobilwirtschaft in China– zwischen Faszination und Irritation. *Personalführung, 11*: 22–29.

Chamberlain, J. (1997). *Chinese Gods* (5th edn). Malaysia: Pelanduk.

Cummings, T. G., & Srivastva, S. (1977). *Management of Work: A Socio-Technical Systems Approach*. Kent, OH: Comparative Administration Research Institute.

Fargel, Y. M. (2011). *Strategisches Talentmanagement in China. Die besten Mitarbeiter finden und binden. Leitfaden für erfolgreiche Personalführung*. Wiesbaden: Gabler.

Fthenakis, W. E., & Oberhuemer, P. (Eds.) (2009). *Frühpädagogik international. Bildungsqualität im Blickpunkt* (2nd edn). VS Verlag für Sozialwissenschaften.

Hebel, J., & Schucher, G. (Eds.) (1999). *Der Chinesische Arbeitsmarkt – Strukturen, Probleme, Perspektiven.* Hamburg.

Herbolzheimer, A. (2009). Coaching expatriates – the practice and potential of expatriate coaching for European executives in China (dissertation). In Reihe: *Forum Beratungswissenschaft 1,* H. Möller & K. Lackner (Eds.). Kassel University Press.

Hofstede, G. (2001). *Culture's Consequences: Comparing Values, Behaviors, Institutions and Organizations across Nations.* Beverly Hills, CA: Sage.

Jing Lihua, Zhou Wenqun & Tse Yuen-ching (2005). *Corporate Governance in China: Ethical and Legal Problems.* University of Hong Kong.

Jullien, F. (1999). *Vortrag vor Managern über Wirksamkeit und Effizienz in China und im Westen.* Berlin: Merve Verlag.

Kluckhohn, F. R., & Strodtbeck, F. L. (1961). *Variations in Value Orientation.* Evanston, IL: Peterson Row.

Kolb, D. G., & Tianjian Jiang (2005). Organizational learning in China: inroads and implications for the awakening dragon. *Reflections by Society for Organizational Learning, 6*(8–10): 15–36.

Liefner, I. (2005). *Ausländische Direktinvestitionen und internationaler Wissenstransfer nach China. Untersucht am Beispiel von Hightech-Unternehmen in Shanghai und Bejing.* Habilitationsschrift: LIT Verlag, Berlin.

Mun Chin Kok (2006). *Chinese Leadership Wisdom from the Book of Change.* Hong Kong: Chinese University Press,.

Özdemir, H. (2010). *Change Management Praxis – Strategische Organisationsentwicklung, ein Leitfaden für Führungskräfte und Berater.* Berlin: Leutner.

Özdemir, H. (2013). *Organisationsentwicklungsprozess in einem deutsch-chinesischen Joint Venture in Wuxi.* Kassel: University of Kassel Press.

Özdemir, H., & Özdemir Lagler, B. (2013). *Coaching Praxis – Ein Leitfaden für Coaches und Auftraggeber.* SARIM Management, edition oezpa.

Rokeach, M. (1979). *Understanding Human Values. Individual and Societal.* New York: The Free Press.

Schwartz, S. H. (1996). Value priorities and behavior. Applying a theory of integrated value systems. In: C. Seligman, J. M. Olson & M. P. Zanna (Eds.), *The Psychology of Values: The Ontario Symposium* (Volume 8, S1–24). Mahwah, NY: Lawrence & Erlbaum.

Selmer, J. (2002). Coping strategies applied by Western vs. overseas Chinese business expatriates in China. *International Journal of Human Resource Management, 13*(1): 19–34.

Selmer, J. (2006). Language ability and adjustment: western expatriates in China. *Thunderbird International Business Review, 48*(3): S347–368.

Shenkar, O., & Ronen, S. (1987). The cultural context of negotiations: the implications of Chinese inter-personal norms. *The Journal of Applied Behavioral Science, 6*: S263–275.

Staehle, W. H. (1999). *Management – Eine Verhaltenswissenschaftliche Perspektive, 8.* Auflage: Vahlen Verlag, München.

Sydow, J. (1985). *Der soziotechnische Ansatz der Arbeits- und Organisationsgestaltung.* Campus, Frankfurt: Darstellung, Kritik, Weiterentwicklung.

Wittkop, T. (2006). *Interkulturelle Kompetenz Deutscher Expatriates in China. Qualitative Analyse, Modellentwicklung und Praktische Empfehlungen.* Wiesbaden: Gabler Edition Wissenschaft.

Xiao Juan Ma (2007). *Personalführung in China: Motivationsinstrumente und Anreize.* Göttingen: Vandenhoeck & Ruprecht.

Yanan, Yu (1996). *Understanding China. Center Stage of the Fourth Power.* Albany, NY: State University of New York Press.

CHAPTER SEVEN

Developing a group relations institution in Lithuania

Jolita Buzaityte-Kasalyniene and Mannie Sher

This chapter describes the establishment of a group relations institution in Vilnius, Lithuania, based on our experiences of two Group Relations Conferences in 2010 and 2011. Via these conferences, group relations methodology was introduced into a post-Soviet society as a developmental instrument for increased social participation by Lithuanian citizens. For fifty years, following the devastation of Lithuanian society in the Second World War, Lithuania fell under the oppressive domination of the former Soviet Union (USSR); for the past twenty years, following the collapse of communism and the Soviet Union, Lithuania struggled to achieve an independent democratic civil society. Against this background, we believed that group relations conference methodology could be a possible positive developmental instrument for conference participants and for Lithuanian society as a whole.

The chapter describes conference design, conference membership, historical, social, and political contexts, relationships with authority, and gender roles.

Design

The 2010 and 2011 conferences were both five-day, non-residential events. The design of the programmes in each conference included large study groups, (LSG), small study groups (SSG), institutional events (IE) or inter-group events (IGE), review and application groups (RAG), and plenaries. As the conference was held at a university, and in deference to its academic culture, two formal lectures were included in the 2010 programme. The lectures were set aside in 2011, based on what the early Tavistock pioneers of group relations had discovered—that lectures served in the main to blunt the emotional experience of participation in an experientially-based conference. In 2011, the IE was replaced with an inter-group event.

Membership

Conference membership was mainly Lithuanian. In 2010, the members comprised mostly university teachers and students, social workers and professionals, mainly from the charity sector. In 2011, there was more diversity in the membership—two non-Lithuanian members, students, teachers, and professionals from both the private and public sectors.

Historical, social, and political contexts

A centuries-long history of being ruled by authoritarian and totalitarian regimes from neighbouring powers (Polish, German, Russian) led Lithuanians to adapt to the systems of their rulers, while struggling to preserve Lithuanian national identity. The struggle, often brutal and catastrophic during the Second World War occupations, first by the Russians, then by the Nazis, and, finally, by the Russians again, and later, between 1945 and 1990, under the heel of the Soviet regime, created huge social, communal, and family divisions, often with family members fighting on opposite sides of the political divide. A proportion of the population still hankers after the "good old times" of tyrannical government, when people knew where they stood. Even if the general level of prosperity was low, it was low for everyone.

Struggling to maintain democratic values, fighting against corruption and the inequalities of wealth, facing westwards instead of eastwards, and worrying about threats from the east, form many of the components of contemporary Lithuanian life.

The conference membership was keen and intelligent, disciplined, co-operative, and refined. But it was also concerned about the development of inequalities in the conference, as these mirrored inequalities in Lithuanian society that flourished following independence and the introduction of capitalist freedom. Nostalgia for the "old days" was accompanied by a fear that *laissez faire* materialism, the absence of visible social controls, would replace core social values, rectitude (outside, church bells were ringing), and knowing one's place in the traditional social stratification of Lithuanian society.

Members spoke about "secrets" alongside references to power and authority. *Animal Farm* by George Orwell was offered as an example of forced equality, as "some become more equal than others", suggesting that Lithuanian history and its experience of domination by foreign powers had led to the present-day attitudes of mistrust towards leadership and authority. This was strongly played out in the relationship between the conference membership and the consultants, whose interventions were frequently ignored, denied, or rejected, as if they were experienced as a new, imposed foreign leadership and authority. Examples of abusive power were frequently referred to in members' places of work—in government, in organisations, in departments, and between individuals, supporting the view that all forms of leadership are experienced as bad and paralysing.

On the other hand, references to "secrets" were also seen as hopeful signs of the membership getting closer to issues of substance. There was discussion about actual abuse of power in the personal lives of the conference participants and in Lithuanian national history. The membership discussed the public debate between a media personality son and his politician father about the war, and the son pressing his reluctant father to publicly acknowledge "secrets" about Lithuanian involvement with both sides—the Nazis and the Communists—in the war. Other "secrets" involved members recalling grandparents being sent to Siberia and their own parents consequently being permanently sad and reluctant to speak; there were discussions about the wars of centuries ago, conflicts between tribes, nations, and religions that are evident in the lives of the people today.

Main themes

Members talked with difficulty about their painful private and personal issues of damaged family relationships and life experiences. Sometimes, it felt that talking about work was defensive against talking about more painful family experiences during the Soviet era of oppression. The German and Polish oppressions were relatively ignored. Geography—the way Lithuania is wedged between three powerful neighbours—hugely influenced interpersonal, intercommunal, and international behaviour. Identity was explained as being less connected with the land (geography) and more with a Lithuanian predisposition for suffering. It was noted with some concern that people's emotional attachment to Lithuania had become weaker, as so many young people with valuable skills had emigrated since independence.

Relation to authority

The memberships' clear dependency on the authority of the conference staff, the memberships' inability or unwillingness to exercise its own authority, was said to be linked to the "history of our country where leaders always get punished". People with leadership potential withdraw their leadership; attempts to lead are often met with passive silence. A healthy co-operation between competitors seemed impossible to achieve.

Differences in relationships with leadership and authority appeared to be generational. The older generation were fearful of it; the younger generation were indifferent or rebellious. This was said to be the result of independence. This kind of rebelliousness was linked to Lithuanian history and people said they felt embarrassed by it being played out in front of foreigners. Several people said they wished to stop talking about it, because they felt shame that Lithuanians seem to develop mainly through the assistance of outsiders. "Why do we do it?" was a question about a shameful history that seemingly could not be confronted. "Sin-eaters" (a reference to Lithuanian gods and demons who ate one's sins) were an integral part of Lithuanian folklore and considered part of the evolving dynamics in the conference—"we need to be punished for our bad behaviour".

Betrayal and loyalty in the conference

An incident occurred in which a member criticised his group to the staff, and later, on returning to his group, criticised the staff. Dual loyalties, disloyalty, and betrayal were considered to be the result of living in a totalitarian regime—a group oedipal phenomenon—in which the father, in warding off the sons' desire to kill him, instead, makes sure that the sons fight each other to reduce their strength in fighting him.

The Lithuanian relationship to leadership is one of lacking trust in leaders leading responsibly. Lithuanian authority is regarded as bad, oppressive, controlling, and uncaring. Public reactions to authority are to ridicule it, ignore it, or acquiesce to it in the hope of obtaining privileges, or sabotaging it through silent resistance.

Gender roles in the conference

Despite females comprising two-thirds of the membership in both conferences, women generally waited for men to take the lead. When men did take the lead, women passively allowed them to deflect the group from its task, and tolerated them messing things up and playing the fool. Men, on the other hand, sat silently watching when women were in conflict with each other. Women appeared more willing to take risks in expressing their emotions. Men, on the other hand, disengaged for fear, it seemed, of exposing their limitations and to be found wanting. Age and gender and intergenerational relationships featured meaningfully—older women seemed less afraid of taking up leadership roles, encouraging their younger male and female members to take more risks, to be more motivated to face issues, to stop "talking about talking" and offer themselves up for shared leadership. However, men tended to avoid leadership struggles, on the whole leaving that to women and then refusing to follow them. This behaviour pointed to general feelings of superiority towards women, leading to female competence and leadership being undermined, spoken of disparagingly, and being not worth competing for. Men said this type of learning (learning-from-experience) that gives importance to emotions and feelings is "women's business".

The role of feelings in organisations

Feelings, as expressed, ranged from discomfort to anxiety, leading to a search for figures who would offer guidance and protection, usually through suggesting some form of action. This was evident in many events in which the defined leadership was that which managed to deflect the group away from experiencing its feelings. Groups vacillated between focusing on what people were actually saying about their experiences and withdrawal. There was almost total avoidance of discussions about the relationships between men and women and between the consultants and members, often resulting in long abstract discussions. A member offered an image of the group being like a sailing boat without a following wind and wondered what other differences, aside from gender, the group might be avoiding.

Motherhood and career

Discussions on themes of children, motherhood, and women's careers were prominent. Many were disinclined to talk about this subject, saying that women giving up their careers for motherhood is regarded as the norm in Lithuania. The membership tended to avoid the subject, but for some it was unavoidable and it was a source of stress.

The membership repeatedly called for equality: "We are equal; we are all the same; there are no differences. Even if there are differences, we are all human." The wish for sameness was expressed mainly by women members—perhaps expressing a wish to avoid competition, to ignore or deny feelings of rivalry. "This is the way I deal with my own and others' rivalry." A statement from a RAG member: "Women are perceived and often treated as incompetent; men get the jobs and promotion; men use the results and accomplishments of women as their own. Women suffer injustice and unequal treatment and are forced to listen to their male colleagues and bosses talking badly about them.'

The topic of female leadership had greater prominence in the conference of 2012, suggesting a positive movement of learning from one conference to the next. Female leadership was placed under the microscope—what type of leadership can women offer? There was a fear of its destructiveness, like destroying "a perfect sand castle", a metaphor that had been offered by an older man. Women's leadership was said to be directive, controlling, even spying—a reference to consultants taking notes during SSG and RAG sessions and wondering if "state files" would be produced on each member. Women's leadership appeared damaging and uncaring; members were forced to endure painful experiences by women.

Collaboration between conference members and staff

Members wondered what prompted the international staff group to work in Lithuania. On the other hand, staff members sometimes themselves seemed intent on projecting into the membership their own preoccupations with totalitarianism, liberal democracy, and the tragedy of the Jews of Lithuania. Collaboration between two groups—members and staff—in a here-and-now learning event means relying on, and using, group unconscious transference phenomena to convey an understanding of what is happening in the session. In this regard, staff rely on time-keeping as an instrument of learning, as punctuality and lateness for group sessions is a means of communicating feelings without using words. The members expressed their dislike of this arrangement by referring to staff time-keeping as "weird", and objected to speaking in English on subjects that are difficult to articulate even in Lithuanian. This was one of several examples of the national historical experience being mirrored in the conference, viz. a sense of being "invaded and a forced reorientation of authority roles". This led to expressions of anti-authority feelings and non-compliance. This would be reflected sometimes in a tendency to "wait"—"waiting for the Barbarians to arrive", for "dragons to emerge", for "the conference to end", and men "waiting for their chance". Collaboration and sullen waiting were linked to two stories: *Waiting for the Barbarians*, by J. M. Coetzee (with an allusion to Samuel Beckett's *Waiting for Godot* and Dino Buzzati's novel, *The Tartar Steppe*). Coetzee's novel is an allusion to the way an empire makes use of an illusory "other" to maintain an oppressive regime. When it emerges that there are no Barbarians coming, and the waiting is pointless, the society that has created a core assumption of waiting for an external invader disintegrates, because it has not managed to deal with its fears of itself—its own internal dragons. The second story referred to William Golding's *Lord of the Flies*, where collaboration turns into a horror story.

By the third and fourth days of the 2010 conference, having spoken about feelings of being trapped in unbearable situations ("attacked by bears with claws"), members were more open about their struggle to get in touch with feelings in contrast to talking about "things". They described how they felt held back by images of "Sunday school" and "kindergarten" and the need to preserve the illusion that "good behaviour" would lead to rewards by a benevolent authority. Images of water—lakes, paddling in the sea, birds, and oases were presented as both challenging and comforting and indicated greater empathy, support for others, and a progression towards relating. Talking about feelings was clearly experienced as taking a risk, but, having taken a risk, people said that they had learnt from it, that making a contribution to the group proved satisfying, as they saw their ideas grow, move around the group, and being built on by others.

Other powerful images were presented that demonstrated difficulties of group membership—a sinking ship with passengers jumping into the water, Guy Fawkes and blowing up Parliament, followed by a bloody persecution of the Catholics, the relationship between fire and water—one destroying the other, and sterilisation—no intercourse, no birth, no pain. Where there was "intercourse", it tended to be same-gendered (two women having an argument while the men sniggered in the background). In these situations, it seemed that collaboration was only possible through suppression of differences, not working across differences; that collaboration was equated in the member's minds with "sameness". These dynamics were interpreted variously in relation to individual, role, group, and institutional differences.

Where there were high levels of reserve and non-collaboration, the groups took on the character of a "collectivity of individuals", where the sole group function seemed to be to oppose the consultants and to stop creativity. "The consultants are putting the group through a difficult time, *and seem to be enjoying it*", one member said.

Dramatic age- and education-related incidents occurred in several groups that can best be described as an unspoken shared group consensus to prevent collaboration. A member would be speaking and the other members would act as if they were listening politely, but actually everyone was staring zombie-like into space and disengaging from the speaker's story. When challenged on the reason and pervasiveness of this type of behaviour, a group of thirty+-year-olds explained it in terms of their school education under the Soviets. Every day, teachers would hover about the classroom before pointing to one child and calling them to the front of the class to be questioned on the previous night's homework. Failure to answer correctly resulted in lower grades and a public humiliation, but the worst part of it was the moment of the teacher hovering before pouncing on a victim. During that time, avoiding eye contact was vital to survival. If one could not answer her questions, the teacher called upon another pupil whom she knew could answer correctly and that pupil would experience a deep sense of self-hatred for betraying a friend.

The system, it was suggested, encouraged a culture of lying and suppressed, hidden identities. Feelings of lost identities or failed creativity were evident because many felt their assumptions about "collaboration" had been destroyed. The intergroup event invites the membership to form itself into groups for the purposes of developing relationships between them and providing opportunities for learning how to lead and take action on behalf of others—representational authority. The process of subdividing and finding subgroup identities and using them to collaborate with other groups initially proved difficult, because many believed that the process could not happen without a centrally-created master-plan which they could not see was impossible.

Mature sexual development involves the growing child being able to take up a position as the "third" in relation to the two parents, without intruding into the parental couple. In organisational terms, this would mean having an understanding of one's role and knowledge of, and respect for, the boundary between one's own role and the roles of others. It also involves an ability to observe oneself while speaking. This general difficulty was addressed when it was noticed that conference members would be either "in" a conversation or "out" of it and uninvolved. Secrets and lack of curiosity characterised many interactions between members, as if their "internal world" of mindfulness, thoughtfulness, and the experience of emotions had to be kept from others. That is common when people have terrible histories that have not been processed, digested, and come to terms with: as someone said, "We are like a people in a coma with our eyes open."

What could the members authorise the staff to do? Where would the membership allow staff to enter and where were "walls erected" to prevent staff from entering? The challenge for staff was as much about understanding group dynamics and respecting the members' need for "walls". Conference staff members were experienced as another form of invasion which made a shared ("collaborative") project difficult to achieve. Faced with this dilemma of the members not being able to comprehend what they wanted from and for themselves, competitive dynamics took over from collaborative dynamics until sufficient "working through" of the differences between the "individual-in-the-group" and the "group-as-a-whole" were understood emotionally. In wrestling with this complexity, it seemed staff and membership were able to access only two out of three layers of experience—material was richer on the personal and cultural levels, but issues of work and organisation were difficult to pick up except in the application groups. It is possible that this difficulty was related to Lithuania passing rapidly from communist oppression to rampant capitalist oppression that created new categories of exclusion, without going through an intervening process to evaluate the nation's mood and desired political and cultural direction.

Another way of understanding the need for "walls" takes the form of an image of two concentric walls between which the conference members feel imprisoned: an outer wall of privacy and secrecy to protect them from possible "invasion" from the outside and an internal wall that alienates the members from themselves. This phenomenon can be related to the transgenerational transmission of trauma: the trauma of being perpetrators both to Jews and to themselves, as well as being victims of the Soviet regime and their collaborators and of the schizophrenia (paranoia) of Soviet times when the default position was that everyone was suspect until proven otherwise. This self-protective dynamic was enacted and, therefore, was not easily talked about; for example, a member who said, "I don't understand. I did not kill anybody. Why should I feel guilty?" There seemed little appreciation of the relevance of the past experience of conference members' parents.

What type of organisation do the members think they are in?

"We feel like rats in a maze; that the consultants are experimenters confusing us and diverting us from our task. It feels very Kafkaesque, being observed like this, but it also has a 'chickens coming home to

roost' feeling. This is what I've done to my students; now the consultants are doing it to me, so that I can know how my students feel being
lectured to in tiered ranks of 100s of students, without concern for
them as individuals and knowing that this method of teaching and
learning is unproductive."

The membership seemed to think it was in a conference organisation
with a paralysed management that could not remove dissatisfactions
or provide for unfulfilled expectations. This internalised picture of
management was translated into the membership's inability to
manage itself in relation to its tasks. Panic developed as the membership fragmented into small groups. This was done on the basis of
previous known relationships which was clearly considered an easier
and more trustworthy way of relating. Attempts at forming groups
based on agreed tasks failed. In other words, sentience appeared to be
stronger than task in binding people together in the conference. This
was based on a suspicion of leadership that is strongly embedded in
Lithuanian culture, due to a history of successive invaders of the land
who appointed puppets to do their work, leading to a lack of basic
trust even towards one's own leaders. Only family and friends are to
be trusted.

> "I feel like the Greeks who first toyed with democracy and the people
> were reluctant to raise their hands when voting, so a system of bean-
> counting was used. In this conference, too, I am reluctant to speak, or
> raise my hand, so my silence is taken as assenting to a male-domi-
> nated discourse."

> "This conference feels like an island surrounded by a rising sea threat-
> ening the people on the edge with drowning; or like having a volcano
> in the middle threatening to erupt and consume the people in the
> centre."

Efforts were made to understand and think about the group
dynamic, but the efforts gave way in the face of pressure to design a
group project that everyone would buy into. Individuals felt threatened and the myth of the men in the group was to create survival
mechanisms that would involve sacrificing individuals ('Lord of the
Flies'). Women struggled with the experience of being in the moment,
joining and taking up membership roles.

"The conference is like a bus full of passengers who are strangers to each other doing the same thing, but not interacting."

Members understood that membership of groups meant working with existential anxieties of not being noticed and risking taking action that might not be noticed. At times, a small number of members dominated the conversation with wall-to-wall speech that was actually depressingly boring and counter-productive. The idea of "thought leadership" seemed new and unfamiliar. A person spoke of fear of having a negative impact on others when speaking; another disagreed and said, "Talking in groups can be positive. We should allow leadership to emerge and stop the tendency to 'shoot' those making a bid for leadership."

A Lithuanian story of a brush was presented as metaphor:

"The brush cannot be bent or broken; but it can be destroyed by picking out one bristle at a time. This is what is happening to us in the conference and is also a metaphor for how invading nations picked off Lithuanian leadership one at a time."

As the conference passed the halfway mark, more members "joined" through speaking. Some spoke of their fear of speaking in groups and linked that to experiences of personal abuse in groups. Speaking determines who feels part of the group and who feels excluded. Tension in the relationship between the individual and the group was evident and was dealt with differently by men and women in the quality and quantity of speech: men, on the whole, seem less concerned about participating and women are more tolerant of the process and any ensuing silences. As the group developed, it acknowledged the interactive dynamics between individual and group. A member summed it up thus: "no man is an island; ask not for whom the bell tolls; it tolls for thee". Another described a moment of weakness and trusting the group to "carry me along safely".

Why was group relations introduced to Lithuania?

The authors are committed to social development and they wished to assist a nation experiencing difficulties in social cohesion and co-operation. These difficulties lie in the nation's ability to reflect, to be authentic, in distrust of one another and in its traditional defensive behaviour towards authority. The nation is critical of itself and is not confident in its judgements of its own behaviour; the nation is quick to take offence when criticised. Its leadership is not trusted.

The authors were concerned that Lithuanian society was letting opportunities for its democratic development to pass by. Our intention was to provide "spaces" where democratic principles, such as transparency, participation, and civil society, could be debated and developed. We believed that group relations conference work would promote democratic processes and people's participation in it without fear. Fear of responsibility comes together with freedom to choose at personal, group, organisational, community, and national levels. Responsibility for outcomes, the results of choices and decisions, belongs to everyone in the nation; if outcomes are disappointing, others cannot be blamed.

In our view, group relations conference work has the possibility of addressing and even resolving some of the political and social problems in Lithuanian society. Working with traditional Lithuanian lethargy was a challenge. The influence of repressed collective memory and the unconscious social dynamics that lead therefrom, and possibilities for learning, excited and encouraged us, despite the presence of tendencies towards massive social defensiveness. People were both critical and encouraging, because group relations work confronts group and social realities, people's responsibilities, and their need for change.

CHAPTER EIGHT

Uneasy on the boundary: reflections on the culture and effectiveness of group relations conference work in the USA, 1965–2012

Bernard Gertler and Charla Hayden

> In *The Bhagavad Gita*, Krishna tells Arjuna that acting with detachment means doing the right thing for its own sake, because it needs to be done, without worrying about success or failure.
>
> "T. S. Eliot once paraphrased Krishna's advice when he wrote, 'For us, there is only the trying. The rest is not our business'
>
> (Kempton, 2004, p. 76)

Introduction

This chapter about the changes in group relations conferences in the USA came out of several conversations we have had about our experiences in USA Group Relations Conferences and Symposia. One such experience occurred when each of us attended an A. K. Rice Institute Symposium in 2008, in which an incident struck both of us as significant. I (Bernie) had organised an event with a presentation as the first part and application work with audience participation as the second. I had set it up with time, space, task, and participants identified in each sequence and shared it with all concerned. At one point, when a participant went over the time boundary, I interrupted him, I thought politely, and said we had to go on to the next section. I was immediately chastised by a seasoned colleague for cutting off the youngest male participating, with a "Don't you see what you're doing—you're shutting out the youth." Yes, I thought, I was aware I cut him off—I was keeping to the time and task we had all agreed on, including you and the member you are talking about. But that was a notable interchange for me. What was the thinking that led to the conflict between this colleague and me? Figuring that out began my engagement with the subject of this chapter.

Charla: My example comes from a recent group relations conference in which I was serving as Associate Conference Director and manager of the training element of the conference. One advanced trainee arrived significantly late to the first meeting of the training group and immediately stated that she was unsure whether she would receive sufficient nourishment at this conference. She was trembling and explained she was late because she had been driving around looking for a grocery store where the kind of food she needed was sold. Unable to find one, she came to the conference with very little food of the kind she said she needed. The other members of the training group and I spent considerable energy inquiring about her dilemma and trying to support her, including considering whether and how her experience might represent a conference dynamic. This effort continued throughout the first half of the conference and was not resolved until midway through, when the trainee found her role and began to work consistently.

After the conference, I was to provide an assessment of what I had observed about the trainee's work to the AKRI Training Committee, and decided to discuss this with her first. We had a cordial conversation, though she disputed whether the nature of her early participation had consumed much of the conference director's and staff's attention. I asked her permission to contact the director and other staff for their perspective on this and she gave it. When I spoke to other staff and the director, I found their perceptions were similar to mine. I met with her again, with her mentor present, and she became less willing to consider the idea that she might need to do some personal work before applying for certification to consult in A. K. Rice conferences. Her mentor continued to work with her for some weeks, but in the end she withdrew from the training programme and from the Institute.

My sadness and confusion in the face of what I considered a clear, though unconscious, attempt to derive a focused therapeutic benefit from the conference were significant. This experience also pointed in the direction of something I have noticed in American conferences for some time: the blurring of the task boundary between exploration of the dynamics of the temporary organisation and their therapeutic use by members and staff.

The issues in these events that concerned us include:

- disputes and confusion about the primary task of conferences;
- privileging group identity and diversity issues over task issues;
- competition between persons holding the various issues, for example, related to power dynamics between senior members;
- focusing less on enquiry and more on pronouncements;
- individual focus *vs.* systemic focus;
- favouring a therapeutic purpose while ignoring boundaries.

Outline of what is to come

This chapter is based on our observations of group relations conference work in the USA over the eighty-two years of collective engagement we have had in conferences. We "grew up" in this work on opposite coasts of the USA (New York City and California/Oregon), and we lay claim to so many years because our paths infrequently crossed during most of them. Bernie's work in the world has focused on psychotherapy, psychoanalysis, and organisational consultation. Charla's work has focused on holding leadership and management roles and on organisational consulting.

Our observations focus on group relations in the USA since its inception in 1965, and how the cultural, economic, and social history of the country has influenced group relations in the USA since then. We pay particular attention to the A. K. Rice Institute and its members, and especially see historical events in the USA from the 1960s to the present as partial explanations for what has occurred within the Institute from an organisational and political standpoint.

We also explore the theoretical frameworks that were joined to develop the group relations learning model we know as "Conferences about Leadership and Authority" and focus on how we understand that model has evolved in the USA over the decades since 1965.

Our thesis is that over the course of these more than four decades, the group relations model in the USA has moved away from a focus on organisational structure/process and psychodynamics and toward a greater interest in the study of groups as groups (and sometimes individuals and dyads)—interests not so obviously embedded in organisational structure and workplace dynamics as might have been predicted by the model's origins. We see this as a consequence related to the adoption of aspects of French postmodern theory (e.g., Foucault, Derrida) in the academy, aspects that illuminate the issues of similarity and difference in group process through the prism of social identity.

While we see these French postmodern influences contributing valuable and uniquely American material and themes to group relations conferences and related intellectual work, we see these shifts as dominating alternate modes of interpretation, particularly those which make group relations learning more directly applicable to organisational life.

We also observe that group relations conferences in the USA have followed the trajectory of many other academic disciplines in moving away from an engagement with the *social* and more toward the engagement of the *personal and individual*. This movement began occurring in response to both the idealism and violence of the 1960s, and probably even earlier—to similar aspects of the Second World War.

Our reflections, therefore, describe how we see the USA's group relations conferences, since 1965, as evolving in directions away from learning about organisational structure and process and towards:

- being impacted, without reflection, by the influence of vast sociocultural and economic changes in the USA (see Handy, 1998, pp. 79–100, on "Proper Selfishness" for concept of the modern "hungry spirit";
- an interest in groups and individuals *per se* rather than their meaning within systems;
- applying a framework of French theory to analysis;
- focusing more on individual development than on unconscious participation in group and system dynamics.

*Evolution in the national ethos and in the intellectual
frameworks influencing group relations work in the USA*

The relevance of the first part of this section of the chapter rests on the
idea that organisations are creatures of their contexts and that in every
subcomponent of a larger system you will find reflections of the larger
context's dynamics. In the USA's conference work, we have called this
"conference as microcosm", since Margaret Rioch and James Miller
wrote about this in 1977 (Miller, 1977; Rioch, 1977).

Part 1: Themes and cultural debates in the USA's history

The continuing struggle to settle on a defining ethos of the country
began with the great constitutional debate among our founders: is
America the land of the self-made, entrepreneurial person, unim-
peded by the demands of the *polis* and unaided by them as well, or is
it the land of individuals who are intrinsically connected as parts of
an entire fabric of effort in which all rise or fall together and social
responsibility equals personal gain in importance. We saw the same
debate enacted during the weeks before the presidential election of
2012.

Let us cite some examples from Daniel Walker Howe's history of
the United States: *What Hath God Wrought: The Transformation of
America 1815–1848*, which is one volume of *The Oxford History of the
United States* Series (2007). Examples:

- *The "myth" of the singular man's triumph.* The Battle of New Orleans
  (1815), in which Andrew Jackson defeated the British Army, was
  regarded as a victory of self-reliant individuals under charismatic
  leadership—a triumph of citizen soldiers over professionals, of
  the common man over hierarchy, of willpower over rules.
  Actually, the methodical gunnery and better cannons forged at
  the beginning of our industrial revolution were what defeated
  the British forces (Howe, 2007).
- *The widespread distribution of land*, especially during the westward
  movement, had powerful consequences, psychological and political: the landowning gentleman did not hesitate to assert his
  rights as he saw them; he was averse to taxation and suspicious
  of all authority beyond his own. This legacy has continued to fuel

a major schism in American political life, causing endless debate over autonomy *vs.* social responsibility (Howe, 2007, pp. 48–49).

- *A cross-current of conflicting beliefs about America's destiny* also emerged in the first part of the nineteenth century when two rival political perspectives wooed American families. Some Americans felt largely satisfied with their society as it was, slavery and all. This was especially so because of the autonomy it provided to so many white men and their communities who wanted their familiar America extended westward across the continent. Other Americans were drawn by the prospect of overarching socio-economic issues and wanted to pursue social reform, even at the risk of compromising some individual and local independence. They envisioned qualitative, not just quantitative, progress for America. In the long run the choice became more than an economic decision; it was a moral one (Howe, 2007, p. 78).

The issues noted above remain unsettled—a kind of permanent struggle over the cultural keystone of America.

How do these continuing themes relate to group relations work in the USA? We believe we see the same tensions and dilemmas expressed, but unexplored, in terms of how these mirror the broader social context in group relations conference work in the USA. Let us provide some examples to illustrate.

Excessive focus on the conference director role—difficulty in valuing examination of the importance of followership and collaboration.

Prominent, charismatic directors and consulting staff draw attention and are mythologised while we neglect recognising the work of effective but less dramatic staff consultants/directors.

National conference dynamics of 1990 and the fact that so many important people left the Institute and did not rejoin was a watershed event in AKRI, a "Hollywood moment" in which holding the stage went to the "understudies". Many who left the Institute and have not returned appear to have enacted the American ideal of the sufficient individual, one whose authorisation is self-derived rather than largely given to him/her through the agency of an organisational sponsor.

AKRI's exercising its authority as a conference sponsor to fire a charismatic conference director might have disabled it over time in the face of the disaffected, idealised characters' departures.

Gradually diminishing numbers of people attending AKRI's "premier" experiential event—its national conference—over the past twenty years.

Difficulty in identifying people who want to actively pursue the Presidency of the Institute and membership on its Board, and the gradual decline of numbers of members of AKRI—from a high in 1990 to approximately half of that today.

Struggles against the implementation of a training and certification programme. During the 1990 conference, Wesley Carr and Charla Hayden, who were staffing the training component of the conference, found there were two members of the twelve-person group we could not recommend should proceed to take consulting roles in the conference at large. This emerged independent of any discussion between us, but when the time came for the trainees to "matriculate", we found neither of us had confidence in the two members. "Why" was the question that emerged for us and led to a paper we presented in 1991 at AKRI's annual "scientific" meeting. It turned out that others around the Institute were having similar thoughts, and eventually a group of us were authorised to design a set of competencies and a mentoring and certification process for those who wanted to qualify to consult in AKRI-affiliated conferences. We did so, but when we took the preliminary plan out to what were then called regional centres, we were met with a great deal of resistance, the nature of which is still familiar today. For example:

> "We select and grow our own consultants here—no intervention of any 'governance' structure but our own is allowed!"

> "We'll secede from the union—that's preferable to having federal intervention in our own backyard!"

> "We like your competencies, but we don't like your certification process—we don't want one—it disrupts our sentient ties to have to make evaluations of each others' work."

> "What matters is between us here in this city/state—we don't think outsiders have much to offer us."

And now, more than ten years after at least twenty people have been certified and most express having a satisfying experience, the programme is still being considered for cancellation, though some of us hope it gets needed improvements instead.

An organisational transformation was attempted in the early 2000s to resolve the tension between the dual tasks of the A. K. Rice Institute: serving members and serving the public. Initially, this was resolved in favour of becoming an educational institution serving the public, but this task was partly undermined by a lack of support by individual members who constructed their own conferences apart from AKRI and by members who felt no connection to the educational mission (Noumair et al., 2010).

Part 2: The influence of French theory on group relations in the USA

When group relations was introduced in the USA in the 1960s, it was primarily influenced by the systems theories of A. Kenneth Rice (Rice, 1965), the psychoanalytic theories of Wilfred Bion on groups (Bion, 1961), and Melanie Klein's theories of the individual (Klein, 1985). Ken Rice, with Eric Miller (Miller & Rice, 1967), provided the elements emphasising leadership and management through his open-systems conception of work-place processes, processes that were intended to accomplish desired outcomes of productivity. Bion (1961) provided the psychoanalytic theory of groups with his emphasis on "group as a whole" and the "work group–basic assumption" distinction, and Melanie Klein's work (1985) provided the more core psychoanalytic ideas of defences against primitive anxiety, defences such as projection and introjection. Rice, in *Learning for Leadership* (1965), established group relations conferences as a specific set of experiential and reflective events intended to train participants for the exercise of organisational leadership. The primary task of conferences was to learn about leadership and authority.

Under the guidance and direction of Ken Rice and Margaret Rioch, group relations in the USA developed in university and medical settings across the country, often led by charismatic professors and physicians. That group relations was deeply connected to universities and medical centres in the USA at its origins is crucial to understanding many of the changes that occurred over the decades.

Group relations in the 1960s and 1970s was connected to two fashionable and prominent intellectual trends of the time: psychoanalysis and systems thinking. Exploration of the individual and society through psychoanalytic and systems lenses helped make sense of the turbulent events of the 1960s.

In the 1960s, the Civil Rights Movement and the Civil Rights Act of 1964, the Women's Movement, leading to the founding of the National Organization for Women in 1966, the Stonewall Inn riot in 1969, which revealed the abuse of gays and lesbians, Native Americans founding the American Indian Movement in 1968, Students for a Democratic Society, with its Port Huron Statement, in 1962, as well as other sub-groups in American society, were all voicing a protest about their position of subjugation to the dominant white, male, heterosexual, European, capitalist class. In the 1960s, the protest took various forms of active civil disobedience. This waned over the course of the 1970s and morphed into a more intellectual shift in the academy, where French theory was a source of inspiration.

Starting in the late 1960s and early 1970s, an American version of French theory became fashionable and prominent .We can look to this as one significant source for the changes in group relations conferences in the USA since the 1990s. French theory gave theoretical support to the developing social consciousness and demands for rights by racial, ethnic, gendered, and other subjugated groups in American society (Cusset, 2003).

French theory proposed that one look into the "hidden aspects" of the supposedly neutral, objective language of texts, and, for our purposes, the social sciences. The Americanised version of French theory would emphasise the political nature of language and literature and how it could lead to the suppression of alternative realities and alternative conceptions. This was a reaction to "objectivity" being seen as the "white, male, heterosexual lens" of the dominant sociopolitical group, and an emerging need to have the subjectivity of "identity groups" recognised and their political suppression understood (Cusset, 2003).

Any universal theory is to be "suspect" based on its potential for domination. Michel Foucault's emphasis on institutions of control and the domination of specific discourses for that purpose is relevant here. In the absence of a clear "absolute truth", an idea of what is right can be imposed by a powerful minority on the majority, and in that way knowledge becomes the use of power as a mental force (Boyne, 1994; Fillingham, 1993, p. 7).

We can add to this Jean-Francois Lyotard's dismissal of looking exclusively to grand and essentialist narratives for meaning (Best & Kellner, 1997). In the 1970s, the dominant American/Freudian ego psychology version of psychoanalysis (which emphasised adaptation) was under serious attack in the USA for its derision of women and for its homophobia. The concepts of "penis envy" in women and that homosexuality was an inversion of the Oedipus complex supported the view that psychoanalysis was part of the "white male" apparatus (no pun intended here). In addition, the lack of empirical support for the theory, as well as for its effectiveness, also made the support of the grand theory difficult to sustain.

Also pertinent is Jacques Derrida's idea of "deconstruction", which has as its aim unmasking the problematic nature of "centres" (Powell, 1997; Wolfreys, 2007). Derrida emphasised that Western thinking often starts from a truth, a fixed centre which provides for an hierarchical inclusion and favouring of one understanding and value over another. In particular, Derrida was concerned with the way centres attempt to exclude. In that way centres ignore, repress, or marginalise others (the Other). Examples of this binary opposition with centres including and favouring are: men/women, white/black, straight/gay, all of the identifiable binary opposites, which end up with privilege/domination *vs.* subjugation as their effects. And the purpose of "deconstruction" is to heighten awareness of the centre and the margin and to possibly subvert the centre so that the margin can become central (Powell, 1997).

So, French theory took the focus in the USA of "unearthing minority identities and the lot of subjugated groups" (Cusset, 2003, pp. 131–132). These ideas gave theoretical support to the already existing political and social movements of identity group thinking in the USA (the Civil Rights Movement, Women's Movement, etc.) and led to the establishment of university departments of African-American Studies, Gender Studies, and the like. This influence occurred in the university programmes where group relations was taught and spread generally to Group Relations Conferences outside the academy.

In the early years of group relations in the USA, race, gender, age, and sexuality were all subjects of concern in group relations conferences. Bernie staffed a "male–female" in authority conference in the mid-1970s. Laurence Gould (1985) held a series of such conferences and describes them in detail in his article, "Men and women at work:

a group relations conference on person and role". The titles of the conferences include "A working conference on women in authority", which had an all-female staff and same-gendered small groups; the later conferences had male–female staffs. This work culminated in two residential conferences entitled "Men and women at work". Small groups continued to be same-gendered and some conference discussions were same-gendered. The primary task of the "Men and Women at Work" group relations conference was to explore the exercise of authority and leadership as it is influenced by gender, sexuality, and stages of adult development.

In discussing these conferences, Laurence Gould uses the person–role–system model for his discussion (see Appendix I). He makes two useful points here: (1) he suggests that when we highlight the person–role issue side (e.g., personal identity characteristics in role) rather than the role–system side, this becomes the foreground while the role–system side (role, group, intergroup, and organisational process) are background (role–system). It is the reverse in the traditional group relations conferences where role–system are foreground and person–role are background. He goes on to say that if the primary task is defined on the person–role side, then focusing on the role–system side is a defence and *vice versa*. Suffice to say, these distinctions do not seem so easy to make. (2) Because these conferences focus so much on the person–role boundary, there is a "pull" toward exploration of typical therapy issues such as family, which make task boundaries difficult to manage. The conferences are intimate and more personal than the usual Group Relations Conferences.

It is our view that current group relations conferences in the USA, whether titled as identity-based or not, focus on the person–role aspect of systems more than the role–system side, and that they tend toward the therapeutic and reformative in their incorporation of French theory.

So, over the course of time from 1965 through 2012, we see a shift in subject and theoretical framework. We see a shift in subject from leadership and authority conferences with a systems-psychodynamic, role–system focus to one more dominated by a person–role focus, which can blur the line between organisational learning and therapy. It is important to note that this shift did not happen everywhere—there were exceptions—and it is also true that conferences themselves often were and are an amalgam of the various theories. Nevertheless, there was a shift from exclusively systems-psychodynamic, role–system conferences to conferences in which person–role was emphasised and where many ideas are in use, and, to our minds, often at cross purposes, as we shall illustrate later.

In the next section, we will describe the shifts we have observed over time:

- The titles of conferences from 1965 to the present have shifted: "Leadership and authority" is the subject almost exclusively in the conferences starting in 1965, but that changed in the 1990s (see Appendix II).[1]
- Group relations readers show an increase in person–role, identity-based work from Reader 1 to Reader 3. In Reader 1 there are no articles with an identity theme (Coleman & Bexton, 1975); in Reader 2 there are three articles (Coleman & Geller, 1985); and in Reader 3 there are six (Cytrynbaum & Noumair, 2004).
- An increasing emphasis on informal, individual role. In several conferences Bernie has worked at recently, staff members in the application groups have used the tool of asking each member what animal represented their role in the conference and had other members suggest what animal they thought they were. We understand this as an individual and interpersonal focus (see Elliott, 2008, pp. 1–24, for overall discussion of sources for concepts of self).
- A conflict between a social identity focus and a systems focus. In another conference, a member barged into the Staff Room declaring himself a plenipotentiary. The ensuing interaction between him and the director focused on her comments noting their similar identity characteristics and how he could be her son. He listened, but did not share his own experience. From a systems point of view, he was the leader of a group that purposefully intruded on many of the other IE groups with the conscious intention of task disruption. He did this also with the staff, physically intruding in the circle and disrupting their work. For Bernie, of course, this issue should have been taken up as an IE dynamic, but instead the person–role question was highlighted rather than role–system. Similarly, in the closing conference discussion, the chairs were configured to focus on the groups that had formed in the IE, but the conversation centred on the lesbian

pairing of the conference director and associate director, rather than the systems view which would have highlighted role–system exploration (see Taylor, 1989, pp. 27–28, for discussion of identity as means to orient oneself to a definable reality).

- The title of the conference did not reflect the identity issues that were being spoken about and had the usual phrases about authority and role in groups and organisations. The primary task of that conference was described thus: "The primary task is to study our own behaviour in the 'here and now' as it relates to the exercise of authority and the emergence of leadership in groups." Sounds role–system, but it was not.

So, we think many conferences are confusing in their combination of person–role issues and role–system issues. It has been our experience in listening to reports of conferences in the USA and in those we have staffed, that the diversity issues are far more prominent. The person–role issues from this identity-based focus figure now far more, and the system–psychodynamic focus of leadership and authority issues are more often background.

Part 3: The increased influence of capitalism as an economic and social system and the consequent prevalence of self-promotion as a "way of life"

This section focuses on the accelerated permeation of American culture by capitalism and the impact of that on group relations conference work.

In his book, *Supercapitalism* (2007), Robert Reich, Professor of Public Policy at the University of California and former US Secretary of Labor, notes that "the last several decades have involved a shift of power away from us in our capacities as citizens and toward us as consumers and investors" (Reich, 2007, p. 5). This very significant shift can be observed in the ambivalence, expressed in polls and interviews, of Americans contemplating their 2012 Presidential election votes: "Do I want to feed my desire to achieve the 'American dream' of growing wealthier, or do I want to take up responsibility for supporting a standard of living that allows all Americans enough resources to sustain themselves and their families effectively?"

Since the 1970s, spanning the life of the A. K. Rice Institute, this growing shift to "Supercapitalism" has been developing. Technologies developed by government to fight the Cold War were incorporated into new products and services, which created possibilities for new competitors in transportation, communications, manufacturing, and finance. This cracked open the stable production systems we had before and forced all companies to compete more intensely for customers and investors. Consumer power became aggregated by mass retailers such as Wal-Mart, which used the collective clout of millions of consumers to get great deals from suppliers. Investor power became aggregated, too, and was enlarged by pension funds and mutual funds that pushed companies to get higher returns.

As a result, consumers and investors had access to more choices and better deals. But the institutions that had negotiated to spread the wealth and protect what citizens valued in common began to disappear. Giant firms that dominated whole industries retreated, and labour unions shrank. Regulatory agencies faded. CEOs could no longer act as "corporate statesmen". Furthermore, as the intensifying competition among companies spilled over into politics, elected officials became less concerned about the communities in their districts and more concerned with attracting funding for their campaigns. Lobbying firms swarmed over Washington, wielding greater power and influence over decision-making. "Thus did Supercapitalism replace democratic capitalism", states Reich (2007, p. 7).

So, how has this movement to "Supercapitalism", growing really from the earliest days of the establishment of European colonies on the North American continent, but burgeoning since the 1970s, affected group relations around the USA? (See Judt, 2004, pp. 11–39, on "The Way We Live Now".)

Cultural impacts on basic assumption life

This last section focusing on shifts in group relations work in the USA deals with the impact of the surrounding sociocultural context on basic assumption life as discerned in conferences. Of course, the original formulations of basic assumption states in groups were laid out by Bion in the 1950s in *Experiences in Groups*: "Dependency", "Fight/Flight", and "Pairing" (Bion, 1961). Subsequently, two others have been added and gained in acceptance by the group relations community. In 1974, "Oneness" was hypothesised by Pierre Turquet (Turquet, cited in Fraher, 2004) and in 1995, "Meness" was proposed by Bain, Gould, and Lawrence (Bain et al., cited in Fraher, 2004).

Because of the enormous shifts in how so many humans now communicate with each other—through electronic means—it has been suggested that it will not be long before another basic assumption needs adding: "Disassociation". Already, a number of conference designers and directors in the USA are conducting conferences in virtual spaces, either synchronously or asynchronously. We mention this because what it means to us is that a grounding aspect of group life as we have known it, which is to experience the visceral aspects of influencing and being influenced by others in the here and now, will be changed dramatically (see Bruner, 1990, pp. 99–138, for discussion of "Autobiography and Self"). We would also like to point out that basic assumption life itself is very much influenced by the sociocultural elements of rapidly changing experiences when once we might have thought of them as immutable.

So, let us explore some of the institutional elements of group relations conference life in the USA, as they seem to be affected by the prominent framework of competitive assumptions represented by capitalism or market dynamics.

- Rise of institutionally based programmes that challenge the authority of the national organisation to enforce any obligations, requirements, or constraints on the work sheltered in universities and private, for-profit, human development companies, all of whom have resources and hope to generate more as a result of providing training in group relations (commodification of group relations learning as a product) (see Bruner et al., 2006, p. 15).
- Lessening or collapse of a sense of loyalty and/or gratitude to the larger organisation and many consumer complaints about what one is not getting for one's dues
- Affiliate organisations reluctant or refusing to pay their share to support central administrative services that benefit them and willing to compete with, or consider pulling out of, the larger organisation as if the local system is sufficient unto itself.
- Generally, it is more and more difficult to articulate and act upon a shared definition of the common good that relates to neglect of citizenship in the Institute.

- Decreasing generosity to contribute voluntary effort toward broader organisational goals.
- Generally decreasing value placed on learning something that does not yield a clear solution or answer.
- Self-reflection often not observable in those striving for power and influence.
- Individual exploitation of the organisation trumps the organisational task: what can I get rather than what can I build for the future?
- Self-promotion as a focus of one's energy in general and, in particular, being seen as potential staff of conferences.
- Self is an object you market—avatar, imago, hashtag, etc.—which challenges the deeply held principle that in group relations work we try to find the courage and self-authorisation to "speak the unspeakable", which usually involves a high level of self-disclosure, and not the pretty parts!

Finding an ending

We are from the second generation of group relations practitioners in the USA. Larry Gould introduced Bernie to group relations just a few years after he was introduced to it, in the mid-1960s. Charla was introduced to it by Garret O'Connor at about the same time. These were charismatic men whose style we have not imitated, but whose thinking we did take in. We valued the application of the group relations model to understanding our personal, work, and societal experience. Appreciation of this enrichment has remained with each of us for over forty years. It is from group relations that we developed the conviction that "no one can take my mind away . . . and no one will".

So why are we writing this paper at this time? We are concerned about the shifts in focus of group relations conferences in the USA. We are concerned that learning from experience for deeper understanding and vision is less important than swimming in the unconscious for its own sake. We are concerned that there is an opportunistic pull for individual gain because of the power of group relations, often by changing it into a derivative, but not the same, pursuit. We are concerned about the return to charismatic models of leadership for followers to engage with—and to add a therapeutic benefit to the potential outcomes to conferences. We are concerned about the uses to which group relations is now put.

We are uneasy on the boundary because we worry that some wonderful and fundamental contributions of group relations are being lost; an organisational and societal focus, a focus on experience, and a "describing and exploring stance" are being replaced by an individual and group focus, a more didactic and reforming correctness, a "telling and explaining" position.

In addition, we are uneasy because we see a strong focus in our Institute on selling, self-promotion, ambition, competition, individual achievement, and an absence of self-reflection on societal influences affecting the behaviour of some group relations practitioners.

We are uneasy because group relations conference work feels more superficial, less profound than it did in our "salad days". Something that gave enrichment and meaning to our lives feels lessened—a richly human element of this work feels as if it is being lost: such as understanding what makes life more worth living. And we think it has to do with an increasing requirement that group relations conferences provide answers—to match the strivings of the culture surrounding our work.

We have asked ourselves, over the course of writing this chapter, why is *having no answer* particularly out of vogue now? Was it ever *in*, even in the beginning of group relations conference work in the USA? Remember how conference directors often stated at the beginning "There is no attempt to dictate what anyone should learn"? As we see it, no outcome from group relations other than individual experience and an opportunity to process it is required, in fact, not even desirable, as an immediate consequence to a group relations conference. Any *answer* is anti-thematic to what we first learnt in group relations. Taking this stance, which is hard to do in current times, is what can liberate deeper enquiry into the nature of organisational life.

We have authorised ourselves to pursue understanding for itself, clarity of "knowing" from experience at the cellular level, exploration without an outcome in mind or striven for. Goals can be derived later by individuals or groups; we do not know what they are until the understanding has been explored, digested, and then applied, or not.

In a book about Wagner's opera cycle, *Ring of the Nibelungen*, titled *Finding an Ending*, Phillip Kitcher and Richard Schact delineate three ways that the question of meaning in human life can be approached:

through fulfilling the purposes of a divine creator; by rejecting the question entirely; and a third that takes the question seriously but contends that the source of meaning is in ourselves (Kitcher & Schact, 2004, p. 51). Our belief is that group relations provides a unique opportunity to search for meaning in ourselves by not providing an answer.

We believe that a certain spirit has been lost over the years. We feel ourselves to be somewhat "outside" at this point and are alarmed at feeling alienated. We regret that and hope for a dialogue with our group relations colleagues.

Appendix I

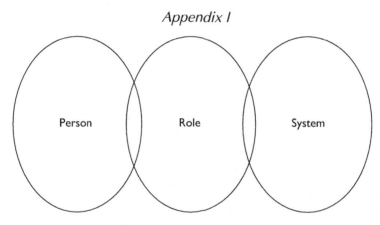

The person–role–system model.

Appendix II

Representative list of United States conference titles.

1965–1973	• All conferences were known as:
	  ○ Group Relations—National
	  ○ Group Relations: A Working Conference—National

1974–1991	• All conferences remained focused on leadership, authority, and organisational issues with titles such as:
	  ○ Group Relations: A Working Conference with Emphasis on Application—National (2 conferences)
	  ○ Group Relations: A Working Conference to Explore Authority and Responsibility in Groups and Organisations

(*continued*)

(continued)

- Group Relations: A Working Conference to Explore Authority and Responsibility in Social Systems (2 conferences)
- Authority and Organisational Effectiveness
- Leadership and Organisational Effectiveness (3 conferences)

1992–1995
- First appearance of conferences with diversity issues in title with authority and leadership conferences also occurring
  - Diversity and Authority: Studying the Reciprocal Effects in Organisational Life
  - Diversity, Authority and Change in Groups and Organisations
  - Authority, Diversity and Leadership in Organisations (2 conferences)
  - Authority, Diversity and Leadership in the Global Community
  - Authority and Leadership in Organisational Life
  - The Dynamics of Authority in Organisational Life
  - Authority and Work: Exploring the Boundaries of Role and Task
  - Learning for Leadership: Exploring Authority, Leadership, and Influence in Organisational and Community Life

1996–2012
- Continuing mix of conferences with diversity issues and authority and leadership titles
  - The Dynamics of Groups and Organisations
  - Diversity in the Year 2000: Are We Lost in the Stars?
  - Leadership, Followership and Organisational Integrity
  - Authority, Leadership and Power in Organisational Life
  - Race, Culture, and Class in Organisational Life
  - Faith, Power, and Authority in Organisations: "Whose God Rules?

Note

1. Note that the source for this is not complete. This representative list was compiled from a list of A. K. Rice National Conferences (Fraher, 2004) and from a search through A. K. Rice Archives, neither of which had all USA conferences. However, the trend is demonstrated here.

References

Best, S., & Kellner, D. (1997). *The Postmodern Turn*. New York: Guilford Press.

Bion, W. R. (1961). *Experiences in Groups*. New York: Basic Books.

Boyne, R. (1994). *Foucault and Derrida*. London: Routledge.

Bruner, J. (1990). *Acts of Meaning*. Cambridge, MA: Harvard University Press.

Bruner, L., Nutkevitch, A., & Sher, M. (Eds.) (2006). *Group Relations Conferences: Reviewing and Exploring Theory, Design, Role-Taking, and Application*. London: Karnac.

Coleman, A. D., & Bexton, W. H. (Eds.) (1975). *Group Relations Reader 1*. Jupiter, FL: A. K. Rice Institute.

Coleman, A. D., & Geller, M. H. (Eds.) (1985). *Group Relations Reader 2*. Jupiter, FL: A. K. Rice Institute.

Cusset, F. (2003). *French Theory*. Minneapolis, MN: University of Minnesota Press.

Cytrynbaum, S., & Noumair, D. A. (Eds.) (2004). *Group Relations Reader 3*. Jupiter, FL: A. K. Rice Institute.

Elliott, A. (2008). *Concepts of the Self*. Gonic, NH: Polity Press by Odyssey Press.

Fillingham, L. A. (1993). *Foucault for Beginners*. Danbury, CT: For Beginners.

Fraher, A. (2004). *A History of Group Study and Psychodynamic Organizations*. London: Free Association.

Gould, L. J. (1985). Men and women at work. In: A. D. Colman & M. H. Geller (Eds.), *Group Relations Reader 2* (pp. 163–172). Jupiter, FL: A. K. Rice Institute.

Handy, C. (1998). *The Hungry Spirit: Beyond Capitalism: A Quest for Purpose in the Modern World*. New York: Broadway Books.

Howe, D. W. (2007). *What Hath God Wrought: The Transformation of America, 1815–1848*. Oxford: Oxford University Press, Nook Edition.

Judt, T. (2004). *Ill Fares the Land*. New York: Penguin.

Kempton, S. (2004). Just let go. *Yoga Journal*, May–June: 75–78.

Kitcher, P., & Schacht, R. (2004). *Finding an Ending: Reflections of Wagner's Ring*. Oxford: Oxford University Press.

Klein, M. (1985). Our adult world and its roots in infancy. In: A. D. Colman & M. H. Geller (Eds.), *Group Relations Reader 2*: (pp. 5–20). Jupiter, FL: A. K. Rice Institute.

Miller, E. J., & Rice, A. K. (1967). *Systems of Organization*. London: Tavistock.

Miller, J. (1977). The psychology of conflict in Belfast: conference as micro-cosm. *Journal of Personality and Social Sciences*, 1(1): 17–38.

Noumair, D., Winderman, B., & Burke, W. W. (2010). Transforming the A. K. Rice Institute: from club to organization. *Journal of Applied Behavioral Science*, 46(4): 473–499.

Powell, J. (1997). *Derrida for Beginners*. Danbury, CT: For Beginners.

Reich, R. (2007). *Supercapitalism: The Transformation of Business, Democracy, and Everyday Life*. New York: Vintage Books.

Rice, A. K. (1965). *Learning for Leadership*. London: Tavistock.

Rioch, M. (1977). The A. K. Rice Group Relations Conferences as a reflection of society. *Journal of Personality and Social Sciences*, 1(1): 1–16.

Taylor, C. (1989). *Sources of the Self: The Making of Modern Identity*. Cambridge, MA: Harvard University Press.

Wolfreys, J. (2007). *Derrida: A Guide for the Perplexed*. London: Continuum Press.

PART III

EXPLORING VARIATIONS IN THEME AND/OR DESIGN OF GROUP RELATIONS CONFERENCES

CHAPTER NINE

Energy, creative collaboration, and wellbeing

Franca Fubini and Luca Mingarelli, with Hanna Fisher, Richard Morgan-Jones, Maija-Leena Setälä, Maria Grazia Siri, and Marianne Tensing

> There is an Indian story, telling how a group of blind men try to describe what an elephant looks like: the one touching the trunk describes something mobile and flexible like a snake, the one touching the leg describes the solidity of a tree trunk, the one touching the belly describes it like a soft boat . . .
>
> Together, through their different perceptions, they get an idea of what an elephant looks like.

Introduction

This chapter is in some way like the story of the elephant. Different voices, from different roles, will reflect on the shared experience of the conference.

Luca, who first had the vision, and Franca introduce and co-ordinate this paper from their roles as co-directors: Maria Grazia contributes in the role of administrator, Hanna, in the role of translator, Richard, in the role of consultant, Maija-Leena and Marianne, in their role as members.

Following the spirit of the Energy, Creative Collaboration, and Wellbeing (ECW) Conference, we are trying here to give voice to the different points of view and explore if and how they can dialogue with, and integrate, each other.

Although there have been two ECW conferences, for clarity's sake and for the sake of the boundaries of this chapter, we shall focus mostly on the second event, which was, in any case, a development of the first.

There is a body of theory behind this work: however, we shall not focus on that aspect, but on the experience itself as it unfolded during the conference.

Energy, creative collaboration, and wellbeing

Energy focuses on the source of energy in the individual, essentially located in the breathing and in the heat which propel us throughout life; it focuses on the awareness of how internal energy links to the use, or exploitation, of the outer energetic resources.

Creative collaboration focuses on how the alignment and interconnectedness of the three "doors" of perception that human beings have for processing their experience (body, mind, and energy), when consciously used in concert, facilitate learning and co-operation within groups. It might help them to tackle complex and critical issues such as climate change, use of energetic resources, etc.

Wellbeing focuses on how awareness of energy and stimulation of collaborative skills may result in an improvement of personal, organisational, and collective wellbeing.

ECW was designed with the idea that the field of awareness within a GRC could expand to cover other essential aspects of life together with authority, leadership, and followership, which are main themes explored and dealt within GRCs.

Many GRCs, including Leicester, have promoted the explorations of new themes and events as a response to the need to develop the original idea and to update it, in line with the new demands of today's world.

Identity, ethnic relationships, trauma, co-leadership, and generational passages have been explored, just to mention a few.

New events, such as social dreaming, the market place, the praxis event, have been created and bear witness to the vitality of GR as an evolving phenomenon.

GR work is, at its core, an ethical socio-analytic enterprise, aiming to make conscious the unconscious forces that hinder the work group and, thus, promote the functioning of the group.

We believe that awareness of human connection to the environment constitutes a fundamental, moral, ethical question, highly relevant, which cannot be avoided at this point in history, and that the GR tradition would be a fertile ground for such an exploration.

The design of the programme is aimed to facilitate awareness of one's inner environment, the external one, and their interconnection. The body seemed to be the obvious focus from which to start, locating the body as a vehicle for understanding the "earth body" we live in as well as its energetic resources.

The capacity to relate learning to the social and physical context where it takes place is an essential element of relatedness.

Sometimes, GRCs are hosted in locations where energetic resources, in terms of water, heating, food, money, etc., are wasted without much thinking about what is going on or the effect it might have on the experience of learning, as well as on the body that learns.

Two simple, and yet highly ambitious, working hypotheses have been formulated for this ECW conference.

The first one is that involving the whole of the complex and interconnected fields of human perceptions—body, energy, and mind—would promote integrated learning; it would act as an effective track to consciousness, reflection, the capacity to think and to take action.

The second hypothesis rests on the assumption that "embodied" learning might facilitate awareness of the connection between one's inner landscape and the outer one. This could lead to a more respectful relationship with the environment and its use.

Franca and Luca chose to work as co-directors as a way of exploring collaboration. They also chose to facilitate the events that focused on movement and sound, as both of them could draw from many years of experience in the practice of movement and voice from a meditative angle as well as a performing one. Working from each one's different background, they collaborated towards the creation of an environment where members could be open to the use of their own bodies as a resource of awareness and presence.

The four-day conference was conceived in 2010, after Belgirate III, by Luca and by Shelley Ostroff, who was the director of the first conference, together with four members of the staff.

It was a pilot edition: Il Nodo Group (Italy) and FINOD (Finland) sponsored the event, and the Tavistock and Portman NHS Foundation Trust and CESMA supported it.

The chosen location was Casa Laboratorio Cenci, an old and beautiful farmhouse in Umbria, a centre for research and experiential learning in the field of education. The environment did offer deep connections to the cultural and natural Italian landscape. It provided very simple accommodation—in fact, Spartan—and wonderful nature for hosting the conference and the outdoor events.

The second location, chosen because there were logistical problems in the first one, was an ex- convent, equally embedded in beautiful nature and in the Italian cultural heritage.

The fee was kept on the low scale, a choice that we hoped would attract young people, people with lower salaries, and foreigners who have to pay their travelling expenses.

Indeed, the membership was international and presented an interesting mixture of professions and age differences (from twenty-two to seventy).

The primary task was: "to offer participants the opportunity to explore how awareness of energetic resources and creative collaboration can introduce wellbeing into the organisations to which they belong".

The brochure stated also that the conference's aim was to extend the field of attention to the unconscious as it manifests itself at the level of the emerging subject matter.

The programme's design included plenaries, SDMs, OE, RAGs, one theoretical dialogue, and it also introduced three events dedicated to the awareness of one's inner landscape as well as of the outer one: morning connections, vocabulary of movement, and night sounds.

The three new events punctuated the rhythm of the conference and somehow supported its containment of it by taking place at the very beginning of the day, in the middle, and at the end. They acted as a thread woven into the fabric of the conference. They were very clearly not events "on the side", but an integral part of its structure (Table 9.1).

Challenge and containment

What follows are the reflections of each of the staff members in relation to the main events. Challenge and containment seem to connect

Table 9.1.   Schedule for GRC Energy Creative Collaboration and Wellbeing, May 2013.

Thursday 9	Friday 10	Saturday 11	Sunday 12
	7.45–8.30 Morning connections	7.45–8.30 Morning connections	7.45–8.30 Morning connections
	8.30 breakfast	8.30 breakfast	8.30 breakfast
	09.30–10.15 SDM	09.30–10.15 SDM	09.30–10.15 SDM
11–12 Registration	10.15–10.40 DRD	10.15–10.40 DRD	10.15–10.40 DRD
11.45–12.20 light buffet lunch	10.40–11.00 break	10.40–11.00 break	10.40–11.00 break
12.30–13.30 Plenary	11.00–12.30 OE	11.00–12.30 OE	11–12.00 POE
13.30–14.00 break	12.45–14.15 lunch	12.45–14.15 lunch	12.00–13.30 lunch
14.00–16.00 OE	14:15–16.00 OE	14:30–18.00 free time	13:30–14:30 AG
16.00–16.30 tea break	16.00–16.20 tea break		
16.30–17.30 OE	16.30–17.30 theoretical presentation		
17.40–18.30 Vocabulary of movement	17.40–18.30 Vocabulary of movement	14:45–15:45 Plenary	
18.40–19.30 RG	18.30–19.30 RG	18.40–19.30 AG	15:45–16:15 farewell
19.30–21.00 dinner	19.30–21.00 dinner	19.30–21.00 dinner	
21.00–21.50 Night sounds	21.00–21.50 Night sounds	21.00–21.50 Night sounds	

the first two contributions. Both the administrator and the translator speak of the deep commitment they felt towards their two key roles and to the task of the conference. They reflect on the experience of providing a container for the conference and, at the same time, of feeling contained enough by the conference to be able to explore beyond their assigned roles, which in some way is evidence of a fertile environment for pushing limitations forward.

The administrator (Maria Grazia)

When I think about my role in the ECW Conference I associate it with "dream" and "interface", but immediately after, "hybrid" comes to my mind. A strange creature that is neither fish nor fowl.

I like the hybrid mind, it is the heart of mental life and, in the administrator role, is the heart of the task.

What does the administrator interface? I think many matters and situations.

The director's project and his realisation

One of the directors called me and offered me the administrator role in a new application of GRC. He explained the idea to me, the embryonic project: words and concepts that sounded very good and interesting to my mind.

But how could I help concretely to bring into existence that idea?

Words: holistic, environment, resources, wellbeing, energy, and creativity.

In my mind "holistic" sounds like "everything": my own and other colleagues' actions had to care about all aspects of the conference.

The ideas and their concrete realisation

The concrete aspects of the conference are the administrator's work field. However, in the ECW, the concrete aspects have the same role that the resources and the environment have in our life.

The administrator has to interface the participants' needs and the concrete location of the conference.

Now, thinking about needs and resources, in my mind the role of interface becomes like the maternal role: the mediation between the baby's needs and the available resources.

The staff and the participants

From creating the brochure to the end of the conference, the administrator has to be hospitable and containing for the participants. Taking care is similar to being in a relationship with the child, but, at the same time, is like being in the couple relationship with the father.

The quality of the relationship between the administrator and the rest of the staff is the ground that represents the means for the participants to respect the environment and not despoil its resources. This is similar to the quality of the relationship in which the parental couple offers the child the way to be fed without despoiling the mother's breast.

In my second ECW experience, I often felt the paternal support of the staff and I could also experience another interface role: to work as a consultant in the DRD and in RAG.

It was a very interesting experience for two different reasons.

Participants, at the beginning of each session, were a little suspicious of my new role. That makes me think about the mistrust aroused by the first women doctors, when the female figure took on a role that until then had been held only by men.

However, after the initial hesitation, members worked with me with commitment.

For me, it was quite an unusual experience: it was like being contained in the container which, up to that time, I had taken care of; I had to change my mental position.

The translator (Hanna)

Being a translator in a group relations conference was, for me, a whole new experience, and my approach was one of openness and strong commitment to the task. I saw my role as a privileged one where I could listen and have access to the complexity of the information exchange, having a real impact on the fluidity and richness of the communication within the group, as well as potentially being at the centre of different forms of demands and expectations from the group.

I spent most of the time during the conference working as part of the staff group, thus representing one of the staff group's "resources", which seemed to trigger rather intense dynamics between this group and the participants activating feelings of envy, admiration, interest, rage, desire, idealisation. The staff group's reflective capacity to name and translate such feelings helped me to manage and dilute their impact on my work, allowing me to observe and contribute to the conference also beyond my specific role.

Translating has often meant being at the centre of pressures and communicative efforts, and the demand seemed to be that I took care of difficulties in communicating and in accessing resources which were easily associated with my role, but also carried the meaning of submerged conflicts and hostility among individuals and groups.

The second OE plenary took place in an open location, under the sun. As a translator, I seemed to become the subject of expectations and requests which, like the intensity of the heat coming from the sun, at one point felt unsustainable. Those who spoke seemed somewhat less aware of my limitations, talking in long and complex sentences that required a rather strenuous effort to be translated. My work seemed to be idealised on the one hand, and, on the other hand, exploited with little awareness of its limits. As Franca astutely pointed out, this recalls the dangers of a collective attitude towards natural resources within the ecosystem, whose unsustainable exploitation possibly originates in the belief that they would ideally be limitless.

The possibility of naming such intense pressures on my role seemed to allow a shift during the last plenary, when I observed a different interaction and the desire to retrieve each one's internal resources, however imperfect and limited. Most participants tried to communicate without my help, creating a different atmosphere, less tense, perhaps mellower in the awareness of its imminent ending, more genuine and creative.

The main events: different languages and their interconnection

The reflections regarding the main events of the conference will be described by Franca and Luca, who, in their role of co-directors, facilitated the three new events; Franca in her role of host of the SDM; Richard in his role of consultant and director of the OE.

We hope that, even in its embryonic shape, it will be possible to see how all the events contributed to the development of the conference and were part of the created system.

Together with many other themes, language became a main issue throughout the conference. It manifested itself in the shape of the dilemma of speaking English and Italian, but the hypothesis was that it became the top of the iceberg for a larger field of action where differ-

ent "languages" had to find their own rightful space and interconnection. Many pairs, not just English and Italian, had to find a bridge
towards collaboration in the service of the task: me-and-the-other,
unconscious and conscious, body and mind, outer and inner context,
to mention a few.

Co-directors facilitating the three new events (Franca and Luca)

Morning connections. Its primary task (PT) was to awake and connect
to one's inner state of being and to the outer context), *Vocabulary of
movement* (PT: to explore the body in action), *Night sounds* (PT:
explores sound and voice; it facilitates the closing of the daily activities and prepares for sleep and dreams).

As a thread throughout the day, these events were designed for the
opportunity, we hoped, to offer a direct experience of energy, creative
collaboration, and wellbeing.

Two of the three events worked at the boundaries between night
and day as a way of bringing attention to what does go on in the transition from the state of being awake to that of being asleep. Linked to
the other more traditional events of the GRC, they supported awareness of the interconnection between conscious and unconscious states
of being, observed not just at mind level, but also at the level of the
"emerging matter".

In line with that task, each of the three events brought elements of
structured work (directions and rules about what to do, both in terms
of movement and in terms of sounds) and of unstructured work (free
movement and improvisation, both of which evoke a world of "multi-
dimensional free associations", where the unconscious can be seen in
action and where creativity is strongly stimulated).

The movement and voice work was kept to its bare bones of
simplicity: exploration of oneself, of the other, and of the group
dimensions (elements of the system); awareness of breathing, and of
the body which moves (energy); awareness of the senses (doors of
connection between outer and inner world); awareness of the hosting
context (environment); listening, resonance and dissonance with the
other (awareness of creative collaboration).

As the four days unfolded, we started to see how the discourse of
the conference, with its own particular themes, manifested itself
throughout the whole range of events. The new and the traditional

were integrated, each contributing to the working through of the emerging themes.

Here are two examples.

Each of the self-constituted groups of the OE, during the Vocabulary of Movement, were asked to move freely in the space while the others watched them. Dynamics that emerged in the OE and got the groups stuck could be spontaneously explored in movement terms and brought back into the OE somehow with seeds of an evolving pattern.

Exploration of authority and leadership, which was clearly taking form within the OE, could be tested not only in the groups and in their interface with the staff, but also in one of the structured "actions" that took place during "Morning Connections" and which required leading colleagues through a determined path.

When one works with movement, voice, breathing, and nature, it is nearly impossible not to experience a sense of alert relaxation, which cannot be kept encapsulated just to the moment of the experience. It seeps through the day with its different tasks and contributes both to the learning experience and to the learning from experience.

As the body is one of the "places" where the unconscious resides, by allowing free movement to take place, unconscious contents can be released and worked through in a creative way by tapping into individual and group creativity.

The social dreaming matrix (Franca)

The primary task: to illuminate the unconscious thinking of the system as it unfolds during the events. The matrix transforms the thinking of the dreams; participants associate as freely as possible to the dreams in order to find links and connections and to liberate new thoughts.

A social dreaming matrix is primarily a door to the social manifestation of the unconscious; within a GRC, it gives access to the social dimension that connects the temporary organisation to the larger context that contains it. It is an event that also contains and transforms, via the dreams, unconscious fantasies, anxiety, fears, and desires; by doing so, the impulse for acting out is both expressed and transformed.

The conference dealt not only with mind, but also with "body matters"—a novel event on the Italian GR scene; the membership needed straightforward, flexible, and safe containers.

Indeed, starting from the very first dream, the hypothesis that the dilemma "body matters" *vs.* mind would be dealt with in the matrix was confirmed.

> . . . it was a nightmare related to the pictures in the cloister [frescoes of saints tortured and killed in various gruesome ways]. There were people shooting, one should avoid being shot in the head; if one could be shot in the body it would be OK.

The theme was explored through the many dreams which followed the first one; they spoke of earthquakes and crumbling houses, revealing the power and the anxiety that can be aroused by encounters with the unknown, which, in fact, underlies the beginning of many matrices, whether the focus is on the body or on anything else; the feelings elicited by the big unknown, which brings major fears and equally powerful movements towards internal freedom, are common.

> I was in my old home which is about to be pulled down, many walls have already gone.

> I was in my home town after the earthquake . . .

> . . . my home was disintegrating by itself, plaster peeling off. I was trying to find a way out from the terrace but the bannister had collapsed.

The integrity of the container "house/skin" seems definitely under threat, whether it represents the inner body–mind identity or the outer context and the perception of a planet under threat, or of a crumbling economy. There is no control over what is happening; it is so basic and elemental—like an earthquake—that nobody can take any responsibility for nature's behaviour (or so one believes).

> . . . the car goes by itself, I am afraid, but then I have to follow and I allow it to happen, letting go, really.

> I drive the car, but from the rear seat. I cannot move to the driver's seat.

Yet, even the very first matrix signals that the internal movements may have a positive outcome.

... after the earthquake everybody in the family is safe.

... there was no disaster though.

... in a bus, unprepared for the journey, I am still wearing my pyjamas; when I get off I am dressed.

... the car goes back on the road and all is OK.

The second matrix started with the dream

A dear friend of mine tells me that she has dreamt of me ...

which makes me wonder whether, as in the Medusa myth, the danger is faced indirectly by looking at the Medusa through the shield *of a friend who dreams of me*; indirect, but still successfully negotiated, as the myth does tell us.

Often, the matrix operates indirectly, in the penumbra of associative thinking and resonance phenomena: "the task of the matrix is to transform the thinking of the dream ...", as the primary task states at the beginning of each matrix.

In the second matrix, dreams enter the human realm: there are bridges, dancing couples, splitting situations, and much water, at times menacing, at times with boats sailing peacefully on the surface.

Then the following dream is told:

Barbarians wanted to enter the castle and rape the women. We wanted to get out, but if we do, they will behead us. We hear that a friend has gone out: they cut off one of his legs and raped his girlfriend ...

Anxiety and excitement, potentially elicited by the involvement of the body, give voice to the risk of crossing boundaries into the realm of violence. Yet, the dream announces the shift in the conference where the contents of the SDM can clearly relate to what is going on in the whole system: connections both with the events and with the larger context disclose themselves and can be acted upon.

The OE sessions were occupied mostly by the difficulty the membership experienced in dealing with the language, Italian–English, an issue which needs very often to be negotiated in GRCs as it underlies the challenge of how to meet the foreigner/other/new idea.

In one of the hypotheses circulated in the OE, it had been pointed out how the problem could be one of the characteristics of Italian society: hospitable, warm country, welcome and tolerant of differences, and yet, also, because of its history, extremely conservative and deeply reluctant to be shaped by foreign/new influence.

In the course of the conference, communication had become stuck; the translator's help was constantly required in a way that resulted in the groups avoiding responsibility for dealing with their task. During the last OE plenary, communication reached a bottleneck: every intervention required translation until the translator became clearly overwhelmed and on the verge of not coping. Images offered by the dream put into words what was going on: Hanna's resources were "raped" and meaningful connections among members "killed" by the barbarians within. It could be seen in the conference system as well as being connected to the deployment of earth's resources, taken for granted as though they could last forever.

After that episode, members and staff started to use their own resources, at times limited and at times more articulated, by communicating in both languages. Mostly, they helped each other towards the task. The closing plenary hardly required the help of the translator at all and she could intervene by reflecting on her own experience of being in the conference.

The third and last SDM opened with a dream, which, as often dreams do, captured beautifully the essence of the experience:

> I am in the cloister, I have knifed someone, one of the members of the group. But it is not so violent, in fact the member was not wounded because the programme of the conference acted as a shield. (like Perseus and the Medusa . . .)

Consultant and director of the organisational event (Richard)

> By the rivers of Babylon
> Where we sat down
> And cried when we remembered Zion.
> On willow trees
> We hung up our harps.
> Those who made us prisoners were so cruel.
> "Sing", they said, "Sing us one of the songs of Zion

> . . . to make us laugh".
> Oh . . . how can we sing the Lord's song in a foreign land.
> (Psalm 137, also found in Giuseppe Verdi's
> opera *Nabucco*, sung to the Chorus
> of the Hebrew slaves)

The playing of the Hebrew slave chorus was prepared as an intervention at the plenary of the OE by the staff. It is a tale of exile and longing for a home; it carries the quality of a yearning so deep that the subjective experience speaks for a collective meaning pushing into consciousness. However it was never delivered as perhaps it was redundant given the increasing awareness of the pains of trying to communicate across different languages and experiences and the feelings of exclusion giving a refugee status of not belonging. In that sense it was part of the collective unconscious revealed in the system dynamics that was in the process of crossing the contact barrier from sensation to dream to feeling to thought described by Bion. This had been further confirmed by many of the dreams reported in the SDM, with car crashes, earthquakes, and personal losses and catastrophes of many kinds being reworked through dreaming and telling the dream experience. This suggested the possibility that the OE could be a vehicle for such unconscious fears of catastrophe to become embodied and worked through as one event in the conference system flowed into another.

The primary task given in the introduction to the OE shaped it *as an opportunity to integrate and experiment with different events and experiences in the conference.*

From adhesion to first moves

In the first two sessions of the OE, when groups had had their first taste of the challenge of forming, there was a clustering of the randomly laid out chairs close around the site where the staff had established their meeting space with visitors' chairs.

It took some exploration of the meaning of this behaviour to understand it as an adhesive response, clinging dependently to staff in a mass for hints at direction, or to imitate their approach. It might also have been a reflection of the seductive aspects of staff leading directly exercises using the body. Perhaps this clinging was in the face of the enormity of the task of integrating the different elements of the whole conference experience in action and reflective enquiry and experiment. Maybe it was a primitive defence of seeking a regressive merger and security in the face of the trauma that threatens when the body gives birth to the mind, or has to cross the caesura, as Bion puts it.

It took exploration of this dynamic for some time before the members found inner resources to begin exchanging between themselves and leaving to find other spaces, contacts, and possible groupings. This was, perhaps, the first of a number of ways in which neediness of dependency and loss that members had brought with them flowed across the skin of the OE for expression, attention, and working through.

Language of the tongue, movement and the body,
and the anxieties of annihilation

Once weaned into the idea that members could experiment with the uncertain anxieties of the unknown of their own authority, four groups formed. Later, two merged, with a lot of competitive friction and seeking consultancy from staff. At one point, the issue appeared to be about the need for translation and the group tried to negotiate to have the resource of the translator.

Initially, the staff decided to send a consultant and not the translator to explore hidden processes. Later, we decided to send the translator in the role of interpreter and consultant, in order to facilitate understanding of what this conflict of language meant while facilitating the use of linguistic resources in the group. This also provided a developmental opportunity for the translator, who was well up to the task of becoming a consultant.

One of the key hypotheses the staff slowly formulated was that there was a particular anxiety and vulnerability, being expressed in anger and frustration, by the leader of the non-Italian speaking subgroup in the conference. We felt that this might be a conflict projected from the Italian speakers. On the one hand, we suggested, there is the ever sociable, welcoming, and hospitable Italian culture that made the venue and the country an ideal place for such an experimental GR conference. The traditional friendly and gentle welcome of Italians towards strangers to their country is epitomised by generosity and shared food and talk at the meal-table. On the other hand, this warm welcome, we suggested, ironed out a buried aggression that in Italian society is reserved for family conflicts and politicians. We suggested that vulnerability about expressing aggression had become projected into non-Italian speakers in the way they felt so deeply alienated.

To communicate this hypothesis. we innovated a systemic intervention. First, we invited two of the non-Italian speakers to hear and discuss our hypothesis. Next, we invited paired Italian representatives from each of the three groups. One of the consequences from this intervention was to increase attempts to communicate between groups. A second consequence was the increased use of metaphors from the non-verbal exercises that held a language of their own, the vocabulary of movement. The task being experimented with was how to transform languages for communication, relatedness, and meaning.

Integration with other events of the conference

During the OE, the staff made several interventions designed to integrate the OE experience with other events on the conference. There was some use of the idea of using embodied metaphors to describe roles by being the mind, the eyes, and the ears of a group, alongside the more familiar political metaphors of ambassadors, messengers, and so forth

During one of the Vocabulary of Movement sessions, each of the three member groups in the OE were invited to express themselves in free movement. The group that had experienced most struggle in forming, then merging with, another group and in battling with conflicts around language, in the event produced the most spontaneous, fluid, and harmonious expression of collective movement that expressed differences.

After-conference thoughts: members' contributions experiencing change

Maija-Leena and Marianne reflect here on their experience as members of the conference. Both witness change in their lives and practices, which they observed as result of the combined elements of the conference where attention was given as much to the design as to the larger container (see the administrator's comments, above).

Maija-Leena

In my work career, I have been in several Group Relations Conferences, as a participant, a consultant, and a director. I see the aspect of the learning as spectacular. In the ECW conference held in Italy, I have experienced some unique phenomena. Their meaning for my later consultant work has been great.

With the traditional events at the GRC, the new elements of the ECW pilot conference were the impact of environment—the influence of food and the body's movements, one's own voice, and, overall, the experience going through one's body. It was important to notice the meaning of the bodily experiences for thinking and the birth, and functioning, of new ideas.

I believe that the most significant detail in resolving the issues was that we were able to reflect the events and our bodies' experiences simultaneously and for a long time. Time had a great meaning. It was important that the event leaders and consultants allowed much time when reflecting the focus of the session and our bodies' experience as well as describing events. Nothing was ignored or skipped. That ensured that the individual's energy could be directed and orientated into remedial action.

Marianne

My participation in the conference turned out to be a significant experience for me. It is seldom that I have such a feeling of gained knowledge after an educational event, as well as a head full of the phenomena produced. I will be able to use the perceptions gained on group dynamics and leadership, as well as my own experiences, not only to benefit myself, but also in my consultation work. When I returned to Finland and then went to my office the next day, a colleague said that I looked different, in some way happier. I believe that she was right, because I felt different. It suddenly felt as if the complex problems of my clients could be steered in a favourable direction. Work issues awakened an interest in me to determine whether matters could be approached differently, and so on. In my opinion, I managed to "press" through my client cases in more detail and was able to wait for my thoughts. I had a greater ability to think for longer periods. The work exhaustion that had built up over the winter had been washed away in six days. I was more peaceful but, at the same time, excited and energetic. I tend to be too rational, but now, on the basis of the feedback from the conference, I plan to re-examine that assumption. Both my mind and my body remember the nature, smells, and sounds: the beauty of the flowers, the songs of the birds, the sounds of the frogs, the heat of the sun, the glances of the people and the approval in their facial expressions—the list is endless.

Conclusions

It is very early days for ECW, it is certainly still in its embryonic shape; however, we do think it bears the seeds of innovation and that the initial hypotheses were confirmed.

There was integrated learning, the new and the traditional events supported each other in service of the task.

Some very traumatic and destructive themes did emerge; they could be expressed and worked through; solutions were found and forms of collaboration were put into action.

It is difficult to say whether this methodology will have an effect on the awareness towards the environment on the large scale; on the small one it certainly showed, and we hope the reader will perceive it.

After all, big changes do happen starting from many small ones . . .

CHAPTER TEN

The experiences of co-directorship in group relations conferences

Ruthellen Josselson, Olya Khaleelee, Mannie Sher,
Mary McRae, Gouranga Chattopadhyay,
Gerard van Reekum, and Susan Long

Introduction

This chapter elaborates on a presentation given at Belgirate IV on the challenges and opportunities offered by co-direction in group relations conferences. We consider the following questions: how did co-direction influence the development of personal authority? What was the impact of the co-directorship on those being led? How were competition and collaboration experienced in the co-directorate and with what effect on staff and membership? How did co-direction affect gender relations? What were the systemic effects of co-direction on the conference as a whole, compared to the experience of paired leadership as in director–associate director or compared to single leadership with a director but no associate director?

Olya Khaleelee and Ruthellen Josselson present a collaborative summary of their joint experiences in co-directing an A.K. Rice International Conference. Mannie Sher and Mary McRae separately discuss different aspects of their experience co-directing a Leicester conference. Gouranga Chattopadhyay writes from many experiences working in co-directorships, and Gerard van Reekum, based on his own experience and relating to the paired presentations, raises questions about what actually constitutes co-directorship. Susan Long, also writing from multiple experiences of being a co-director, offers and explores a conceptual framework of some of the main themes of the other presentations.

Co-direction at the A. K. Rice conference 2011

Olya Khaleelee and Ruthellen Josselson

The co-directors decided on the title of this conference—"Changing Authority: Collaboration and Interdependence in a Diverse World"—in 2010. With its emphasis on "Changing Authority", it proved prophetic for 2011, with the conference taking place as the Arab Spring took hold in several different countries. This revolution emphasised major changes in authority relations, with a rejection of hierarchical leadership and the possibility of developing new, perhaps more creative and collaborative, ways of working together. The global timing had the effect of making this conference a very exciting experience for all—for participants as well as for staff. Ruthellen Josselson had made the decision to explore the possibilities of co-direction and she invited Olya Khaleelee to take the co-director role. From the time Olya accepted, in the late summer of 2010, all decisions about the conference were made jointly.

The co-directors took very seriously their plan to collaborate on the directorship and they met frequently and intensively before the conference, reviewing all decisions that that they could foresee needed to be made. This meant bringing together in the co-directorship two strongly related yet different models, that of AKRI and of the Tavistock Institute, together with differences of culture (USA–UK) and of style. All this pre-planning, plus their natural affinity for one another, led to an almost seamless collaboration.

At the conference, they differentiated their roles so that staff were clear about who they should look to for leadership at specific times; for example, it was made clear at the outset who would run particular staff meetings. They differentiated in other ways when it made sense to do so. For example, Olya Khaleelee took a consulting role in the large study group and became more embedded in the system, while Ruthellen retained a management function by attending meetings of the small study group team, the large study group team and the administrative team. This also enabled her to maintain a more "macro" perspective on the total system.

One consequence for members was to regard Olya as the "visible" and Ruthellen as the "invisible" director, linking this also with "warmth" or "remoteness". This was a very moderate form of "parental" splitting compared to how strongly members could have tested the boundaries of this pair had they really wished to do so. However, perhaps because of the collaboration emphasised in the title, the tendency was to preserve rather than to attack the pair. Pairing as a dynamic was very much in evidence, naturally embodied in the co-directorship; the co-directors tended to walk together in break times, sit together at meal times, and often be seen together. Much of this time they were actively working on their experience of the conference. As a result, both felt enriched by this experience of sharing directorial authority, partly because they learnt from one another, but also because working together was simply more enjoyable than working alone. It minimised the loneliness of the director role, an aspect of organisational leadership not often acknowledged. Furthermore, creating a system headed by two women seen to be collaborating had important effects on the resulting system-in-the-minds of the members.

Political and global context

We chose the title, "Changing Authority: Collaboration and Interdependence in a Diverse World" because we are living in an increasingly global society where, inevitably, we interact in more complex ways and where it is clear that the nature of authority is indeed changing. Our need to collaborate with each other correlates with this change, making us more interdependent. This interdependence necessitates collaboration with people who are different from us; working together brings us face to face with the dynamics of difference and diversity and the enriching possibilities they offer. So, one question was: how can we make difference a resource rather than an impediment?

Given the upheavals in the Middle East taking place just before the conference, we were highly aware that the use of personal authority by the individual citizen is increasing. There is no longer the same hierarchical attitude to authority that existed before the arrival of Facebook and Twitter. It seems that the top-down exercise of authority is not part of leadership for the future, even among those people who are used to a more authoritarian culture. Simultaneously, political events in the UK had resulted in a coalition government and the pairing of David Cameron, a Conservative, with Nick Clegg, a Liberal Democrat, so there had been an opportunity to experience their paired leadership over the past year. In the USA, citizens were experiencing the powerful pairing of Barack Obama and Hilary Clinton. So, one question was: working collaboratively, can we do better?

The group relations context of the conference

As far as we know, this was the first (AKRI) group relations conference to be co-directed by two women. When Ruthellen Josselson first proposed this collaboration to Olya Khaleelee, the latter initially found it hard to conceive of how this paired leadership would work. We are all products of our culture, and she came to realise the extent to which she had also internalised a hierarchical concept of authority and leadership. She wondered about the impact on those being led. Would it be confusing? To whom would they look for leadership? She considered whether co-direction was similar to a partnership model, and came to a view that co-direction probably was manageable so long as each of the roles of the co-directors was clearly delineated.

Despite this clarification, in practice at the outset, in her many Skype discussions with Ruthellen in 2010, Olya found herself taking up more of a comfortable associate director role, easy to do because, being UK based, she was distant from the USA and because it made sense for Ruthellen to be managing the boundary with the sponsoring organisation. Ruthellen had also taken charge of producing the brochure. Eventually, with encouragement, Olya began to use her directorial authority more and found that nothing problematic resulted from doing so. This description of the beginning, however, provides some flavour of her pre-conference anxieties, which are probably quite representative of the kinds of concerns that many co-directors have as they take up their roles, particularly where there is the threat of disturbing sentient relationships. A counterbalance to these feelings of uncertainty, or even pessimism, was Ruthellen's enthusiasm for innovation, which made Olya feel that co-direction might also be a fascinating and developmental experience for everyone.

Although the idea of co-direction seemed extremely innovative at the time, paired leadership is in fact a very old concept with a long history. Apparently, the Spartans had dual kingship and two royal houses. The Romans elected two consuls to serve for a one-year term, each with veto power over their colleague. They alternated on a monthly basis. Dual or paired leadership also existed among the Aztecs, who split the leadership between the Divine King, with brother succeeding brother, and the cities, each of which was ruled by a king selected from relatives. The Cherokees and some other Indian tribes also had paired leadership. So, although we experienced this co-direction as something new, in fact paired leadership and dual kingship is an old concept and practice.

Of course, leadership, paired or otherwise, also requires followership. Recent political events had clearly demonstrated that there are no leaders without followers. It is the followers who give authority for leaders to lead. This is a very important and underrated role. Without followership, this conference could not have taken place despite the formal authorisation from the A. K. Rice Institute, the sponsoring organisation, and from the staff who confirmed Ruthellen and Olya in their roles as co-directors.

We were also wondering whether there had been a more general loss of trust globally in hierarchical authority, which leads to a greater dependence on a horizontal "peer" authority or "sibling" attachment, evidenced in social networking and blogs, whereby any individual can comment or offer advice without having a specifically recognised expert authority to do so or, indeed, any personal knowledge of or relationship with the other. Certainly, paired leadership, co-directorship, partnership, or distributed leadership seem to be more in focus today. Perhaps this is a manifestation of a longing in society for a different kind of leadership.

The experience in the conference

From the feedback we received, the conference was a success in terms of providing members with opportunities to experience and learn. As far as the element of co-direction is concerned, this success was due to a number of factors. First, the powerful desire to make it work.

Second, a clear delineation of roles. As Ruthellen did not wish to consult to any "here and now" events and Olya did, particularly as large group consultant, it meant that Ruthellen had more time available and took primary responsibility for liaising with administration. At one point, Ruthellen said, not complaining, that she had never done so much administration in a conference before. This was partly to do with the complexity of staff–member relations and how that affected group allocation, partly to do with the nature of the role as she developed it, but also to do with our desire for perfection.

Third, we welcomed difficulties as opportunities to learn about the dynamics of collaboration and had the capacity to talk about them. An example of the differences between us and some of the inevitable tensions occurred in the Institutional Event, where a number of issues were interacting: one was the differences in method between AKRI *vs.* TAVI, for example, working in the IE with a differentiated model of management separate from consultants, *vs.* a "together" model. Then there were cultural differences in how management manages the event: for example, the desire actively to obtain data from the membership *vs.* waiting more passively—as in the medical model—for the data to come to you. In addition, there were style differences, with Ruthellen being more proactive than Olya, a more active manager, as it were. The only moment that there was a difference that could not be resolved by discussion came in an IE event where Ruthellen wanted to find out what the consultants (who had not reported to the management) were doing and Olya wanted to wait and see if they came of their own accord. Clearly, there was no way for anyone, as representative of management, to both go and stay at the same time. Either management went to the consultants or it did not—the first true binary in the conference. Ruthellen tried to persuade Olya to change her mind, but Olya simply said, "You are a director of this conference." Somewhat hesitatingly, because she had never acted alone in regard to this conference before, especially in the face of a different view from her co-director, Ruthellen went to the consultant group. (As far as she was aware, there was no reprisal for this.)

Staff were very supportive of the co-directorship, eager to experience it, and fearful of splitting it. This meant that perhaps some of them, particularly some of the men, did not allow themselves their full authority to challenge the directorship. This may have had an impact on the men in the conference, who were equally non-challenging, although considerable rage and competition was expressed, certainly in the large group (LG). So it might be the case that in order to preserve the female pair, the men may have felt "castrated" at times.

One implication of the directors' collaboration was that, institutionally, it seemed that hierarchy needed to be abolished or obliterated at all levels. The small group (SG) team and the consultant group in the IE tried to work without delegating leadership, by trying some kind of rotating leadership, which led to somewhat inefficient and confused functioning in these teams. On reflection, the directors thought about the invisibility of their own preliminary collaborative work to staff, wondering whether it might have seemed to staff that one could simply decide to collaborate or rotate leadership roles. Then, when this did not work so well, there was considerable frustration among them. Eventually, both of these subsystems appointed clear leadership and their work together went more smoothly. So, while the co-directorship was a conscious choice of pairing at the work task level, the basic assumption pairing that developed elsewhere during the conference, among both staff and members, was more to do with the difficulty of keeping at bay issues around fight and competition.

While the co-directors offered what was perceived as an enviable model of collaboration, and while the staff generally worked together harmoniously both among themselves and with the co-directors, the system was awash in suppressed competition. This mostly found expression in the LG. Of the four sessions, two were characterised by anger, competition, and sexual aggression. Splitting was evidenced between the angry, competitive, and ambitious majority of women with the male minority sitting back, peacefully awaiting the outcome of the fight. Fear and attraction dominated. Murderousness was overt and was linked to an exploration and testing of the authority in the conference as a whole and how to relate to it. Staff in the LG system wondered whether co-directorship might be experienced by LG members as a single-parent system, with boundaries to be tested to the limit, and they debated whether this was normal rage or whether it also related to the revolutions taking place around us globally.

How the IE developed in the light of the theme of changing authority, collaboration, and diversity had a flavour of the Arab Spring, a sense of creativity, trying new things, with participants treating management very much as equals, thus not being in a BA dependency mode, rather more in a pairing mode, mirroring the directorship.

Asked about the systemic effects of the collaborate directorship, one of the consultant candidates, Jenna Bernstein, summarised succinctly that the men felt marginalised and the women were freezing. (Indeed, the air conditioning in some rooms was frigid, yet there were other implications of the temperature as well.) Perhaps the self-sufficiency of the co-director pair led everyone to struggle with how they could become objects of desire; the strength of the pair seemed to be too much to overthrow or enter. These dynamics, while they seemed to exist in the membership, were not detectable in the staff. Again, though, there seemed to be a strong dynamic of making everything work and wanting to make things work, so there might have been many issues and anxieties of which the directors were not apprised.

Another effect of the collaboration is that it raised many questions in the system about how to differentiate without hierarchy. The role of experience was often under attack as the least experienced or capable people were sometimes put forward to lead, both on the staff and in the membership. We saw this as some effort to create a world where the last would be first. (This was partly a result of there being two training functions in the conference, with the resulting questions about how and when inexperienced people could take up new roles and gain experience.)

In sum, we learnt that one can change authority and try to build a more collaborative universe, but this throws into different forms of expression the inevitable issues of competition (for affirmation, for recognition, for existence); it does not obviate them. That we seemed like a "perfect pair" in the system seemed to exacerbate the need to "get it right" and increased anxiety even as it provided a well-bounded container that made it possible for everyone to work. In the end, while there is no utopia, there was a great deal of learning. The task of the conference was fulfilled.

Co-directorship of the Leicester conference 2012

Mannie Sher

Our (Mary McRae's and Mannie Sher's) co-directorship of the Leicester conference broke with the traditional concept of leadership as individual endeavour and was more in line with our belief in leadership as shared effort, making leadership as much an institutional process as it is an individual trait. Because of the increasing organisational complexity of the Leicester conference, shared leadership became almost a necessity. We have seen this in our work with organisations that have grown so complex that it is felt to be entirely unreasonable to expect one person to "hold in mind" the entire organisation.

We were aware of the resistance to the notion of shared leadership that stems from centuries of cultural conditioning based on the Platonic view that leadership is a rare trait, typically possessed by only one person in any society, an individual who has a unique perspective on wisdom and truth. We felt a greater affinity with the Aristotelian view that truth is not singular and wisdom never the sole province of one person. We set out to challenge the dominant model of one-man-rule leadership.

It is commonly assumed that the biggest problem of co-leadership is dividing up the work. We found that to be only one determinant of success. Much depended on how our co-leadership roles originated, how complementary were our skills as directors and the emotional orientations we each possessed as individuals, how we worked together before the conference and during it, and how we involved others in the management of the conference. We self-selected as a team and not as two individuals; successful co-leaders typically choose each other as partners and are not foisted on one another. We were careful and lucky in this, as we worked to balance our relationship against a background of one of us (MS) being a director and employee of the Tavistock Institute and the other (MMc) being an invited professional associate.

Our co-directorship was built on a basis of trust—a quality that needed to be created slowly from the beginning, decision by decision. Working in tandem, each co-director picked up different parts of a problem. This was determined by the fact that one of us (MS) held executive responsibility on behalf of the sponsoring organisation and was, therefore, on the scene most of the time, and the other (MMc) was located at a distance and was outside the direct line of accountability.

Shared leadership models work well where they are extended down the line to all subsystems. The two administrators of the Leicester conference formed a team of co-administration. Later, in the conference, the unconscious evolution of the alternative leadership dynamic and many other instances of partnership and co-leadership emerged as pairs that we saw as mirroring the co-directorship pair.

Different roles

Shared leadership involved the two of us playing different and complementary roles, where "emotional leadership" was matched by "task leadership". Shared leadership made it easier for us to switch focus to meet changing conditions, as when we found our authority being questioned (by pairs of people, mainly) and the boundaries of the different subsystems were under threat of becoming unstable.

There was also fragility in our shared directorship. At different times and in different situations, one of us usually became more equal than the other and that needed to be accepted and worked with. As co-directors, we believe we were able to manage and value our complementary skills, temperaments, and perspectives. We recognised the importance of combining talent and chemistry and worked hard at achieving this.

Working together

Ideally, co-leaders should be able to choose each other. Once selected, we needed to work together, and we learnt to do so. For the sake of accountability, tasks had to be divided, but more important than the division of tasks was handling the division of credit. The hardest thing we had to consider in our joint directorship was that the biggest challenge was not practical or technical. Instead, it was managing our feelings and emotions—pride and arrogance. There were different moments when one stepped back and let the other take the credits.

Roles and tasks in our co-directorship were divided by interests (innovation *vs.* operations), skills (technology *vs.* people) or personality (strategy *vs.* implementation) and there were some very dramatic moments in the conference when these differences had to be knitted together and deployed. Roles and tasks were divided along the lines of individual skills and interests on one axis and organisational needs and opportunities on the other.

At times, we found the most effective approach to task division was to have a fluid approach to who takes responsibility for leadership tasks. It did not matter so much how responsibilities were divided. It mattered more that we were clear about our roles and honest with ourselves and each other about our respective contributions and needs for acknowledgement and power.

The questions we, as co-directors, asked when starting out were: what are we each good at? What areas in the Leicester conference would need our direct leadership in order for it to succeed? How were we going to co-ordinate and communicate with each other so we did not step on each other's toes? How could we make sure we arrived at agreed positions and sent the same messages? Co-ordination and alignment involves communication. As we were only two co-directors meeting several times a day, communication was often spontaneous and constant.

Working with others

We found that we needed to discuss our respective responsibilities and allocation of tasks and resolve many of our ambiguities ourselves; otherwise these would interfere in staff relationships. Staff sometimes felt otherwise: that we had become too joined-up and therefore terrifying to deal with, except by enrolling another person to form an opposing pair. We expected staff members to deal with issues of the membership in their respective group settings, and not with political issues caused by the co-directors' role ambiguities. We expected that the more interdependent the work of co-directors, the more we could expect the staff to co-ordinate between themselves. This sometimes proved more difficult than we had hoped.

In the shared directorship of the Leicester conference, people at all levels—directors, administrators, consultants, and members acted with more responsibility for participation and managing themselves in role, took initiative to solve problems, accepted accountability for meeting commitments and for living the values of the group relations conference and its theme of "coalition, co-operation and sustainable society", and created, maintained, and adhered to systems and procedures designed to promote learning as the conference's primary task.

Conclusions

Despite continued assertions that co-leadership does not work, there are enough examples of successful co-leadership combinations to make it possible to identify the factors that lead to successful co-leadership: joint selection; complementary skills and emotional orientations; mechanisms for co-ordination.

These might seem to be common sense, but not common practice. In our case, the co-directors

- "owned" stakes in the success of the Leicester conference, were concerned to groom successors in group relations, and were able to combine our different skills into a combination of complementary skills;
- had our own special way of bringing skills and talents to bear and did not compete for credit; had realistic assessments of our own skills; worked hard and talked together to maintain an agreed position on major issues; where there were differences, the directorate meeting was the appropriate forum for discussion and resolution; chemistry and trust between us was important. We did not leave that to chance; we worked hard to do nothing separately; all reporting relationships were directly to both of us;
- each took certain lines for decision-making and certain support functions;
- when problems arose, we worked on group process and communication. This sometimes left staff unclear as to how they should be treated in terms of decision making and communication. Where that happened, we tried to make clear what was a staff group activity and what was director-to-director activity.

We believe we were perceived as being fundamentally co-ordinated with respect to the direction of the conference and we brought to bear different skills in directing and consulting in order to maintain that direction.

Mary McRae

In my opening comments at the Leicester conference 2012, I (Mary) stated that I was honoured to be invited by Mannie Sher to be the first American of African descent to take up the role as director of the conference. Mannie and I had decided to list ourselves as directors, not co-directors. I was proud to follow one of my mentors, Kathy White, who was the first of my nationality, race, and gender to take up the role of associate director at Leicester; she had encouraged me to attend as a member about twelve years ago. My attendance at that conference introduced me to a group of international colleagues that I have developed wonderful working relationships with.

I use the concept of person-in-role as a lens for my own analysis and understanding of my first experience of co-directorship. Roles are occupied by individuals and are related to perceptions of who is appropriate for a given role. In predominantly white institutions, where white men and women have held the role of leadership, it can be difficult to authorise a person of colour in a leadership role. There is often a perceived lack of fit or a discrepancy between the person and others who have held the role. This has been the case for women chief executives who take up roles traditionally held by men.

Person-in-role is about representation, what the person-in-role might represent to those she or he is working with. What I would like to focus on is what I might have represented to the staff and members at Leicester in terms of nationality, race, and gender and how this representation impacted my co-directorship. Visible identities carry hidden assumptions, stereotypes, attitudes, and perceptions. These assumptions are often not in our conscious awareness, but deeply ingrained in the way we think, see, hear, and touch those around us. I found Obholzer's (1994) work on the different levels of authority helpful in exploring the concept of person-in-role, especially from a systemic perspective. He states, "clarity in matters of authority, leadership and organizational structure is essential for the competent functioning of any organization". He identifies three levels of authority: personal, from above, and from below.

Personal authority: When I spoke of my honour in working with Mannie, it was my intent to be more personable in role, which has to do with my style of working and finding more comfort in my person and skin. I felt ready and able to take up the role of director and co-director. It seemed that all the work I had done prior to this conference as conference director, associate director, consultant, and administrator had prepared me to take up the role of director and co-director in the Leicester conference. Mannie and I had done some interesting work prior to the conference, working on our own dynamics and expectations as we did the nuts and bolts of conference preparation. So, I entered the temporary educational institution feeling excited, creative, and ready.

Authority from above: Pre-conference work with Mannie was very satisfying. We spoke often and seemed to complement each other well in our work tasks and styles. It was understood that because of Mannie's role as Director of the Group Relations Programme at TIHR he would take care of several tasks that were done best by the sponsoring institution. Mannie, the conference administrators, and I touched base more often as the conference approached and I received copies of emails regarding membership and other issues that did not need my direct input. I was engaged in all major decisions regarding the conference brochure, design, hiring of staff, member recruitment, and general conference issues. I felt fully authorised by Mannie and the Tavistock Institute to take up my role.

Authority from below: From day one, the staff questioned our authority. One concern was whether we were truly co-directors, since Mannie hired me, how could he hire someone to take up an equal position with him? It would have been better if the executive director of Tavistock had hired both of us. I experienced this comment as a challenge to my authority. In my mind, the task was to study the "temporary" institution formed on the first day of the staff meeting and then with the members. Yes, the pre-conference work and relationships have an impact on the temporary institution, but the focus is on what we all create together. Hence, I was suspicious of the comment about whether we had equal authority in the temporary institution, especially since I am aware of a number of directors who have invited someone to co-direct with them with no question of who did the hiring. A group of members, consisting of mostly white businessmen at one point offered a plan to sustain the Tavistock Institute, as if the sponsoring institution was in trouble. I began to wonder what I might represent to the staff and to the members and what it was about my pairing with Mannie that might create tension or concern.

My scholarly work involves putting a multi-cultural lens to group relations concepts. The concept of person in role examined with this lens could be: what does the person represent in terms of nationality, race, and gender for those she is working with? How might her representation affect her authority and how she is authorised in role?

Nationality: A citizen of the USA announcing the status of her role and her pride in doing so might have conjured up international competition in regard to institutional affiliation. Why did the Tavistock Institute choose an American to take up this role; why not someone from one of its other partnering organisations? So, here again, I wondered what I represented in role as an American. I also wondered about my institutional affiliations as a professor at New York University, an A. K. Rice fellow. The USA is a global power and NYU is a global university. What about the USA's aggressive role in the Middle East and other parts of the world? What might that represent? What did the choice of an American citizen mean for members and staff from Europe and other parts of the world, who were more highly represented in the conference than members from the USA?

Race and gender: Race is an issue and it does matter. I do not believe my authority in role would have been questioned if I were a white male or female. My evidence for this is the history of previous co-directorships that were same or mixed gender pairs. The strong reactions of the staff and members to the co-director pair created some difficulties for us but it also pulled us closer together as a pair. We felt pressured to meet privately to air some of our concerns rather than work them publicly. While this allowed us to work together more effectively, the staff experienced our work behind closed doors as parents abandoning their difficult children. So what helped us to maintain role was perceived as a divisive threat to the staff. I think that maintaining role became very important to us. I am known to be quite creative in the director role; at Leicester I felt as if I used all my energy to contain, to hold the ship steady, a stereotypical role for African-American women. African-American women are often perceived as strong carers. Dumas suggested that Black women in leadership are perceived either as "the mammy" or the "bitch". The dilemma for Black women is the dichotomy of a no-win situation. I do not take up "the mammy" role well, so I tend to be perceived as the "bitch" or the angry Black woman when I take up my role in an assertive and task orientated manner.

So, in reflecting on this experience, I learned how difficult it is to work with person-in-role, especially when one of the co-directors is from a different national, racial, and cultural background. I think that my taking the co-director role heightened concerns about succession and who will take up the role of director of the Leicester conferences if not Eliat Aram and Mannie Sher. Will it be an American? Will it be a person of African descent? How does this speak to the traditions of the institution and leadership roles? What will those in leadership roles look like at the Tavistock in the new global world and how would we deal with changes when the person-in-role looks different from what we have seen in the past?

In summary, I think that the issue of person-in-role as it relates to nationality, race, and gender needs more in depth exploration and thought. The dynamic is intersectional, with multiple identities stepping into roles that are new and different to those who have held them before. How do we manage and understand this change that is very much representative of the global world that we now live in?

Reflecting on my experience of co-directorship: challenges and opportunities.

Gouranga Chattopadyhay

Most of my co-directing experience has been with Rosemary Viswanath, currently Managing Trustee of Group Relations India. The first time that I co-directed with her, the decision came about rather late. The sponsor of that GRC was Tata Management Training Centre (TMTC) at Pune. They had authorised me as director. In that role I had negotiated with Rosemary and appointed her in the role of associate director. Then, on the way from Mumbai (Bombay) to Pune with a non-Indian staff, we got into a discussion about co-directorship as against associate directorship. Since we arrived at the venue two days in advance, first I checked with the Director of the TMTC if I could consider converting the role of associate director into that of co-director. The TMTC Director had attended a GRC many years ago and after some discussion, he agreed to the idea. Rosemary arrived at the venue next morning and we discussed the idea of her becoming the co-director. We were a bit vague about sharing responsibility and authority and generally agreed to allocate longer time for directorate meetings to monitor how co-directorship worked. Our next task was to get the staff to agree to the change. By then I had introduced the practice in all GRCs that I directed of not only confirming the director in his or her role, but a process of peer authorisation of all staff in their role to underscore sharing plenipotentiary authority. To this we added confirmation of the co-directors in their respective role. The next step for me was to inform the members in the opening plenary of our rationale for this introduction of co-directorship.

During the conference, though, we discovered that, somewhat spontaneously, we distributed our areas of responsibility. While Rosemary looked after the administrative boundary, I concentrated on the rest of conference boundaries. While Rosemary introduced the IE, sitting in the management territory (it was a comparatively small conference so we did not have a separate territory for consultants) I began to explore how much directorial authority I had emotionally been able to delegate to Rosemary. My yardstick was the nature of my anxiety while I waited with my colleagues for her to come to the management territory after opening the IE. Further, during the event too, in relating to members coming as PP and delegates, I discovered that I was being quite careful about not hogging enough time to rule out leaving space for not only the rest of the staff, but especially the co-director.

This experience further helped me in reorientating my approach to my colleagues in my back home work place, as well as at home. My wife and I were, by then, married for almost fifty years, two of our sons were in their early forties, and the youngest one was in his late thirties. We also had two daughters-in-law and two grandsons by then. With my background of economically belonging to Bengali middle class and, in the back of the mind, being the scion of a Raja, a Prince, and a very well respected intellectual-cum-philanthropist, I had always been very careful about not becoming a "bossy" person. As a student of social anthropology, I knew that while in the rest of India much patriarchal or, in pockets, matriarchal culture existed, those were somewhat diluted by the ancient inheritance law known as *Mitakshara*. In this system, a male infant born in patriarchal families became a co-parcenor of the family property, meaning a joint heir to the property or estate. Here, one could see hints of co-directorship. However, in Bengal and some of the adjacent territories, there used to be a different system known as *Dayabhaga*. This ancient inheritance law had left its mark on how authority in family, and, by extension, authority in work organisations was used. But in the *dayabhaga* system, the male head of the family owned all the property and he could leave it to anyone of his choice. Although now both *Mitakshara* and *Dayabhaga* systems have been replaced by a common inheritance law, a lingering unconscious impact of the *Dayabhaga* system is that Bengali heads of families and enterprises find it extremely difficult to delegate or share authority, as authority is so vested in the head of the family or the leader. As a Bengali, therefore, I have been always acutely conscious of the possibility of my unconsciously withdrawing authority from the co-director.

I had previously co-directed, with a male colleague, in only one GRC. I think in that GRC the well-known phenomenon of envy operated. In that international conference the male co-director sided with a foreign staff member to challenge my authority. The issue came to a head in the IE when the foreign staff, as part of the consultant group, refused to accept my choice of the head of that group, left the territory, and wrote a long note to members and stuck it up on the notice board. Luckily, the administrator saw the note and removed it. I put it to the staff that in deserting the consultant group, the person had gone out of his role as staff and therefore he had no role in the GRC. They agreed and I sacked him. During that meeting, the co-director realised that he had become the lackey of a "foreign invader in the mind" and had sided with him. This is something imported from Indian history and the continuation of that process takes place even now as colonialism-in-the-mind. Since he did not agree with the idea of envy also playing a part in his siding with the foreign staff, I dropped the issue.

Co-directorship is challenging, as the directors need to work out new authority relationships. One issue here is role-making *vs.* role-taking. In role-taking, there is an assumption of following some set ideas, set guidelines, fixed ideological orientation, and, last, role definition set up by a charismatic person who had been in that role. But role-making has the element of using one's personal authority to freshly explore the organisation–role–task relationship.

A particular challenge in co-directorship was what the members were projecting on the two co-directors and we were aware of those projections to the extent that our roles remained within the process of our making rather than unconsciously influenced by the membership. Leader–follower collusion in all situations exist in organisations. But the challenge is becoming aware of this collusion when it starts corrupting the task.

When co-directing with a woman, I have been acutely conscious of projection of both envy and phantasy of the pair as a sexual pair. I think the envy is related to the latter to an extent. This envy is so powerful that after co-directing with Rosemary several times, I received an email from a colleague in another organisation who also directs GRCs. His email contained innuendos of other covert issues lying hidden behind the pairing of co-directorship. Upon receiving that email, I wondered if we had missed out many unconscious projections of the members, since apparently our successful co-directorship evoked such a strong emotional outburst in a colleague with whom I had last worked several years ago.

In most of the GRCs in India and the only GRC in Australia that I have directed, my co-directors were women. My experience was that, in plenaries, and more so in the LSG, the women members were more forthcoming and took greater risks than the men. By and large, the systemic impact of co-directorship has been to create and maintain a container that made way for greater task orientation for both staff and members.

Conference director, not co-director

Gerard van Reekum

In my mind, there is a big question mark jotted behind the role title "co-director". I have never been one. Both times I was a conference director I have been authorised in that role simultaneously with a colleague. We were deployed "with equal authority and accountability for jointly directing the conference and assuring its quality." And the letter of authorisation continued, "The two directors might want to take up and fill in their roles differently from each other at a later stage. When this would occur the board expects to be informed in a timely fashion about the impact this change in roles would have. The board expects a willingness from the directors to explore the continuous innovative character of both the conference and the way it is being directed." So there was no limit imposed on my authority and we as conference directors were free to differentiate between us—if at all— any way we would find useful or necessary during and in the service of the conferences we were invited to direct. Here I must emphasise that I am the sole author of this part in the chapter, just as I was also invited as an individual conference director to participate in the panel discussion at the Belgirate conference. As far as I know, my colleagues were not invited; we are talking about three different persons here and I cannot speak or write on behalf of the other two. What I *can* say is that, in both instances, the other conference director and I felt in tune about maintaining a questioning attitude, also with regard to the doubling of the role we were in.

During both conferences I experienced the usual episodes of confusion about the direction we were moving in, the inevitable confusion among staff as well as among members, and other subsystems that emerged. I do not think the confusion was less or more intense from what it would have been if the conferences had had a single conference director.

Some confusion resonated with the uncertainties, mysteries, and doubts that each of us encountered and managed according to the way we understood our role, including issues related to the fact we were not the only (al)one. Yet, these issues never drowned the conferences.

Against this background, what does "co-directorship" mean? I associate the term with co-dependency, and am unhappy with that. It could be true that a development away from locating the seat of direction in one person is a reaction (reversal) to the image of the narcissistic director, which, as we know, is an attractor for co-dependent responses. But even then I do not think the decision to authorise more than one conference director would justify the use of another role title.

Undeniably there is a certain amount of confusion and then excitement about the idea of having more than one authorised director, first in the staff and then also among the other participants. To me, it seems it is precisely this emotional experience that is denied by and hidden behind the use of a new role title. I think we should not do that in GRCs, I think we should try to confront our anxieties directly, based on our best understanding of how and by what they are provoked: the discovery that there are more conference directors than one (or a single set of co-directors).

A conference director is on the receiving end of authorisation by the permanent institution/sponsor, and, prior to the opening of the conference, he or she will share that authorisation with the staff in order for them to become plenipotentiaries so that all staff can jointly act as management. This puts an associate director—if there is one—in the same position relative to the authority of the conference director as other staff. Obviously, it will be different when two (or more) conference directors simultaneously receive authorisation from the source. Both of them will have an equally direct link with the permanent institution that authorised them. This difference highlights a particular illusion in the staff and in the conference, that the issue of authority would have been more manageable when handed over to one individual and less clear now it is no longer one unit of person and role that may be held ultimately accountable for whatever happens with or in the conference. I think it belongs to the task of GRCs to explore the nature and origin and corollaries of such illusions, regardless of whether conference management is modelled in correspondence with the proverbial belief that "two captains sink a ship", or not. We should not first encourage members to project "leadership" on one person (or on one construct, like "co-directors") and then shower them with hypotheses that depart from an understanding of role as something that is temporary and produced continuously, in a dynamic social process. I think our own management structure and practice should evidence this last understanding of role. At least we, as a staff, accept the task to work with the difficulties connected to our own concept of role, emotionally and politically, consciously if possible: the conference director is not necessarily the one who leads all the time, and the members of staff and of the conference are not necessarily the ones "being led" all the time.

Having listened to the other presentations on the panel which are now related in this chapter, I discovered that in all other examples of "co-directorship" only one conference director had actually been invited by the authorising body, and had decided on his or her own authority to invite a second director to "co-direct". Therefore, I thought these examples were not so different from the tradition of inviting an associate director that they would justify the use of another role title. The assumption that such "co-directorship" presents an innovation is illusory. When we choose to invite more than one conference director, we should not change the role title, but allow the emotional impact of discovering multiple conference directors to come to the fore and make that experience as such available for reflection and learning.

My conclusion was that changing the role title into co-director is a conceptual defence against this emotional impact. Yet, this conclusion did not go down very well during the discussion. At one moment, the whole idea of working with more than one conference director was rhetorically questioned: why would you want to do it in the first place, what is the relevance for the members anyway, and are there not better ways for training directors? I interpreted these deflective and offensive reactions as challenges to the text that introduced our panel discussion in the Belgirate brochure. Indeed, for me, promoting the idea of working with more than one conference director is not related to revolts against undemocratic male leaders, or to an increasing emphasis on the use of personal authority by individuals. On the contrary, I believe it has to do with the unmasking of single-mindedness in society and a growing tolerance for people in authoritative positions who publicly admit they need ambiguity, contradiction, and redundancy in order to arrive at more valid inspirations for action. To what extent this is merely talk for the stage remains to be explored in each particular case, but at least there is a broadly recognised shift in culture to which we must adapt.

Co-direction

Susan Long

I distinctly remember a conference that was co-directed by Alastair Bain and Larry Gould in Australia in 1991. I was a staff member, given the role of selecting consultants to work with groups in the institutional event. One particular group came with a request. Both Alastair and Larry claimed my attention wanting to be the consultant to the group. They had previously agreed that, as they were both directors, only one need stay in the management room at any one time to take up the director role. The competition was obvious as both gave reasons why they should be the consultant. Finally, Larry turned to me and shouted "Choose!" The room, with many observers, was tense. It was as if the question that sat in the whole membership was projected on to me. I had to choose who was the "real" leader: Alastair or Larry?

It seems the conference systemically was caught in the question that should never be asked of a child—who do you love most: Mummy or Daddy? It did not matter that they were both men. And the question was laced with an underlying threat—who will you have to live with after the choice? I learnt a lot at that conference about how I could or could not use my own authority in the face of a powerful pair. I could not look to my leaders alone to direct me, but had to live through and interpret a dynamic of choice rather than simply enact it (as I initially did). The structure of co-directors opens the possibility to move beyond dependency.

I think the pairing phenomenon of a co-directorship (following Bion's ideas of pairing as a basic assumption) is both its strength and its weakness. Co-direction is a special form of pairing. At best, it is a marriage of equals where the leadership is contained within and between the pair. Competition need not be absent in the pair, but it must be worked with constructively. The pair is emotionally connected to the group through a dynamic of hope. It is hope, both realistic and idealistic, that underlies the pair and its relationship to the group, including the work group. In the conference mentioned earlier one hope (I think) was that the conference work in Australia might pair with other group relations work internationally through the co-directorship of an Australian and an American. It was early days for us.

The question of leadership in co-directorship is enacted in relation to the membership in many ways. The pair may be split so that the multiple conflicting aspects of leadership do not have to be reconciled and just one is seen to be the so-called "real" leader at any one time. Alternatively, the pair may be seen as monolithic, impossible to differentiate. This seems to happen when the pair is seen as a couple (sexually or in terms of a strongly bonded relationship). In both these dynamics the *relationship* between the co-directors becomes a focus, sometimes rather than the role and accountabilities of each. Exploring the fantasies surrounding the relationship is inevitable at both a conscious and unconscious level. As always, the exploration of the enacted "unthought known" is fundamental to group relations work.

I have worked in a co-directorship several times with both men and women as my co-director. Often, working with a man led to us almost comfortably falling into stereotypical gender roles or, alternatively, fighting such stereotypes. Certainly, the co-directorship led to exploration of gender differences. In my experience, the male–female co-directorship seems to be experienced as less threatening than a single female director. The single female director can provide for powerful learning about women leaders, but often the defences mobilised by the group prevent learning for some participants.

Two female co-directors might also at times seem less threatening than the single female director. It is as if the power of the mother is dispersed. I think in fantasy the two females come to represent more than two—a group if you like. (The positive image would be a group of protective aunts or of muses; the negative image is that of the furies or witches.) In one conference, where all the staff members were women, albeit with a single female director, the fantasies centred round them being either nuns or gorgons. Fusion between the female leaders seemed to occur. Two male co-directors generally appear to be differentiated more readily. In this male–male configuration, the unconscious image is often that of brothers. Cain and Abel as arche-types come to mind, but also the brothers in Freud's story of the killing of the despotic father. Each brother is differentiated and gains separate strengths and capacities.

The opportunities in co-directing are many:

- two heads to make decisions;
- emotional support;
- alternative perspectives that can enrich the understanding of a situation;
- someone to hold the capacity to think when projections are des-troying the thoughts of one leader;
- the two can work as different containers for different kinds of projections into leadership (for example, as with male and female co-directors, or with co-directors with different professional backgrounds, religions, ethnicity etc.);
- leadership functions can be shared either jointly or by dividing the functions between the pair. Because a large part of the work of a director and the directorate occurs before the conference, I have always experienced much anxiety in the lead up to the conference.

Will the conference go ahead? Will we get the membership? Is the venue suitable and how can we manage the demands for payment that contemporary venues require many months before the conference is held? This is the business side of the conference and although the conference administrator carries a lot of the work, much of the anxi-ety lies with the director or co-directors. Having a co-director at this stage is invaluable to share the work and the concern.

The challenges are also many. One challenge is how authority and accountability are distributed. For example, are different events directed by each of the two, or are some of the events co-directed? Who does staff turn to for final decisions? Does the pair rely too heavily on one another rather than engaging other staff—or indeed members? Having co-directors raises envy of the pair. They might appear to be self-sufficient. The challenge is to see how co-directorship can work as a creative pair that appropriately includes or excludes others in accordance with the task. All such dynamics must be explored in a transparent way in the staff group and in the conference.

I want to raise just one more question—why have we now become interested in co-directorship? Of course, it appears more democratic, in so far as all power and authority is not in the hands of just one person. And it stimulates hope for a better future by bringing in a leadership with more diverse skill and knowledge. However, as I have said, the drawbacks are that a pair also stimulates envy, splitting of leadership functions, and poses questions of divided loyalty.

I have a hypothesis that pairing provides the fundamental basic assumption for our time where the market rules as a major social institution. The prime pair in this is the consumer–provider pair: roles at the basis of the market; roles that are now emphasised and seek to overshadow the non-market roles of, for instance, doctor and patient, or teacher and student. I argue this fully in my book, *The Perverse Organisation*, and further with Burkard Sievers in our book, *Towards a Socioanalysis of Money, Finances and Capitalism*. Fundamentally, it is recognised that leaders and groups create and need each other—not so much in a dependent way, but in an interdependent, co-creative pairing. I now wonder if increasing co-leadership, supported by basic assumption pairing (in positive and negative ways) reflects this social dynamic.

Conclusion

Ruthellen Josselson and Olya Khaleelee

We have placed Susan Long's paper at the end because, without having heard or read the other presentations, she summarises accurately the main themes that are presented in these diverse papers on co-direction. She articulates clearly both the advantages and challenges of co-directorship that the other writers elaborate in their contributions. Her list comprises the issues that the other writers selectively detail in relation to their particular experiences. All of the presenters comment on the importance of the sense of authorisation to direct, whether it comes from a sponsoring organisation, is self-authorised, or one director authorising the other to co-direct. All of these scenarios (including the fantasies around them) affect the sense of the authorisation of the pair and how they may work together.

All of the presenters (with perhaps the exception of van Reekum) detail the ways in which their experiences with co-direction were valuable to their own and others' learning but none herald it as a solution to any problem in leadership. With the search for alternative models of leadership, co-directorship is one possibility, but still an arrangement that has its advantages and disadvantages. At a theoretical level, as several of the authors state, co-directorship privileges a pairing basic assumption and conference dynamics are affected by enhancing this unconscious propensity. One could argue, however, that a single director may encourage dependency—and that any leadership arrangement privileges particular basic assumptions.

All agree that for co-directorship to succeed, some differentiation of role functions is necessary within the structure of the conference, or the leadership is seen as merged or perhaps fluid and, detrimentally, invites scrutiny of the persons of the co-directors rather than their roles.

For the most part, the panellists were enthusiastic about the opportunity to try out a new model and this seemed to energise their conferences. Co-direction provided a novel twist to authority structures, raised interesting questions, gave staff and members a new order to experience, and generally stimulated learning.

Reference

Obholzer, A. (1994). Authority, power and leadership: contributions from group relations training. In: A. Obholzer & V. Z. Roberts (Eds.), *The Unconscious at Work: Individual and Organizational Stress in Human Services* (pp. 39–47). London: Routledge.

CHAPTER ELEVEN

Group relations and twelve-step recovery: mixing oil and water?

Jeffrey D. Roth, Colleen Brent, Vivian Gold,
Seth Harkins, and John B. Robertson Jr

Introduction

T his chapter describes the development of a series of group relations conferences designed to compare and contrast two different models of authority and leadership as they might apply in the process of recovery from addiction: the group relations conference in the Tavistock tradition and the Twelve Step model first developed in the fellowship of AA. As the conference director, I am an addiction psychiatrist and group psychotherapist with more than twenty-five years of experience in both group relations conference work and Twelve-Step recovery. The vision of mounting such a conference was inspired by a series of conferences directed by Garrett O'Connor in the late 1980s with the theme of recovery from alcoholism. Two events nearly twenty years later catalysed the first conference in Chicago on "Authority and Leadership in Recovery from Addiction" in 2011: first was my attending the 2009 Leicester Conference as a member, and second was the initiation of a new programme for social work students at Loyola University Chicago to become certified addictions counsellors. The Leicester conference featured a structural innovation of a Yoga Event, which I would change into a Twelve-Step Event in these conferences. The new programme for social work students provided a foundation for a membership for the fledgling conference.

An extensive literature is available on Twelve-Step programmes. Two of the most studied programmes are AA (*Alcoholics Anonymous*, 1985) and Al-Anon (Al-Anon Family Group, 1997), a mutual support group for the families and friends of alcoholics. Twelve-Step programmes function according to the Twelve Steps and Twelve Traditions, the importance of which is briefly summarised as follows.

- The Twelve Steps outline a path of recovery for each individual.
- The Twelve Traditions outline a path of recovery for each group and the fellowship as a whole.
- These steps and traditions are guidelines, not rules.
- While the sequence of the steps logically progress from surrender, to internal examination, to external change, and then to maintenance of the recovery process, the steps may be practised in any order.
- The traditions protect the group from three covert processes (Roth, 1991) described by Wilfred Bion (1959) that may interfere with the work task of the group: *fight/flight, dependence, and pairing*.

One may hear in a Twelve-Step meeting that the steps were designed to prevent us from killing ourselves, and the traditions were designed to prevent us from killing each other.

Table 11.1 describes some of the differences and similarities of group relations work and Twelve-Step recovery.

Other than facing the challenge of studying the group and organisational dynamics of recovery from addiction, the issue of special relationships between and among staff and members played a pivotal role in both conferences. Both the staff group and the membership contained a number of current and former patients of the director, and the relationships among staff and among members were characterised by analogous authority relationships of varying complexity. These special relationships mirror the experience in the world outside of the context of group relations conferences: for instance, when people attend a Twelve-Step meeting for the purpose of recovery and encounter friends, neighbours and potentially those over whom they have authority outside of the meeting.

Table 11.1.   Differences and similarities between group relations work and Twelve-Step recovery.

Group relations	Twelve-Step programmes
Differences	
Temporary	Enduring
Closed system	Open system
Free interaction	No crosstalk
Staff–member roles split	Member roles equal
Authority defined by outside agency	Authority from higher power
Group focused learning	Individually focused healing
Exercise personal role authority	Surrender self authority for
to accomplish work of the group	authority of group
Similarities	
Experiential learning	
Self-exploration	
Self-discovery	
Self-expression	
Acknowledge the power of irrationality	
Interdependence and collaboration	
Belief in groups as systems	
Whole is greater than sum of parts	
Recognise the power of the group to	
facilitate growth and transformation	
Concern with leadership and authority	

Recruitment of members was successful for both of the first two conferences. By the time of publication of this chapter, a third conference was held in January 2013, a fourth conference was held in January 2014, and a fifth conference was held in May 2014 in Beijing. The addition of Twelve-Step meetings was the only structural innovation for what were otherwise standard, non-residential weekend conferences. Members and staff attended these Twelve-Step meetings in the same role as would be practised in any Twelve-Step meeting: as a person hoping to learn about their attachment to addiction in themselves or others. The impact of introducing these Twelve-Step meetings into a GRC is the continuing object of study. Therefore, these conferences are in a process of development, and some of the disruptive influences of this structural innovation might become clear only as these conferences continue to be offered.

Upon losing one's group relations' voice: Colleen Brent

This section is a discussion of the difficulty that I had in consulting to the first addiction and recovery conference in 2011. I have been involved in GRC work for over thirty years, and have learnt to be sceptical about much of what is accepted dogma in any field, including group relations and religion. I find that dogma often supersedes compassion and humanism towards others. Because of my experience with treatment of addictions, I was initially enthusiastic about working on a GRC with addiction and recovery as a focus. Although I believed that AA was not the only form of recovery to be explored in the conference, it was the only paradigm that I saw considered. It has been two and a half years since the first group relations: "Authority, Leadership and Recovery from Addiction" conference. I retain four very strong images from the conference.

First, religion was present and dominant without being analysed at this conference. On Friday night, during a staff dinner meeting, there was a flurry of activity and I heard "Where are the candles?" Candles were lit, the associate director sang a song in Hebrew, and the rabbi on the staff said a prayer in Hebrew. This service was not mentioned and, in retrospect, this is when I lost my capacity to speak to these unstated paradigms of the conference.

Second, a "coffee klatch" occurred when the conference director, the associate director, and the administrative director held their staff meeting during breakfast; as the other staff members were only observers, several of us drifted outside to have our morning coffee. The four or five members of this "coffee klatch" were neither Jewish nor members of AA; we mused about that, but did not take discussion of this dynamic back to the other staff.

Third, the membership included both a de-licensed therapist who had sexually seduced a patient and the seduced patient, both of whom interacted throughout the LG meetings, thus acknowledging their struggles to the membership. At one point, these two hugged in a verbal exchange about caring while the entire LG watched silently. This interaction between perpetrator and victim might have reflected a conflict between group relations and Twelve-Step ideology.

Fourth, my application group contained a member who stated that AA had saved him from a life of crime and destruction. The director had made an explicit sexual statement early in the large group. The provocative consultation disturbed this AA member, who had learnt to apply rigid control to his destructive impulses, causing profound anxiety. His verbalisation of this struggle brought this man to shaking and tears.

Unfortunately, when belief in the Twelve-Step method might have been questioned, the staff not involved in that method remained largely silent. The question for me was: how did I lose my group relations interpretative abilities, and what did this represent in this conference? The most obvious issue was that the conference director's patients and supervisees were in both the staff and the membership. This was acknowledged, but no attempt was made to consider the effects of this on the work of the conference. As usual in conference work, there was a wish to have the director of the conference be either the supreme therapist or perhaps even an all-powerful deity. His position as LG team leader with two new LG staff members and one well-known Twelve Step colleague made this role difficult to resist. During the conference, in a staff meeting, I became filled with anxiety, sadness, and an overwhelming concern about the blurring of boundaries, the religious-like acceptance of the Twelve-Step programme, and the unconscious issues that were not being worked. I brought this up in tears and said that I thought I was carrying something for the conference, but was not sure what it was. My invitation to work the issues of voicelessness on the staff was not taken up.

In summary, my experience in the first Chicago conference was that both Twelve Step and group relations work were truncated and distorted, and that the consulting staff members were largely silent in this struggle. The relationships among the members were unexamined and undiscussed, in direct contravention to group relations' principles. If there is to be an exploration of the possible relationship between the two approaches, a more integrative approach will need to be employed in the future.

Finding our voices in a new arena: group relations conferences and authority and leadership in recovery from addiction: Vivian Gold

These conferences extend the Tavistock approach beyond our usual networks as an opportunity to explore the issues that occur in any

GRC in a new arena, that of addiction and recovery. They are an application of group relations' principles, where we offer a systems perspective and a view of unconscious processes at work within the systems that maintain addictions. Two aspects of the 2011 and 2012 conferences created specific areas of chaos and conflict: (1) spirituality *vs.* religion as conference phenomena, and (2) the multiple relationships within the staff, the membership, and across the boundaries between staff and membership.

The issue of splitting between those in the Twelve-Step recovery programmes and those not committed to these programmes was rife from the very beginning of our telephone staff work. My desire to help contain the chaos led me to accept the role of associate conference director that Dr Roth had offered. That the issue of spirituality became prominent within the conference is not surprising, since all conferences are microcosms of larger social issues, and the split between those who are religious and those who are secular is one of the most cogent issues dividing people today. We often assume that most consultants who work in this field are secular. However, I believe that we see the conference dynamics in the light of our overt or covert spiritual beliefs, and that as these beliefs emerge, they are present to be studied. The religious aspects not only created conflict at our conferences, they are part of ongoing conflicts within and surrounding the Twelve-Step programmes. Other approaches exist for secular people who prefer not to engage in any programme invoking a "higher power". In my opinion, these issues were both enacted, interpreted, and studied in the 2011–2 012 group relations conferences presented here.

Many of us were shocked and troubled when we discovered that among both the staff and the members were people recruited from among Dr Roth's patients within his practice, as well as the student and patient populations of other staff members. This was a controversial dynamic that had to be worked through in both conferences. The relationships were not held in secret, and the enactments that occurred were in the open, giving the staff and the membership an opportunity to work deep issues of favouritism, envy, rage, and gratitude. The Twelve-Step programmes have an ethos that we are all equals in our common humanity, culpabilities, and vulnerabilities. That this equality can exist while issues of authority and leadership are explored is what created much of the tension that pushed the staff boundaries, generating both stress and creativity. Members and staff experiencing being silenced, and a member finding her voice in a scream in the large group in 2012, were some of my most poignant memories of the conferences. In this chapter, we have a variety of voices with different views on what happened. In my view, these conferences were like others I have attended, definitively group relations conferences, with a twist.

Group relations and Twelve-Step recovery as a lived experience: Seth Harkins

I attended my first group relations conference at Northwestern University in 1985. The experience was profound and career changing. Without it, my career in educational administration would have been short-lived. Simultaneously, I was struggling with progressive alcoholism. I attended my first AA meeting in August 1988, convinced I had walked into a religious cult. While I did not immediately buy into AA, I stopped drinking after my first meeting and kept going. Although unwilling to accept God as my higher power, it was easy to accept the group and AA as my higher power.

In 1996, I attended a nine-day residential conference at Vassar College in New York. I went to the conference solo. I found myself linking with a subgroup of three Chicago area members, all in recovery and associated with Dr Jeffrey Roth. I was keenly aware that alcohol was used by members and staff at the Vassar Conference, as I had experienced it being used at other conferences as well. It simply was not talked about. This struck me as the "no talk" rule in alcoholic families.

In 2004, I was invited to be a small group consultant in a group relations conference directed by Dr Jeffrey Roth. The conference theme was authority and power in social systems and the family. This conference marked my early attempts to integrate the worlds of group relations and recovery in my consulting. The group relations concepts of splitting, projection, projective identification, and group-as-a-whole began to merge with Twelve-Step concepts of higher power, surrender to the group, group conscience, fearless and searching moral inventory, character defects and spiritual awakening. I began integrating my roles as group relations consultant and a person in recovery.

As a consultant in the 2011 and 2012 Loyola University group relations conference: "Authority, Leadership and Recovery from Addiction", I had the opportunity to further my enquiry. The overarching question for me was: could the language and cultures of group relations and recovery actually be integrated to enhance learning about authority, leadership, and unconscious phenomena? Searching for ways to consult from the group relations and Twelve Step parts of my brain, finding my voice as a consultant in recovery was a challenge. Was an empty chair about a member having "gone back out"? Was basic assumption process evident in the group behaving as if it were an addicted family? Could I attend an AA meeting with members and retain legitimate authority as a consultant? In the 2011 conference, I sometimes could not find my non-recovering colleague in the large study group. In the 2012 conference, I was challenged with the unconscious location of the previous year's conflict involving a recovering therapist and multiple special relationships in my small group.

Hoping to learn as much as possible from the 2011 experience, I took copious field notes with the thought of writing auto-ethnography of my conference experience. I ended this conference experience convinced that research into the lived experience of the conference needed to be undertaken. With Drs John Bair and Shelley Korshak, I examined the qualitative data and wrote a comprehensive article (Harkins et al., 2013). Similar studies of the 2012 and 2013 conferences are under way to better understand the intersection of the two different languages, cultures, and traditions. What I found in the 2011 and 2012 conferences is that, despite the differences, these two different approaches to group learning could indeed inform one another and enhance the recovery of persons and systems challenged with addiction. I found I could speak with a new level of authority, enhancing my role as a consultant and deepening my recovery.

Does violation of usual group relation conference boundaries between staff and members corrupt the GRC experience?
John B. Robertson Jr

Transference and countertransference are powerful experiences in every GRC. Analysing these responses, both individually and as group phenomena, provide much of the transformative learning. The issues of transferences within the boundaries of the GRC might become less clear when data about the staff or membership are available from sources other than within the boundaries of the GRC. Unique to this GRC was an opportunity for membership to experience staff in a non-staff role, which was integrated in the form of Twelve-Step recovery groups. During these Twelve-Step groups, staff and members became equal participants. For me, there were two broad take-home points from the conference.

First, transference was clearly affected by the introduction of Twelve-Step groups into a traditional GRC. This resulted in significant changes in the member and staff experience. However, the achievement of the primary learning task was not diminished.

Second, recruitment for these conferences has been successful despite many other GRCs during this time having to be cancelled due to lack of membership. Clearly, the Twelve-Step recovering community offers enormous membership potential for GRC work.

I anticipated that the addition of Twelve-Step group process would be like grafting a branch on to the primary group relations conference plant. Instead, my experience was that this marriage of two powerful methods of doing groups gave birth to something unique and very different from either parent, with its own DNA structure equally contributed by both parents. Like a child from parents of mixed race or ethnicity, the unique blending creates shared characteristics of both, yet distinctly differs from both.

So, what do you get when you marry Twelve-Step programmes and group relations? Group relations conference work is about learning how groups function, and especially about the role of authority. Twelve-Step learning is about how the individual functions, especially about improving that function by substituting higher power authority for self-authority. For me, the resulting event is softer and gentler emotionally than usual group relations conference work with less regression psychologically and a more therapeutic component.

Two main attributes might account for my experience of this marriage: (1) the larger than usual number of special relationships within Twelve-Step recovery groups and, therefore, within our conference and (2) the distinct differences in authority structure between the two different models, Twelve-Step recovery and group relations. For Twelve-Step groups, confidentiality and anonymity, as well as having memberships that are both open and non-hierarchical, results in groups that tolerate multiple special relationships. This is different from most groups, which are unable to tolerate and function well with multiple special relationships.

The other primary reason that transference energy is diminished is related to the healing goal of Twelve-Step work and its use of transference to a personal higher power. Transference is transformed by at least two factors: (1) focus on self, and (2) focus on personal higher power. Replacing the usual triangulated relationship among the individual, group, and designated authority structure, the individual in recovery from addiction may use the group and designated authority structure as components of a personal higher power. In essence, the personal higher power modulates the compulsion to locate a higher power in the director and staff with regard to significance for that person's experience and learning.

Because of the comforting relationship with a personal higher power, there are fewer and less intense paranoid projections and unrealistic expectations regarding staff authority. Over and over during this GRC, individuals made reference to their higher power with the effect of diminishing conflicts with the role of conference staff authority. Often, in my role as small group consultant, I experienced fewer attempts to deify me. Indeed, interpretations regarding my small group consultant role and its relationship to the authority of the director were largely ignored. By contrast, I saw a combining of authority of higher power with that of our director. More than once participants made the comment that "Dr Roth saved my life", indicating a great deal of almost supernatural attribution of his gifted ability as a clinician to affect them personally.

Conclusion

Even as group relations conference work and Twelve-Step recovery represent two very different cultures, languages, and traditions, including different conceptualisations of authority, role, task, and boundaries, the integration of these two models has generated a series of stable conferences. The diversity of experiences of the consultants participating in the writing of this chapter accurately reflects the tensions that these conferences embody. We return to their voices:

"I was seriously considering withdrawing from the staff due to some pre-staff work that seemed to be dominated by Twelve Step references. Jeffrey assured me that other voices needed to be and would be heard."

"I see the 2011 and 2012 conferences as the creative work of Dr Roth, his staff and others deeply involved with and interested in studying authority issues in addiction and recovery. Dr Roth stretches the boundaries of group relations work in an exciting and important arena. In Jewish tradition, a fruit tree takes three years to flourish. May the 2013 Group Relations Conference on Addiction and Recovery have a fruitful year, and be the forerunner of many more.

"How could I incorporate the language of recovery with the language of group relations?

"In Tennessee, the southern part of the United States where I live, we have a saying, 'There is more than one way to skin a cat.' What I have learnt from my experience participating in a group relation conference that integrated Twelve Step recovery groups is that each group model brings with it a rich tradition and learning that is powerfully effective educationally and therapeutically. Having membership and staff with a variety of experiences, some with and some without prior experience in both group models, created a wonderfully creative tapestry rich in the depths of colour and opportunities for learning and healing at various levels."

References

Al-Anon Family Group (1997). *Paths to Recovery: Al-Anon's Steps, Traditions, and Concepts.* Virginia Beach, VA: Al-Anon Family Groups.

Alcoholics Anonymous (1985). New York: Alcoholics Anonymous World Service Organization.

Bion, W. R. (1959). *Experiences in Groups.* New York: Basic Books.

Harkins, S., Bair, J., & Korshak, S. (2013). Group relations and twelve step recovery. *Alcoholism Treatment Quarterly, 31*: 296–412.

Roth, J. D. (1991). *Application of the Tavistock Model to Group Psychotherapy with Recovering Addicts.* St. Louis: MO: Proceedings of the A. K. Rice Institute Scientific Meeting.

PART IV

POST-CONFERENCE REFLECTIONS

CHAPTER TWELVE

Oral envy and networks

Anja Salmi

F inland is a country located in the Arctic Circle. This means that in the winter we have a period of total darkness when the sun does not rise and, equally, in the summer, a period of total lightness when it does not set. In Finnish mythology, Kalevala, the wicked woman from the North, stole the moon and the sun and locked them inside a mountain. This is how all became dark (Anon., 2004).

The Tavistock was, in the 1980s, the buttress of my mental image, like the axis of the globe. This invisible structure allowed my life to spin on its orbit. At the Belgirate IV, I took part in the group that was studying the theme of "co-directing".

This polar axis and its vertex—the Leicester conferences—represented a place in the world where one was not able to survive by relying on half-truths or lies, or on one lap where one always would be safe: Tavistock. This idea of security rested on my general conception of life, the good and evil of mankind, the powers of destruction, and the urge to construct (Graves, 1992).

Our generation was building up Tavistock to be very important and intended to make it strong. It symbolised our values, as does Mount Everest for mountain climbers, Robben Island for Africans, or the church of St Peter for Christians. We happily laid the bricks of harmony, unity, closeness, security, and unanimity (Burleson, 2005). These were the building blocks for constructing togetherness.

Idealisation

The affiliation was vertical. Each had his or her own bond with Tavistock (Bion, 1948). We were holding in mind the wish to be the most talented child of the wise mother. Idealisation was the prominent defence against envy. At the time, this vertical structure provided benefits in various ways, as similar phenomena do elsewhere. It made it possible to preserve the feelings of security and to place the evil outside us (Bion, 1948). It made it possible to locate the feelings of helplessness and incapability in those who did not understand the psychoanalytical group processes or in the ones who had not been to Leicester. Evil is something that separates us, leaves us isolated, as in the Bible: God turns his face away from us.

It was not difficult to negate the awkward feelings of envy through idealising, as so often happens in the dependent groups (Klein, 1957). The Tavistock–Babel was imagined growing higher and higher towards the sky. Inevitably, we continued growing. We learnt more, developed gradually, matured, and went forward. The unspoken ambition was to rise as high in wisdom as the wise mother, Tavistock, and even higher. The struggle for the place on the lap led to the aspiration to grow inwardly. It activated the intention to climb up the ladder. By climbing higher, the space was diminished (Aram, 2012).

Back home, the basic idea of the Leicester conference was repeated and taught to the colleges. Many were building their own working conferences in their own cities. We wanted and achieved the opportunity to establish our own Leicester, exactly how we wanted, where we wanted, and precisely according to the vision we had. The house was occupied. All of this was now ours (Armstrong, 2005).

Interdependence

The vision turned out to be more difficult to achieve than had been imagined. It was not possible to put knowledge in one's pocket and bring it home. Not everybody was interested in these unknown theories that we were so excited about. The freedom to build and to create was equally within everybody's capacity. None of us knew how to build alone (Poundstone, 1993).

We twiddled our thumbs. Some innovative people started to collect splinters from the floor. They manipulated them this way and that, trying to see what could be put together of these fragments of Leicester conferences. How one looked in the eyes of the sagacious mother no longer seemed significant. It became meaningless to look better than one's siblings in those eyes. Gradually, it became more important to learn how to co-operate with the littermates and how to build out of nothing. The survival and success of the venture turned out to be dependent on our helping and supporting each other.

It became vital to understand whom to trust or to work with. Regarding the desire for security, we were tossed on a stormy sea and had to rely on each other in creating the life-rafts.

We became a handful of die scattered out throughout the world: the Tower of Babel destroyed by God (Kahn, 1962). We belonged to different nations and races and spoke various languages. The common task was to create a connection to one another. It formed a general aim to fight against loneliness and separateness.

It became crucial to empathise with the associates with whom one was dealing. Previously, it had been possible to trust the approximation of the prudent mother. In the past, it was possible to be lulled into slumber by the entrance qualifications. The Leicester conference was operating like a gatekeeper who sieved the evil away. Despite the fact that we had learnt to understand at Leicester that evil is in all of us, the thought that it was possible to escape it by creating new defences still persisted. There still was less evil inside than outside the gate. The ones who wanted to recognise the evil in themselves were less evil.

Paradoxically, we did not know at the time how important it was to undergo acceptance of one's own helplessness and incapability. It was difficult to see what to do with this treasure of knowledge. Some wanted to formalise it as a degree and add it to their personal curricula. Others were happy with making it part of a portfolio. It was like walking on the crest of the wave of the world's development and then sinking into the water for some unknown reason. Speechless stagnation smothered the effects of joyful play. New challenges were brought up on the journey. The deaf were listening to words that did not come out of the gagged mouths. We had to face each other. We had become significant to one another. We reached out our hands to each other, but found that the hands were disconnected from the limbs (Cooper & Lousada, 2005).

It became important to learn how to evaluate each other's abilities. Who is reliable? Who is capable of keeping boundaries? Who is able to direct a conference? Who knows how to mutually exchange?

Oral envy

The exceptionally difficult part was the fear of being utilised. Suppose the significant other steals our precious ideas? How is it possible to trust the other while fearing being used? We were arguing strongly that this might not be merely a groundless fear. In life, sometimes, ideas do get stolen. There was a longing for the sheltered environs of Leicester. The distribution of justice and even-handedness was ruefully missed. Climbing up the ladders had turned into rolling down the stairs. It was like the Three Bears in the fairy tale who were questioning the intruders: who has stolen my ideas? Who has taken my thoughts? The rivalry had degenerated into the green sludge of oral envy (Klein, 1957).

Like the blind touching and grasping to be able to form a picture of the surroundings, one had to learn to trust one's own instinct. One had to learn that one's eyes did not always see correctly (Totro & Hyyppä, 2012). There was a lot of disillusionment in the associates. Although many felt betrayed by agreements, one was responsible only on one's own account. It became all the more depriving since there was no omniscient mother to accuse of the sudden lapse of attention. One had only oneself to blame for one's own blindness and unwise judgement.

Sometimes, evil was seen in places where it did not exist (Kernberg, 1994). It was humiliating to be confronted with being blinded by one's own envy. In those processes, one sometimes lost necessary resources or burned bridges that should have been left intact. Sometimes, one felt about to be crushed by shame.

There was quiet longing for the mother's consolation: never mind. One simply had to gather together the tatters of dignity and stand up again. Tavistock had been overpowered. The limits had been broken.

We had founded the global group relations network, but who knew what it really was?

Competition

At least it was wonderful to be inside. It felt worthwhile and prestigious to belong to the global group relations network. But who was outside of the network? For some to belong, there have to be others who do not (Klein, 1945). Who does not belong to a network that is expanding? How could the world be brought to understand group relations through exclusion? Or was it just about an inner circle? (Riesman, 1961). Was it about the qualification for some specialist know-how or a graduation certificate after all? If not that, how does one differ from those who do not belong to the network?

The scattered fragments of the Tower of Babel needed to become integrated. The Belgirate conference was founded. Belgirate was the place to safely disclose the creation of knowledge and thoughts. Evil could be located in the world outside the walls of the idyllic Italian hotel. At Belgirate, it could be possible to strive for the place in the lap of the good mother. At Belgirate, it could be possible to compete.

The success stories of hard work were proudly presented to one another. Many accomplishments in the outside world were described and the number of conferences attended was explicated: how many of these conferences had been directed, by whom, and what exotic places these conferences had taken place in. The education programmes were construed and the challenging work on which we had consulted was presented. We were eager to learn more.

At Belgirate IV, we started the group with enthusiasm about intelligently studying the subject of "co-directing", chosen by us from the given possibilities. I chose this group because of my earlier studies in co-directing. We have a peculiar political situation in Finland, since the power of the president has been diminished to an extent that gives the impression that the prime minister and the president have been allotted an equal amount of power. This leads the large study group of the Finnish nation to be "co-directed". In my article, "Who is directing Finland—or is anybody?" (Salmi, 2010), I am looking in depth at its influence on Finnish society, particularly from the point of view of its paralysing and destroying effects.

Deprivation

The atmosphere seemed to promise us that we were the bright children of the prudent mother. We wanted to tell this to each other.

At first, we did not really want to let it enter our consciousness that the group did not have a consultant. We had only each other. Carefully, we tried to gaze around: who has stolen the mother?

There is a thief here!

Quickly, we locked the door of our thoughts and pulled the curtains in front of our eyes (Maslow, 1972). We wanted to guard our ideas. We were afraid of thieves. We all wanted to be wise mothers or prosperous directors. But did we want to be co-directors? How can one share motherhood or be just a half a director? How can one be a gifted child of two mothers? How can one direct if one has to share the governance? Sharing is not directing.

We groped to perceive the theory of pairing as the basic assumption (Bion, 1948). No recollections reverted. We made an effort to discuss what we ought to talk over. The words just did not come out of our mouths. Co-directing—it was as if we had heard the idea for the first time and we understood nothing of it.

For some inexplicable reason we were paralysed and afraid (Menzies-Lyth, 1988). Is there a thief here?

Rage

Gradually, the stagnation passed. This was heard in the discordant protest about how Belgirate has turned into such an arduous place. People do not want to come here any more. This was agreed upon. We started enumerating the people who were not with us. This was nothing short of awkward: co-directing. We spoke about those of whom we had heard rumours of not wanting to come to Belgirate any more. We felt guilty. We were mourning. What went wrong? Why did we suffocate fresh new creativity? Part of us felt envious of those who had stayed at home. They had indeed been right. We were ashamed to be stupid enough to come and to believe in this. This nonsense is never going to work.

We refused to understand that we did not want to understand.

Co-directing means one ought to share the leadership. How can we know while co-directing which one of us is better? Who is going to justify us rightfully? The thoughts felt not so much unpleasant as impossible. Defensively, we claimed that we did not want to compete; we just wanted to show how skilful we were. Sometimes, we were overcome by indisposition. Where can we lodge the green mud of envy if we volunteer to surrender to exploitation? None of us wanted to admit any desire to take something from somebody else: a brochure, a programme, an idea? We happily projected this out of ourselves and whispered in the corridors like the three bears in the fairy tale: there might be someone here who just came to look for something to steal. We thought rationally about how indeed there might be such people somewhere, but we had to keep on building regardless of it. How could we direct anything at all if we allowed our thoughts to be cloaked in secrecy? Anyhow, these fantasies were all too risky to be expressed aloud in the group and not one of us was able to say anything.

The air between us was thick and black like smog.

Utilisation (paranoid–schizoid position)

At Belgirate, we were people from all over the world. In short-lived light moments in the co-directing group, we spoke of South America, Australia, Italy, and the USA. We flew with the power of our thoughts from one variegated culture to another. Our grey, ordinary, everyday life was transformed into the shimmering wings of a colourful butterfly. We almost felt how it might feel ascending, flying into the air as if lifted up by the thoughts of our group members. Unexpectedly, however, our feet became heavy, like stones. We felt as if we were sitting glued fast to our chairs like the broken pupa of the larva, which falls to the ground empty after having delivered joyful life from itself.

We had been defeated (Klein, 1957). We had become hollow.

Mourning (depressive position)

Co-directing supposedly means to direct together, to share the leadership. Who will take the credit? Our intelligent study of co-directing had resulted in painful feelings of loss. Our envy had made us feel empty.

One member of our group claimed to be feeling like a discarded peel. The work in the group was like giving life to a carefree butterfly. It would neglect us and fly away (Ogden, 1988).

Another member of our group smiled and said, "Hopefully."

A ray of sunlight pierced our thoughts. The wings of a dragonfly were illuminated. Life is born out of love. Love means giving and sharing, not keeping it to oneself (Klein, 1957; Sauer et al., 2010). We discovered that this is how it is meant to be. The prince gave life to Snow White, who was poisoned by the apple of envy, by kissing her. The blood started to circulate in our feet again. We felt alive and able to dance joyfully. We started talking, giving and taking, exchanging ideas and thoughts.

The air in the group was full of little butterflies, flying up and down, back and forth with their tremulous wings. The ray of light had refracted our feelings into all colours of the rainbow.

Sharing is prohibited by early feelings of envy (Klein, 1957). These early feelings are introjected in our desire to grab from others and projected in our fears of being molested. How can we share if we are afraid of thieves? How can we co-direct if we are afraid of sharing? How are we able to contain our inner and outer integration under pressure in groups?

When the structure in groups turns from hierarchical into vertical, a major amount of oral envy is always released into interpersonal relations. At this time, envy often transforms the atmosphere from idealisation into the fear of utilisation. How can it be possible to get the group working if interaction is prohibited by the ambivalence created by the fear of utilisation and the urge to steal? The solution and outcome through competition was frustrated since there was no clear management to evaluate and deliver imaginary credit. This is a major challenge in all the non-hierarchical organisations that are so popular in our postmodern society. My background is in healthcare organisations. They always contain both hierarchical and vertical elements in their structures. There is deep complexity in all networks that are constructed in horizontal forms.

Working

Our "co-directing" group was deprived because it had no director or consultant. Among other difficulties, the group had to deal with the feelings of oral envy while trying to work. The subject we were talking about was co-directing. It contains a complex form of competition. The co-directing pair as a director is a complex structure in groups in many respects. It affects the basic assumption of pairing. Co-directing is not supportive to the outcome of the group to deal with its envy by working via constructive competition. Our group had at least three major aspects to look at.

1. The group needed to see itself as working without a consultant.
2. At the same time, it had to empathise with a complicated form of directing: "co-directing".
3. Simultaneously, it was necessary to keep in mind Bion's basic assumptions, both within the group working here and now and, imaginarily, how co-directing in general would influence the basic assumptions of the group.

This resulted in the group becoming largely paralysed.

What was particularly interesting in our work was learning that there was very little splitting, just some isolated comments. (This happened when Eliat Aram came to observe our group. Just this imaginary drop of "directing" got us to work by splitting (Kohut, 1996).) In relation to frustration, it was notable how the flight/fight aspect was generally absent in the study group.

In the end, the key solution in our group was not so much the studying of the subject given to us, but observing ourselves and our own working in a group without a consultant. After facing our own primitive envy and the emptiness it brought us, we accepted the inevitability of giving if one intends to work (Klein, 1957). By experiencing our own loss and helplessness, we overcame our stagnation and regained our creativity.

We went on working with the problems of how we contend with our envy. How is it possible at the same time to encourage and support the co-director we are taking on?

The stagnation of thoughts and the silence in the words: at times, we felt it to be the art of the impossible. How do we build and how do we provide input to the joint constructing? We are predisposing ourselves to the threat of abuse while working by creating, whether or not we are co-directing. How do we tolerate our own urge to steal from one another? How do we combat our fierce urge towards rivalry? How is it possible to keep all these controversies alive and integrated in us at the same time? How is it ever possible to grow through all this? How do we construct the essential confidence in one another, to love, to create, and to keep on building.

No longer were we screaming, "Where is our wise mother?" We now had each other (Klein, 1957).

Continuity

We spoke about the next Leicester conference. Mannie Sher and Eliat Aram would be responsible for it. We exchanged information about the future working conferences in Spain, Germany, or Finland. We reached out towards each other. We were structured around an axis: Belgirate. At least for one moment we had reorganised ourselves into a structure that had both vertical and horizontal elements: our mother Tavistock and our interdependence on each other. We felt content.

We had rammed into the wall through our own urge to compete. We had collided with our own quality requirements and our appetite for exclusion. We had faced our feelings of abuse and stealing. We had confronted the feeling of our own emptiness. Inside us, we felt like the beautiful phoenix rising from the ashes. We had conquered our own urge to destruction.

Conclusions

In the aeroplane, flying back home, I felt the wings of the plane shaking. I was reminded of the little shivering wings of the swarm of colourful butterflies that filled the air in our group.

References

Anon. (2004). *Kalevala, The Finnish Mythology*. Juva: WS Bookwell Oy.
Aram, E. (2012). "Climbing fast up the ladder?!" The lived experience of directing. In: E. Aram, R. Baxter, & A. Nutkevitch (Eds.), *Group Relations Conferences, Tradition, Creativity and Succession in the Global Group Relations Network (Volume III)* (p. 9). London: Karnac.
Armstrong, D. (2005). *Organization in the Mind: Psychoanalysis, Group Relations, and Organizational Consultancy*. London: Karnac.

Bion, W. R. (1948). *Experiences in Groups*. London: Tavistock.

Burleson, B. W. (2005). *Jung in Africa*. Cornwall: MPG Books.

Cooper, A., & Lousada, J. (2005). *Borderline Welfare. The Feeling and the Fear of Feeling in Modern Welfare*. London: Karnac.

Graves, R. (1992). *The Greek Myths, Complete Edition*. London: Penguin.

Kahn, H. (1962). *Thinking about the Unthinkable*. London: Weidenfeld and Nicolson.

Kernberg, P. (1994). Mechanism of defence development and research perspectives. *Bulletin of the Menninger Clinic, 58*(1): 55–87.

Klein, M. (1945). The Oedipus complex in the light of early anxieties. *International Journal of Psychoanalysis, 26*: 11–33.

Klein, M. (1957). *Envy and Gratitude. A Study of Unconscious Sources*. New York: Basic Books.

Kohut, H. (1996). *The Restoration of the Self*. Madison, CT: International Universities Press.

Maslow, A. (1972). *The Farther Reaches of Human Nature*. New York: Viking Compass.

Menzies-Lyth, I. (1988). The functioning of social systems as a defence against anxiety. In: *Containing Anxiety in Institutions* (pp. 70–77). London: Free Association Books.

Ogden, T. (1988). *The Matrix of the Mind*. London: Maresfield Library.

Poundstone, W. (1993). *The Prisoner's Dilemma*. New York: Doubleday.

Riesman, D., with Glazre, N., & Denney, R. (1961). *The Lonely Crowd*. London: Yale University Press.

Salmi, A. (2010). Kuka Johtaa Suome—Vai Johtaako Kukaan? [Who is directing Finland—or is anybody?] *Uusi Suomi Blogi*: online magazine.

Sauer, E., Salovaara Perttu, M. A.-M., & Ropo, A. (2010). *Johtajuuden uusi taide* [The New Art of Management]. Sastamala: Tampere University Press.

Totro, T., & Hyyppä, H. (2012). *Vailla muistia, vailla pyrkimyksiä . . . Todellisuuksien kohtaaminen—W. R. Bionista keskiajan mystiikkaan* [Without Thoughts, Without Desire . . . Facing Realities from W. R. Bion to the Mysticism of Middle Age]. Jyväskylä: BookwellOy.

CHAPTER THIRTEEN

Intergroup process at an international level: reflections from Belgirate

Gordon Strauss

"Group Relations without an ethical . . . agenda is an empty form"

(Western, 2012)

This chapter is a reflection upon the experience of attending Belgirate IV: "Exploring the Impact and Relevance of Group Relations Work Within and Beyond Its Network" (hereafter referred to as Belgirate IV). This was the fourth international gathering of those who work in GRCs. However, as someone who attended the three previous Belgirate conferences, it would be naïve, if not disingenuous, to imply that this reflection is not influenced by those experiences as well. (My comparison of my first two Belgirate experiences appeared in the second volume of this series (Strauss, 2009).) For example, I "discovered" a number of ideas and relevant thoughts from Belgirate III (Aram et al., 2012) which, while too late to influence my experience at Belgirate IV, have nevertheless influenced my thinking for this chapter. In this reflective essay, I hope to connect some of my learning at Belgirate IV to my experiences there, but also to both group relations in the USA and to developments in group relations internationally. I believe this will link to the title theme for Belgirate IV.

The relevant group relations concept I wish to start with is the intergroup. As I hope to demonstrate, what my experiences at Belgirate IV have allowed me to do is to think about intergroup phenomena where the "groups" are GR organisations within and across national boundaries. In addition, as the epigraph from Simon Western signals, I have questions and concerns about whether and how an ethical perspective fits in as GR organisations expand, compete, and stake out new territories.

The intergroup experience

Within a GRC, the intergroup event (IG) often represents a key transition. Often, the experiential learning events up to that point have been only the small and large study group. But with the start of the IG, the two theoretical models underpinning group relations—Kleinian psychoanalytic theory and open systems theory—are given equal emphasis. It is common for GRC consulting staff members to be instructed to keep the IG groups from veering too much to either extreme: settling into an isolated in-the-room process as against going out to test and explore boundaries without first establishing who they are, what they represent, and what tasks they wish to pursue (beyond exploration for its own sake).

At Belgirate, the exploratory event is set up most like the IG and/or an institutional event (sometimes termed the world event). Conference members are invited to form groups of their own choosing to explore a theme or topic for up to five ninety-minute sessions, followed by a plenary session to discuss and review what the groups did and some of the learning. As with a GRC IG or IE event, there are opportunities to send representatives to other groups to observe, to seek specific information, or to invite interaction between groups. Unlike a GRC, however, there are no staff consultants either assigned to the available rooms or sitting separately as a staff group available for consultation or group interactions. Inevitably something of shock to anyone attending a Belgirate conference for the first time, this absence of familiar structure and tangible authorisation "from above" does serve to signal that Belgirate is not a GRC in the usual sense.

The exploratory event lends itself to great variation in the tasks pursued by the groups and considerable anxiety—off and on—about "doing it right" (especially in the absence of staff consultants) and whether and to what extent the shared models of small group, intergroup, and institutional event are the appropriate models for the event at Belgirate. Perhaps ironically, there is ambivalence about using the experiences that qualify any of us to attend Belgirate: having been part of the staff of one or more GRCs. Ask any experienced GRC staff member what to do when faced with uncertainty in a conference, especially when the director is not available to advise them, most would instinctively rely upon self-authorisation (plus previous experience).

If it were only that simple! First, as Hogberg and Larsson (2012) and I (Strauss, 2009) have pointed out, no amount of experience immunises us from the very group dynamic processes we teach about in GRCs. Second, as Bion himself stated (1961, p. 88), there is a certain hatred of learning from experience. Finally, further complicating the experience of a participant in the exploratory event at Belgirate is the notion, also in Hogberg and Larsson's chapter, of "tradition as a prison". The dilemma here is articulated well by Western: "If the only lens you have to look at conferences is groups, roles and tasks, then all you will find is groups, roles and tasks" (2012, p. 262). While these concepts (along with authority and boundaries) have been a rich source of ideas for 50–60 years, they represent the established paradigm and might constrain creatively fresh ideas.

My roles at Belgirate IV

What follows is a somewhat selective survey of the events I attended at Belgirate IV. It is "selective" because I have chosen to highlight those aspects of Belgirate IV that most contributed to my understanding of my learning in intergroup terms.

I came to Belgirate IV earlier and left later than I had for the three previous Belgirate meetings in order to "shadow" Dr Robert Baxter as part of one of two transitions on the management and administrative team (MAT). He had been the representative of the A. K. Rice Institute for the Study of Social Systems (AKRI) on the MAT since Belgirate II; the AKRI Board had authorised me to take that role beginning with

Belgirate V in 2015. Dr Josef Triest was in a similar shadowing role *vis-à-vis* Dr Avi Nutkevitch; Dr Triest was destined to become the Belgirate V MAT representative from the Israeli Association for the Study of Group and Organisational Processes (OFEK), a role Dr Nutkevitch had held for all four Belgirate conferences. (The other two members of the MAT, Dr Eliat Aram, representing the Tavistock Institute of Human Relations (Tavistock) and Ms Rachel Kelly, administrator for Belgirate IV and also from Tavistock, were expected to continue in their MAT roles at Belgirate V.)

So, in ways I had not really appreciated until writing this reflection, I was primed to experience Belgirate IV in terms of IG experience: the MAT itself could be considered a stable IG working group to begin with, and then Dr Triest and I created an additional "IG-ness", our presence perhaps representing future leadership interacting with, and learning from, past and present leadership.

On the evening of the first day, I attended the open space session, an informally structured event where participants were invited "to discuss their research findings or topics from their work". There were four to choose from and I chose the one on "the psychodynamics of inter-organisational collaboration". Professor Sandra Schruijer from the Netherlands presented her research on "developing collaborative relationships across organizational boundaries" (Schruijer & Vansina, 2008; Curseu et al., 2011). (Again, I can now see foreshadowing of the IG focus for much of my Belgirate IV experience.) During her presentation of her research findings, she offered what were, in effect, the lessons she had learnt.

1. Bring the stakeholders together.
2. Legitimise their separate presence.
3. Create conditions for trust
   (a) have some ground rules;
   (b) establish boundaries (but minimally).
4. Do not suppress conflict.
5. Reconnect subsequently "face to face".

I shall return to these "lessons" when I take up the issue of a moral framework for intergroup relations among group relations organisations.

On the morning of the second day, we heard a keynote address from Hüseyin Özdemir entitled "Exploring group relations work in

China: challenges, risk, and impact". (It is found elsewhere in this volume.) He described how he used his business and organisational consultation work in China as a springboard for creating and directing the first GRC in China. In his presentation and in the discussion that followed, there was much to think about in terms of adapting GR to and in a developing country, a non-Western country and a country that, while increasingly engaging capitalism and free enterprise, is certainly not a democracy. The challenges were easy to see. I think I was not alone in also wondering how feasible GRCs could be—given their organisationally subversive qualities—in a totalitarian society.

Later that same morning, I chaired one of the "parallel presentation" sessions, during which a paper was presented titled, "The confusion of tongues between the East and the West—the need for a new language". Two parts of the paper (not yet published) resonated for me, then and after Belgirate IV. The authors, Shankarnaryan Srinath, Arunita Biswas and Manab Bose ask:

> While the philosophical underpinnings of group relations are universal, is its spread hindered in the East because a Western paradigm—a psychological and social construct with origins in the Western culture—is being applied uncritically to understand societies that are structured differently psychosocially and culturally?

While the "East" of this paper is India and South Asia, the question surely applies equally to the "East" defined by China.

In that same paper, the authors offer another observation:

> . . . one could say that Indian society is based on an obligatory system in contrast to the contractual system in the West. We see this in the group relations conferences in different cultural contexts, how people prioritize boundaries, tasks and relationships. The word "obligation" in the East is predominantly moral, while in the West it is largely seen in legal and other terms.

I shall return to this theme of moral *vs*. legal obligation when considering the "intergroup" of group relations organisations in the USA and internationally.

The second half of the second day of the conference was devoted to the first three sessions of the exploratory event; two more sessions occurred on the third day and a final plenary meeting occurred that evening, bringing the event to a close. As was the case in all but the second Belgirate conference, I was indecisive about which group to join: some topics just did not appeal, or the topic sounded interesting but so many people joined the group that I thought it likely that thoughtful reflection would be difficult (not to mention the likely competition just to express one's thoughts); I also did not wish to be in a group heavily loaded with others from the USA. Perhaps inevitably, the group I joined was one of the last few to form and leave the room where everyone had initially gathered.

I find it somewhat shocking that I cannot now recall what the original topic or focus for my group was. We were a group of 12–14 with a mix of men and women from a number of different countries and group relations organisations: I was one of two men from the USA, there were several from the UK, at least one woman from Australia, as well as individuals from Israel, Scandinavia, India, and several other European countries. Given the experience with GRCs in the room, it was striking that we never did feel the need to differentiate in terms of formal roles within the group (e.g., designated leader, door keeper).

The early sessions were very like a GRC small study group (minus a staff consultant): a rather desultory exploration of who we were and what we wanted to focus on/learn about in and through *our* exploratory group experience. For example, it was not until the third or fourth session that we "discovered" who in the group had had experience of directing a GRC. Eventually, we got out of our room and began to see what was going on elsewhere in the exploratory event. (I went out on behalf of our group, authorised to observe and interact with either of two groups. One room was empty—the group had left, but it was not clear if they had abandoned the space or were simply all out "exploring". The other room had a group of fourteen as well as representatives of one or two other groups. I heard reports about other groups (e.g., "there was not a sense of purpose . . .") as well as, in answer to a question about what this group had been working on, "We've been talking a lot about group relations.".)

But for me, the seminal moment in my own group came in the final session prior to the plenary. A member from Australia was talking about the dilemmas faced by Group Relations Australia (GRA, the GR organisation in that country that would correspond to AKRI in the USA or OFEK in Israel). In a manner that seemed to reflect a mixture of emotions—distress, anger, chagrin, almost an embarrassment at revealing this—she disclosed that in recent months (? years) a GR organisation from outside Australia had mounted GRCs which had been marketed very effectively and were well attended. However, she indicated that these conferences' success had resulted in a decreased attendance at GRA conferences to a degree that threatened the financial stability and perhaps even the viability of GRA.

Many of the members of my exploratory event group were quite struck by this new (to us) information. For me it seemed to crystallise quite suddenly what our group had been struggling to find: some link between what our group contained and the broader Belgirate IV meeting, particularly its title/theme. Here, it seemed, was an example of a GR organisation moving beyond its usual network and having an impact. Like the GRC in China that had been presented in the keynote talk, a European-based GR organisation was taking its approach to group relations and putting on GRCs in another continent, but, unlike the China example, the result was competition with the "native" GRC.

This brought to mind the situation in the USA where, over the past two decades, attendance at GRCs sponsored by AKRI have declined while certain other GRCs have remained very well attended. (To illustrate the decline in attendance at AKRI's own annual GRC, when I attended as a member in 1976, there were 50–60 members, whereas in the years 2007–2009, when I directed AKRI's GRC, our membership ranged from twenty-seven to thirty-five.) AKRI has several affiliate centres—GR organisations which operate from a metropolitan or regional base—and, while most continue to mount GRCs, the number of such conferences has also declined. In contrast are the GRCs that are part of a college or university department's curriculum. Those GRCs, with large numbers of students who attend the GRC as part of a class, often also recruit non-student members of the public; membership totalling 50–70 is not unusual.

I do not believe the university-based GRCs set out to compete with AKRI or its affiliated centres, and I certainly acknowledge that there are factors beyond the success of the university-based programmes that account for the fiscal straits in which AKRI now sits (summer of 2013) and has for the past several years. Similarly, I do not believe the UK-based GR organisation that has mounted conferences in Australia did so to compete with GRA in a manner that would threaten its survival. Intended or not, however, the consequences are there. To my mind, the issue becomes how do we think about these intergroup relations where the groups in question are GR organisations? What models guide how we think about these developments?

Is an ethical agenda germane?

Here is where I wish to introduce the question of whether an "ethical agenda" is germane. One might argue that the apt model is a Darwinian "survival of the fittest": GR organisations must "evolve", must meet the demands of their environments in order to survive, let alone thrive. This view resonates in part with the open systems notions of all organisations operating like living organisms and interacting with their environments in order to survive. Similar, but slightly different, is a model based on capitalism, where competing for "market share" would be viewed as not just unavoidable but a necessary and desirable way for GR organisations to deal with each other. Success would be reflected by GRC membership size and would be assumed to reflect something about the quality of the GRCs competing with each other.

While I cannot say that either of these models—or a mix of the two—is incorrect, they do seem to lack the ethical agenda referred to by Western in the epigraph to this chapter. To focus on the situation in the USA, because I am most familiar with it, there is a value in having a GR organisation like AKRI that, among other functions, represents the history, values, and accumulated wisdom of group relations within a country. Certainly, the vitality of university-based GRCs can be temporary and is often linked to the academic status of specific faculty; I know of at least four university-based courses with GRCs that once thrived and are no more. Similarly, I can think of at least four AKRI affiliate centres that have gone out of existence over the past thirty-five years.

So, is there a better model in thinking about GR intergroup relations within and across national boundaries? "The network" might seem at first to be an appealing model, but, as Hogberg and Larsson (2012, p. 224) point out, "a network has no centre and, dynamically, it operates on the binary logic of inclusion/exclusion". They assert that while networks "are value-free and neutral", they lack the "recognition of the Other that transforms the most basic element of GRT (group relations tradition)—that of relations". This view of "the network" makes it appear more a part of the problem than the solution.

As "retro" as it may sound, perhaps *the family*, especially the *extended family*, might present a useful starting place. Here, we might want to incorporate some of the ideas about "obligation" in the moral, rather than contractual or legal, sense, as Srinath and his colleagues suggested. I also think the "lessons" of Sandra Schruijer's work could be a practical way to operationalise such an obligatory system. What else is needed? Leadership, most obviously, is required, along with the capacity to hold—dynamically as well as concretely—the group and its place in the larger (GR) environment in the mind. I do not believe this is an impossible task, though it may have to wait for Belgirate V in 2015.

References

Aram, E., Baxter, R., & Nutkevitch, A. (Eds.) (2012). *Group Relations Conferences: Tradition, Creativity and Succession in the Global Group Relations Network*. London: Karnac.

Bion, W. R. (1961). *Experiences in Groups and Other Papers*. London: Tavistock.

Curseu, P., Schruijer, S., & Boros, S. (2012). Socially rejected while cognitively successful? The impact of minority dissent on groups' cognitive complexity. *British Journal of Social Psychology, 51*(4): 570–582.

Hogberg, B., & Larsson, M. (2012). The chains of tradition: escaping, endorsing or exploring? In: E. Aram, R. Baxter, & A. Nutkevitch (Eds.), *Group Relations Conferences: Tradition, Creativity and Succession in the Global Group Relations Network* (pp. 217–226). London: Karnac.

Ozdemir, H. (2015). Exploring group relations work in China—challenges, risks and impact. In: E. Aram, R. Baxter & A. Nutkevitch (Eds.), *Begirate IV: Exploring the Impact and Relevance of Group Relations Work within and Beyond its Network* (pp. 103–125). London: Karnac.

Schruijer, S., & Vansina, L (2008). Working across organisational boundaries: understanding and working with the psychological dynamics. In: L. S. Vansina & M.-J. Vansina-Cobbaert (Eds.), *Psychodynamics for Consultants and Managers* (pp. 390–410). London: John Wiley.

Strauss, G. (2009). Learning from experience: The two international group relations meetings in Belgirate. In: E. Aram, R. Baxter, & A. Nutkevitch (Eds.), *Adaptation and Innovation: Theory, Design, and Role-Taking in Group Relations Conferences and their Applications* (pp. 243–248). London: Karnac.

Western, S. (2012). Remnants, Quakers and group relations. In: E. Aram, R. Baxter, & A. Nutkevitch (Eds.), *Group Relations Conferences: Tradition, Creativity, and Succession in the Global Group Relations Network* (pp. 259–274). London: Karnac.

CHAPTER FOURTEEN

Cobblers' children or creative flux?

Kay Trainor

O n my return from Belgirate IV, I was full of ideas, and also found myself reflecting, as others have I am sure, on whether I had found the design of the conference "requisite" (Jaques, 1996) for the primary task of the conference: *to provide opportunities to learn about, and explore, the impact and relevance of group relations work both within and beyond the group relations network.* In this short chapter, I will explore two different responses I had to the conference. It is a difficult task to design a conference to facilitate a primary task such as the one above and my thoughts about the design are offered (consciously at least) in a spirit of collaboration and creativity. It is a chapter in two parts.

"Cobblers' children", from the saying "Cobblers' children go un-shod", refers, in this context, to the lack of the sort of reflective space, particularly small group reflective space, in the conference (spaces in which we might have been able to work through our own experience and understand this experience as "data" from the wider system of the conference), the psychodynamics of which might have been inhibiting the capacity for "learning" and "exploring" as invited by the espoused primary task.

"Creative flux" speaks to a part of my experience at the conference to do with the nature of creativity and when and why it occurs where it does. I will describe the genesis at the conference of what I consider to be a creative idea in terms of my own potential contribution to group relations design. The design of the Belgirate IV conference seemed to facilitate the emergence of this idea. I shall explore what I think might have made this possible at the conference, citing Bion's Ps↔D formulation of thinking.

Cobblers' children

Probably like many colleagues, on my way back from Belgirate IV, I wrote some notes on my laptop—an *aide memoire* to the conversations I had had and what emerged from them. When I received an email from Rachel Kelly inviting proposals for chapters in this book, I looked them up. They are reproduced below (including typos) without any elaboration, apart from the substitution of an X where conference delegates or other colleagues were mentioned by name.

X Robert Reich super capitalism
Psulkrugman syndicated columnist
X for business development at TC
Work is a resource – it should be shared. X etc
GRC – find out how it has been described in course literature. Speak to this. Co creation. But speak to obligatory in opening lecture.
Commission X to understand why the numbers are low
GRC should we make courses visible in opening plenary.
Israel – which GRC for X
Otto scharmerliz
Conversion rates D10 X's sense that it is X
D10 interviews change the format
Keep X close to tc for next year
London insight for meditation
X (email address) for ma programmes around the world. A meeting X
PCCA Partners confronting collective atrocity—past in the present conferences
GRC ideas—a third role for the training group in the IE could be to join the management group.

Intimacy as a product—X GRC as deep team building.
X, X and X the book
X cant make partnerships because they don't know who THEY are.
X premises we could share

Something troubled me about these notes. They made little sense (certainly at first), were full of spelling mistakes, cryptic. This differs from the usual sort of notes I make after such an experience, which would, typically, have been much fuller. I had been exhausted when I wrote them but this did not sufficiently explain the paucity of elaboration. There was something to be understood, as I sometimes say to students presenting case work, about the writing. What this was became clearer as I worked on the idea for this chapter. I eventually concluded that something may have been left with me, something I could not, at the time, process, and this had resulted in the cursory, stuck note taking. I had wanted, on my way home, to abbreviate the experience, as it were, to move quickly away from something. Partly, anyway—as I shall explain.

As a starting point for this first part of the chapter, I need to describe a disturbing, repeating, experience I had at the Belgirate IV conference (the stuckness).

I have disguised the key dynamics of the experience, and my own childhood experience, to which I eventually realised this aspect of my own (post natal) groupishness related. The essence is kept, but the characters, roles, and events are changed.

Three times during the conference I found myself drawn to male colleagues whom I knew to be close to female colleagues with whom I was experiencing difficulties professionally. "Found myself" is the right description. The experience was powerful, as if I was compelled to try to win their approval, which did not work and which left me feeling exposed, rather foolish, and rejected in a particularly painful way. How I understood these experiences later relates to my own childhood experience, which I "capture" as follows: a mother who died when I was young and who was quickly (my siblings and I thought prematurely) replaced by a stepmother whom I resented and whom I experienced as vindictive and unfair. I never understood what my father saw in her, and told him so repeatedly, though I failed to convince him of the justice of my complaint. I came to understand that the situation I "co-created" at the conference was a version of this group where I try, in vain, to persuade my "father" to prefer me to the "interloper".

What sort of experience was this? A compulsive repetition (Freud, 1914g) of my own traumatic "group"? Still unresolved at some level, had it been reanimated by the presence of certain male colleagues at the conference in combination with whom I and the absent "rival" made a dynamic three, from which I felt excluded? In an analytic session after the conference, I was stunned to realise how the painful incidents related to my own story—already much discussed in analysis. In this respect, I found these re-enactments useful and was able to work at understanding the familiar story in a different way—another level of the narrative was revealed. All to the good, but why did these re-enactments happen, three times, at this conference? Was there a wider relevance or meaning that could have been explored, or did it *just* relate to my own past experience?

Had I had this repeating experience during a GRC, the small study group (and/or end of day review group in certain designs) might have offered the opportunity to process the experience and seek a systemic understanding. My repetition compulsion might then have been understood as valency—a willingness to take up a particular (unconscious) role on behalf of a system. The experience might have been understood, in other words, in terms of something wider, of which it was a symptom. Small group reflection of this sort was not part of the Belgirate IV design, however, so the experience of the dynamic remained my own—personal.

After the event, I decided to do some thinking and experiment in developing a hypothesis using the experience with my male colleagues as data. Could my experience, of seeking out a "three" from which I then felt excluded, have had a wider meaning? Might the macro have been in the micro? Might it have been an expression of the organisation-(or conference)-in-the-mind, in other words? The hypothesis I developed was that my experience of an excluding three *might* have related to the "three" at an entirely other level of the conference; it might have been a reflection of the interplay between the "three" sponsoring organisations of the conference. Was it possible that one of the three felt excluded by the other two? Might excluding three-ness have been a characteristic of the system, which I had absorbed?

I do not know and whether or not my hypothesis might be convincing is not really the point. I also realise I might (at least partly) be involved in the exercise of making myself feel better about a difficult experience. But what I wonder is whether the processing of such experience in real time, as it were, as data from the system, might have enriched the conference, enhanced our understanding of the system psychodynamics of our collective experience, and freed our thinking.

Regarding the design, perhaps small, consistent membership reflection groups might have been included, facilitated by consultants. Perhaps the exploratory event, also, might have benefited from "consultancy" in order to help us make sense not just of our discussions, but of our experience at the conference, the enacted? Need cobblers' children (to return to the title) go unshod, in other words? And if we did at the conference, might we need to probe a bit deeper about what inhibits us from allowing each other to take up the role of consultant (cobbler) for each other, on behalf of each other, and in the service of the task *to learn about, and explore, the impact and relevance of group relations work both within and beyond the group relations network.* We are an organisation, after all, with organisational defences, which sometimes get in the way of thinking.

Creative flux

What helps ideas emerge? As well as the experiences described above, I also had an experience at the conference of being able to be particularly creative with colleagues. A design idea for a new, differentiated, role at GRCs emerged during the exploratory event—an idea which has further evolved and been piloted during the year since Belgirate IV at the ISPSO conference in Oxford, July 2013, where the role of "conference artist" (the new idea) was integrated into the design. I have proposed introducing the role into the Tavistock Clinic's in-house GRC in December 2013. The "conference artist" is neither conference member nor conference staff, but will interact with and involve both members and staff, working across the various boundaries of the conference to help reveal the system to itself using a different medium, that of performance.

In terms of creativity, I am interested in the moment at which this idea formed. It seemed to form at a moment I would describe (personally) as "disintegrated", following one of the difficult encounters described in the first part of this chapter. I was feeling anxious, unravelled, at the "lonely end" of an excluding triangle (description courtesy of Stephen Briggs). The idea itself could even be seen as related to the pain of this experience (an oedipal reaction), the creation and championing of a legitimised "third role" (Oedipus, the artist!) in the group relations canon—a sort of manic reparation. But even if it was, was it just that, or might this process tell us something about creativity and the conditions under which we might expect to "be" creative?

It is something which has preoccupied me in my own practice as a writer and which I sought to operationalise in co-founding a consultancy company (Kube) which had, as part of its portfolio, the possibility for clients to work with artists. The role of the artists, broadly speaking, was to "promote creativity" through various sorts of improvisation work using (for example) performance, movement, mark making, and music to develop new ideas in relation to particular client issues. This corresponded with, and built on, my own practice as a writer, using improvisatory or "free" writing—the practice of "keeping the hand moving" and seeing what emerges (Breton, 1933; Cameron, 1994) which, in my research, I relate to the practice of free association in the psychoanalytic dyad. I also suggest (after Bollas, 2002) that the practice of free association is often defended against, as we found with the process of improvisation.

I have explored elsewhere the problematic of the Kube experiment (Doctoral research 2011 and 2012 ISPSO Symposium). Artists were idealised while clients defended themselves against the actual practice of improvisation that the artists modelled. There are many reasons (explored in my research) why clients may have defended themselves against working more freely with the artists (and consultants) with) with whom they, avowedly, wanted so much to work. For the purposes of this chapter, I will concentrate on one aspect—the disintegration that I propose is at the heart of "evolutionary creativity" (Halton, 2004), that is, the sort of creativity that moves beyond "reparative creativity" into the painful creation of the "new idea".

The differentiation between reparative and evolutionary creativity is implicit in Bion's work, but not explicit. He describes the process of thinking in terms of a conversion process of raw unprocessed elements (beta elements) that require an alpha (containing) function in order to be converted/combined in to alpha elements—that is, thoughts (Bion, 1962). He relates this capacity to the infant's ability to bring two objects together and is explicit that the nipple of the mother and the mouth of the infant are the site of discovery for this bringing together, as long as the frustration of the "no breast" or "bad breast" of the sometimes absent mother can be borne. This equates, essentially, to the process described by Halton as reparative creativity—the PS↔D of Bion's formulation.

It is Bion's further elaboration of Ps↔D which, in my opinion, relates to evolutionary creativity. Ps↔D, and in particular the D→Ps part of the process, I propose, relates to a dissolving of the maternal container caused by the arrival of father on the boundary of the dyad, re-exposing the infant (with echoes for the adult "creative") to the confusion and terror of the paranoid–schizoid position. For Klein, the oedipal situation is primitive and corresponds to the developmental stage when the infant relates primarily to part objects (Bell, 1992). It is my proposal that evolutionary creativity (the new) relates to this developmental period. It has a primitive oedipal quality, a maelstrom of feelings and disorientation unleashed, from which a new idea may be forged. The two objects that are brought together in this context relate to the parental couple rather than the nipple of the mother and the mouth of the baby. Evolutionary creativity depends on a capacity to bear the dissolving of the container and, eventually, the internalising of a creative parental couple in the mind of the infant.

While Halton identifies clearly the need to go beyond the depressive position (of reparative creativity) in order to encounter the "new", he regrets Bion describing "creative flux", as he calls it, as "a state of mind analogous to the paranoid schizoid position" (Halton, 2004, p. 113).

However, in reviewing my experience of free writing as a creative process, over the past ten+ years, I find it corresponds closely to Bion's description of an oscillation between disintegration and reintegration. Like free association, the "fundamental rule" of which it shares (Freud, 1916–1917, pp. 448–463), it temporarily dissolves the container in order to enter a regressed (paranoid–schizoid) state of mind. I could provide many examples of this process from my own free writing.

Returning to the Belgirate IV conference, how might my experience of the conference relate to the different forms of creativity and thinking cited above? I conclude this chapter by exploring this in the context of Belgirate IV and of group relations more broadly. What sort of creativity characterises group relations? In a conventional group relations design, created to explore both personal and organisational authority, members are encouraged to explore the pictures in their minds—of other groups of members in various events, of the conference staff in different events, etc. They are helped by conference staff (in consultant role) to travel along a continuum that could be described as Ps→D, that is, reparative. Members might typically say *We've been behaving "as if" the group in room A/the management were monsters, were irrelevant, were deviant.* With help, they might understand this as a picture in the mind, related to anxiety, related to the system. Understanding it helps to relieve it, helps to take in the other. It is perhaps this sort of reparative understanding of the system that I was seeking in order to help me make sense of my experiences (of the excluding threes).

But what of the primary task of Belgirate IV? What sort of creativity did it require? And, consequently, what sort of design? I experienced both the sort of disturbance typical (if that is the right word) of a member at a GRC—a disturbance which needed to be understood (Ps→D), but also moments of exciting creativity. This creativity happened, as I have said, in a moment of "disintegration" (D→Ps). In my opinion, it is this process of disintegration during creativity which is hard to bear and which, along with other pressures, caused Kube's clients (and all of us sometimes) to defend against it.

Had my painful experiences at Belgirate been understood (Ps to dPs→D), would I have had the idea (of the conference artist) which resulted, potentially, from a capacity to bear D→Ps without any real knowledge that I would travel the other way and a new idea be formed? My capacity to bear it was, if not facilitated, then certainly not blocked by the design of Belgirate IV. What might have been revealed is the design dilemma faced by the management team.

References

Bell, D. (1992). Hysteria: a contemporary Kleinian perspective. *British Journal of Psychotherapy, 9*: 169–180.

Bion, W. R. (1962). A theory of thinking. In: E. Bott Spillius (Ed.), *Melanie Klein Today: Developments in Theory and Practice. Volume 1: Mainly Theory* (pp. 178–186). London: Routledge, 1988.

Bollas, C. (2002). *Free Association*. Cambridge: Icon Books.

Breton, A. (1933). The automatic message. In: F. Rosemont (Ed.), *Andre Breton. What is Surrealism? Selected Writings* (pp. 132–147). USA: Pathfinder, 2011.

Cameron, J. (1994). *The Artist's Way*. London: Souvenir Press.

Freud, S. (1914g). Remembering, repeating and working-through. *S. E., 12*: 147–156. London: Hogarth.

Freud, S. (1916–1917). *Introductory Lectures on Psycho-analysis. S. E., 16*. London: Hogarth.

Halton, W. (2004). By what authority? Psychoanalytical reflections on creativity and change in relation to organizational life. In: C. Huffington, D. Armstrong, W. Halton, L. Hoyle, & J. Pooley (Eds.), *Working Below the Surface: The Emotional Life of Contemporary Organizations* (pp. 107–124). London: Karnac.

Jaques, E. (1996). *The Requisite Organisation*. Arlington, VA: Cason Hall.

Trainor, K. (2012a). An exploration of the impact of unwork. Paper presented to ISPSO Symposium, 13 July, Oxford.

Trainor, K. (2012b). Exploring the meaning for clients of the arts-related organisational consultancy offered by ABS: what are we doing here? PhD thesis, University of East London.

CHAPTER FIFTEEN

What happened to authority?
A reflective dialogue

Gerard van Reekum and Barbara Williams

Our starting point for submitting this chapter was a series of Skype conversations during which we exchanged and discussed some diary notes about how we experienced various authority issues in the 2012 Belgirate conference, and how, for us, reflection on this most central concept in the group relations theory and methodology was insufficient, where authority issues seemed obscured and hidden.

The notes deal with the following episodes of the conference:

- the opening plenary, where it was announced that a next Belgirate conference would be planned and managed by a different team;
- the open space event, where presenters had no moderators, where sessions took place in one room simultaneously, and participants were encouraged to move freely from one session to another;
- a parallel session on "co-directorship", where it appeared that the conventional manner of single authorisation survives under the guise of a different role-title;
- the exploratory event, where management did not provide the containment that is normally provided to participants of GRCs;
- a parallel session near the end of the conference on group relations work within an organisation in transition, where the authority

of the moderator, the presenting institution, and management in general was attacked;

- finally, after the conference was over: although we made several attempts, we could not obtain a copy of a relevant keynote presentation, parallel to our effort of grasping what was happening to authority.

Our conversations around these notes ended in a reflective email correspondence, that we offer here in a slightly edited version, both as a contribution to a record of the conference and for further exploration into the subjects of authority and authorisation.

G: Have you also noticed how optimism was promoted as a new cultural norm in this conference? People seemed to understand that the task was "to have a real good time here", like a vacation. Some even brought their family members, possibly encouraged to do so by management who communicated this as a feasible arrangement with the hotel. We mingled with them during breaks and meals; the conference in the mind included the "spouse in the room". Yet, despite the drive for optimism, I came away from it profoundly confused about the methodology in use and deeply pessimistic about its relevance. My sense is we're colluding in a hidden enterprise to do away with the entire body of knowledge, techniques, and skills that was developed and handed down to us by previous generations of group relations practitioners. The framing of the conference made it difficult to remain faithful to the legacy.

I don't think we have developed any other technological sophistication besides talking and listening, yet I felt we gave each other a hard time believing or taking seriously almost anything that was said. No matter the publicly promoted beliefs about role as a property of the system and invitations to openly explore the processes of attribution, I found only a handful of colleagues willing to actually try this, and instead I felt I had to deal with the constant risk of becoming the kill-joy. Under these circumstances, I experienced the "net" aspect of the network as a conceptual tool, a weapon almost, meant to catch me. I'm not worried about myself outside this network (beyond it, if you wish), but within it I really think I can no longer contribute. You've been there too at Belgirate; where are you now?

B: I am not sure there is any other technology beyond "talking". It's the only possibility for me, for putting the body of knowledge we have under investigation as well as the limits and troublesome problematics of the knowledge itself. In my view, we are stuck with the problem of authority (and by that, I mean knowledge) authorising its own deconstruction. You felt yourself a kill-joy in these discussions at Belgirate, potentially at least. The particular vignettes we worked with suggest frustration with both the lack of containment (in the sense of providing a psychical frame for the Unc explorations and explorations of Unc processes) and with the obdurate presence of "constrainment" (in the sense of an unwill-ingness/refusal/derision to actually explore). I'm not sure it is the knowledge itself that is at stake (not for me anyway). I wonder, rather, if the sense of addiction or discursive repetition to close exploration, rather than open it, actually arises from an uncon-scious distrust and fear of the "coming to know", which cannot be known in advance and perhaps not at all in a final way. So, in this sense, you might be right. I think the limit may well be in "the dream for a knowledge" and in its unthought application that must be worked toward. But maybe this is the new paradigm?

G: Of course, we do not have much working for us besides talking and listening. There is no way we can feel what someone else feels or know what other people think (with sufficient accuracy and certainty, that is) except by how we talk about it between us. And even when we stretch the technology of "talking" to include the motor language of our body, it is still doubtful what becomes really "known".

Empathy or the allure of empathy as the ground for optimism about the emergence of true understanding between subjects remains a problematic issue within social theory. For me, the 2012 Belgirate conference showed how this is equally true for psycho-analytically informed professionals, versed as they are in alter-native readings of human relations due to their understanding of dynamic processes such as projective identification, extractive introjection, and the like. Our methodology holds the ingredients for a critique of humanist psychology and in particular of the notion of empathy (the notion that one can feel what the other one feels); this is why we arrived at our particular concept of role, isn't that right? What we offer in our conferences is a series of opportu-nities to discover how behaviour (including the use of speech and language) is behaviour "in role", also derived from, and effected in and by, the systems of which we are part, rather than only inter-personally activated and propelled by individual drives and intent accessible through cognition that we consider "solely our own".

To make some headway into that unknown territory we're developing and applying a method. And because we have no other instrument for our explorations than the one we're exploring, the method must consist of more than the dexterity of our voice alone (or the words we use to report our thoughts, as in our writing here). This is exactly my point: that although no limits should be pre-established in the subject under study, there is no excuse for failing to establish boundaries within the frame and setting of our work. That's how and why management and consultancy enter the picture, and why authorisation and authority are such indispensable elements of our method. When that is denied or even actively sabotaged, I want to explore how and why, and expect to be recognised as someone doing the task instead of being the kill-joy. All right, I won't always have my way, but even when I am put, or put myself, into the role of kill-joy, I want to explore how and why, and expect to be recognised as someone doing the task instead of ... well, you get my drift, but I'm slipping into explanation mode again. What am I trying to defend here?

B: I'm not sure, but I think what you are saying is that the Belgirate conference fails to exemplify or amplify a group relations understanding of role. The group relations method offers opportunities to discover how behaviour is mobilised by others (behaviour in role), not simply by our own drives and intentions. And because we have no other instrument for our explorations of behaviour than the one we're exploring—that is, we have no ways of enquiring *into* role except *from* role—it is all the more imperative that the boundaries we know to be essential for enabling that exploration are in place. That's how and why management and consultancy enter the picture, and why authorisation is such an indispensable element of our method. When authorisation and authority are, or appear to be, denied or obfuscated or abrogated, you think we should explore how and why. And I agree. Even when you do so from the role of kill-joy, you wish and expect to be recognised as someone doing that task, instead of being reduced to just a kill-joy and nothing else.

G: Right.

B: It occurs to me that your reference to empathy may also indicate that you felt disregarded in the task you were trying to take up. You were mobilised to kill the joy that seems perhaps to have come from "wanting to have a really good time", not wanting to do the work of "learning about, and exploring, the impact and relevance of group relations work both within and beyond the group relations network" and not being able to enquire into the obstacles. What if you actually identified as/with the kill-joy as an important role in this new paradigm? What do you think?

For now, I want to work with something else. Perhaps the difficulty is that there is a wish or dream for a method that can work at (or beyond) its own limit: a method of enquiry that interests itself in what lies beyond what it knows or what it presumes to know. I don't understand the strong—what seemed to me—disinclination to work on questions of authority and authorisation, to see what these might mean for the work more broadly. And, alternatively, why it seemed that utilising the boundaries of consultation or management or authorisation was thought to be unnecessary. Could it be that "boundary-lessness" prevented that work? In which case, it would prove the point you are making about the need for "authority" as well as its exploration, rather than disprove it.

What are some other hypotheses: we really don't trust the method? Or perhaps, we did not want to work along the method and face the consequences of its limit? Then this would be a question of faith or confidence or politics, which might go with your feeling of some sort of betrayal? Or, alternatively, is it that we are wisely (or perversely) afraid of the envy and aggressions that arise toward authority when taking up that role with peers and colleagues? One way of seeing your experience is not so much of being extruded (though I might not understand this term well), but that you hold this limit in application and are indeed representing a loss of faith—in the theory, the method, in the application, the network as a whole.

I have been aware of the competition for participants in various group relations conferences and have been thinking about the experience in Belgirate from a larger frame, that of the survival of group relations generally in a hostile post-psychoanalytic, hyperglobalised and highly competitive economy where it seems it is impossible to work together to build a broader shared strategy. Together.

G: What you wrote about this possible other layer under my reference to empathy has set me thinking. Indeed, I did feel disregard and disregarded, but I wasn't suffering because of a lack of empathy I think. Rather the opposite, I perceived an excess reliance on the notions of empathy, moving—from a norm that ought to be questioned or interrogated—towards a value above critique. It made me anxious, overly careful, and also sad in a way, like the deep sorrow when you realise you've lost something forever. I'm not sure about betrayal, I don't feel cynical or anything, but it is true that I am disappointed and losing confidence. Losing confidence in what? Well, you said it beautifully; I think I've lost confidence in the possibility for "my" group relations to survive. Just when we need it the most, intrinsic inconsistencies prevent effective application and render it useless and irrelevant.

Bringing this back to the subject of authority, I think the psychoanalytic paradigm is to blame. There is something in the stance of the analyst, coming from deep in its origin (probably through Freud's own psyche, in the role he assumed under the influence of projections he couldn't work through without a supervisor) that has contaminated the *modus operandi* of group relations practitioners. It is the confusion between establishing authority and establishing dependency in the relationship.

I was in a conference the other day where a participant defined authority as the ability to trigger the other person's autonomy. I think it is exactly this application (and explication) of authority that was lacking in Belgirate, causing my suffering.

B: I suspect this might have a lot to do with "whose psychoanalysis" or "who's psychoanalyst". Paradigms don't carry blame in my mind. But could we (does Pollyanna now come to group relations) develop a shared de-constructivist orientation—of mind and feeling—to explore what blame we *want* them to carry for us and what enactments we employ in their name *to what ends*? Knowledge and the so-called authorities of knowledge and theory hold (but cannot contain) intrinsic inconsistencies and contradictions. To work with these is the work; it's my work whatever paradigm I make use of.

G: I don't think I'm guilty of reification, because I am speaking about Freud and his role. Of course, I would agree that you can't blame a paradigm, but you can blame an institution, or an institutionalisation. The difference between establishing authority and establishing dependency is illuminated by the following quotation. I was mildly shocked by reading this description of authority according to group relations theory:

> Authority is the claim of legitimacy, the justification and right to exercise power and the ability to influence others to do something that they would not have done. Authority is the capacity or a relationship, innate or acquired, for exercising ascendency over others. It is sanctioned, institutionalised power. (Aram & Sher, 2013, p. 267)

B: I do think the notion of authority is very complex and over-satu-
rated now with meaning. I mean by this that it is quite difficult to
know what we all mean when we use this term, when we try to
interrogate its implications and study its applications, not only for
ourselves (in role) but for the other (in role also)—even if/as we try
to define it. Author, authority, authorise, and authentic derive
from the Latin roots *aug* and *augere*, meaning to increase or
expand, which sounds closer to your thought about authority as
an enabler of autonomy rather than as an influencer.

It seems to me that a thread throughout this dialogue that we
have not made explicit is that psychotic elements do inflect our
work—at least that is a premise from which I begin. "Authority"
of the other and "containment" or desire for the other are inextri-
cably linked to understanding, working with, working through
these psychotic elements. But as I suggested earlier, these are
"affected undertakings" (Britzman, 2011) and, therefore, this line
of enquiry always provokes resistance against whatever new may
be created. I wonder if that is also your disappointment: that little
"new" can emerge at or beyond this limit. And when or if it does,
it is not even recognisable.

G: I loved your reference to Polyanna, just hits the nail on the head;
in my perception, some group relations events develop towards
being a kind of Glad Clubs (Porter, 1913) (perhaps "clubs" in
several respects). I want to tell you that I woke up from a dream
on Sunday morning, I believe the day you started in the pre-
conference meeting in Spain. Here's the dream:

I was in a church, where every Sunday a particular ritual was
performed: before the start of each service, the best singers from
the congregation offer one hymn from their choir bench, while
other members wait in the aisles and listen until the end of the
singing before finding a seat of their own. When I was there in my
dream, the church received a large delegation from another
church. Upon entering the building, these people enjoyed hearing
the singing—which was beautiful—and in their innocence
proceeded to find a seat. Confused and surprised, one after the
other choir-member fell out of role and stopped singing. Not a
word was spoken, no explanation given. In this moment of alarm,
although unfamiliar with the ritual, the visitors noticed that as a
group they were the only people seated and guessed an error on
their part. Now one after the other visitor returned to the aisles
and with the last of them rising and joining the crowd, the choir
resumed.

My question was: how is this ritual established and how is it maintained? If something happens that disrupts the liturgy, if unexpectedly the trusted and celebrated structure (the singing) is disturbed, how does that inform us about the task the choir is doing, about the authority of the conductor on the basis of which he or she selects the best singers from among the members, about what causes their collapse, especially at such a moment of pride and already by such innocent intervention? And then the relief when we as hosts are saved the embarrassment by the compliance of our visitors; we can continue to believe that we are understood and can understand. Yet, like our "visitors" we cannot but err in our learning together—but if we allow ourselves to do so, may we then still trust to be welcomed or will we be stifled? For dealing with such anxieties I think we need containment. And authority.

This is all very different from what I read in the quotation above on authority. For the sake of contrast, compare this with Bruce Reed while teaching the clergy, and mark his emphasis on freedom:

Role transforms power into authority. . . . A person's actions can be authorised by others only if they are considered as working within prescribed limits, limits (boundaries) which enable the actions to be understood as carrying out the aims of the authorising body by accepting accountability for their actions. Hence others also functioning within these limits experience freedom if they can take the role to exercise their own authority. (Reed, 1999)

B: I was struck in your dream by the image of the beautiful music and its connection to "joy" as it came up earlier in our conversation. I was also struck by the question of who "erred". I wondered if there was some connection between the joy you didn't want to be the killer of, your own joy lost, and the problem of error. Of course, there are rituals in group relations work (or traditions) and there are also errors in the work, such as boundary errors resulting in loss of containment, inappropriate and perverse interactions, and staff incompetence. But to sustain the ritual can't be in itself such a bad thing. Perhaps what makes the experience in Belgirate disappointing for you—as someone who has had such a lengthy time creating and working in this ritual—is that you want to continue, not simply to repeat, the legacy. You want to push it toward new possibilities. That might be unwelcome.

G: Yes, in Belgirate I felt the push is in a different direction: this system does not easily face and explore its own needs for authority and containment. I'm learning to accept that.

References

Aram, E., & Sher, M. (2013). Group relations conferences. In: S. Long (Ed.), *Socioanalytic Methods, Discovering the Hidden in Organisations and Social Systems* (pp. 257–277). London: Karnac.

Britzman, D. P. (2011). *Freud and Education*. New York: Routledge.

Porter, E. H. (1913). *Polyanna, the Glad Book*. Boston, MA: L. C. Page.

Reed, B. (1999). Organisational transformation. In: J. Nelson (Ed.), *Leading, Managing, Ministering—Challenging Questions for Church and Society* (pp. 243–262). Norwich: Canterbury Press.

INDEX

Printed in Great Britain